202

WAYS TO
SUPPLEMENT YOUR
RETIREMENT INCOME

Other titles by James Stephenson

- *202 Things to Make and Sell for Big Profits*

- *202 Things You Can Buy and Sell for Big Profits*

- *202 Services You Can Sell for Big Profits*

- *Ultimate Homebased Business Handbook: How to Start, Run, and Grow Your Own Profitable Business*

- *Ultimate Small Business Marketing Guide: 1,500 Great Marketing Tricks That Will Drive Your Business Through the Roof*

- *Ultimate Start-Up Directory*

202

WAYS TO SUPPLEMENT YOUR RETIREMENT INCOME

JAMES STEPHENSON

EP
Entrepreneur.
Press

Managing editor: Jere L. Calmes
Cover design: Beth Hansen-Winter
Composition and production: Eliot House Productions

This publication is designed to provide accurate and authoritative information in regard to the subject matter covered. It is sold with the understanding that the publisher is not engaged in rendering legal, accounting, or other professional services. If legal advice or other expert assistance is required, the services of a competent professional person should be sought.

Library of Congress Cataloging-in-Publication Data
Stephenson, James, 1966–.
   202 ways to supplement your retirement income/by James Stephenson.
      p.   cm.
   Includes index.
   ISBN 1-932531-66-1 (alk. paper)
   1. Retirement income. 2. Retirees—Finance, Personal. I. Title: Two hundred two ways to supplement your retirement income. II. Title: Two hundred two ways to supplement your retirement income. III. Title.
HG179.S8347 2005
332.024'014—dc22   2005013406

Printed in Canada

11 10 09 08 07 06 05   10 9 8 7 6 5 4 3 2 1

CONTENTS

CHAPTER 2

Legal and Financial Issues _ _ _ _ _ _ _ _ _ _ _ _ _ _ 17

CHAPTER 5

Sales and Marketing _____ 85

CHAPTER 6

CHAPTER 7

202 Ways to Supplement Your Retirement Income_ _ 129

PREFACE

Truth is, at time of writing I am 39 years old. You're probably thinking, and rightly so, how can this young punk possibly know anything about the financial and income issues and challenges facing people aged 50 and over? Obviously, you're not completely off base. I am not yet aged 50-plus, but I do have many years of small business, sales, and marketing experience under my belt and have written numerous books on small business, sales, and marketing topics. Combine these experiences with my many hours of research on the challenges facing people aged 50 and older, and I can say without any hesitation that you are reading one of the most comprehensive and authoritative books available today about the best ways to supplement your retirement income.

My objectives in creating this book are to identify the best ways that you can supplement your preretirement or postretirement income and to give you the information and tools that you need to get started in a simple-to-use, step-by-step format. Let's face it, there's no shortage of books available about how to save or invest for your retirement, and most are very helpful, that is, if you are 20, 30, or 40 years old. Why? Because all of the investment and savings strategies require 10, 20, 30, or more years of consistent saving and investing to realize the full financial benefits. But what do you do if you are one of the millions of people over the age of 50 who need or want to supplement their retirement income right now, not years or even decades from now? *202 Ways to Supplement Your Retirement Income* is one of the few books available that is solely focused on what you can do to start generating income right now; it is also the most up-to-date and resource-packed. The information and ideas featured here have been specifically developed to walk you through every step that is required to start and run a business for maximum success and profit.

After completing this book, you will have acquired valuable information and knowledge on all the critical topics, including choosing the right income-producing opportunity for you, satisfying the legal and financial challenges, planning all aspects of your business to ensure success, setting up your business, sales and marketing, and, of course, the best 202 ways to supplement your retirement income with big profits!

Getting Started

Inside, I explore reasons why you might need or want to supplement your retirement income—to keep up with inflation, to maintain your preretirement lifestyle, to fulfill a dream of owning your own business, to escape the impact of downsizing, and many more. You'll also learn what you can do to supplement your retirement income, including providing services, selling products, or manufacturing simple products, all for big profits and in many instances from the comfort of your home.

Of course, the $64,000 question that everyone wants answered is, "How much money can I earn?" It varies, but I'll help you to determine your income wants and needs, and throughout the book, I'll provide you with the information and tools you need to meet—and exceed—your income goals. I'll also help you to find a good business match, taking into consideration issues such as doing something that you love, capitalizing on your current skills and knowledge, using the amount of money you have to get started, and allowing for your health as well as your short- and long-term business and income goals.

You'll also learn about business options, such as starting a business from scratch, buying an operating business, or purchasing a franchise or business opportunity, and the advantages and disadvantages of each. Just think, you will discover all of this valuable information to put you on the path to successfully supplementing your retirement income, and that's just in the first chapter alone!

Legal and Financial Issues

When starting or buying a business, there are always lots of tough legal and financial issues that need to be demystified and satisfied. So to help, you will learn how to register a business name and select a legal business structure—sole proprietorship, partnership, limited liability corporation, or corporation—that best meets your needs. You'll also find out what licenses and permits are needed to start and operate your business, and how and where these can be obtained. Do you need insurance to sell products and services? In most instances, yes. So you will learn what insurance coverage is needed to best protect your assets and where you can get it.

It also takes money to start or buy a business, and I'll show you how to calculate how much money will be needed, what funding sources are available to you, and how you can get started on a shoestring budget. Money management issues are discussed. You will learn how to set up your books, work with accountants and bookkeepers, and open commercial bank accounts. You will also discover how to establish merchant accounts so you can provide your customers with convenient payment options, including credit cards, debt cards, and electronic money transfers.

Business Planning

A business can only be as strong as the research and planning that goes into it right from the start. To establish a rock-solid business foundation on which to build, you will find out how to develop a business plan in step-by-step detail, one that can be used to secure start-up funding, and also act as a road map to guide your new business and marketing strategies so you can minimize financial risks while maximizing the potential for success and profitability. Who is your target customer? In this book, you will learn how to identify your target customers—who they are, where they live, how many there are, how they make buying decisions, and how to build lifelong selling relationships with all of them.

Depending on your venture, your business and marketing plans do not have to be highly sophisticated. Even a few well-researched and documented pages covering the basics are often sufficient to reveal the information you need to describe your business, identify your customers, reveal your product's or service's advantages, develop your sales goals and marketing strategies, and create your action plan. To assist in this endeavor, information is provided in a workbook format requiring you to answer critical business and marketing questions. Your responses can be used to develop a basic business and marketing plan to help reach your business and income goals.

Setting-Up Shop

Every business also needs a base of operations to work from, and in Chapter 4, you will learn how to select the right operating location for your business; home-based, office, and storefront locations are discussed along with the pros and cons of each. An operating location can also be on the web, so I'll show you what you need to know to get on the internet and start doing business there. Topics such as building your web site, selecting the right domain name, and registering with search engines are covered. Once you have chosen your operating location, you also need to know what type of equipment and technology is needed and how to organize your workspace so that you can maximize efficiency and productivity; these topics are discussed in detail.

Setting up shop means building a team to help operate your business for its greatest success and profit. Your business team can include family members, employees, professional services, sales agents, suppliers, subcontractors, and business alliances. I'll teach you how to build the best business team possible. You also have to create a business image, one that over time and with consistent use causes people to visually identify your image with your business and the products and services you sell (referred to as branding).

Sales and Marketing

The lifeblood of every business is sales and marketing. Think of it as oxygen; businesses simply cannot survive without it. In fact, sales and marketing is so important that I have dedicated an entire chapter to it, with information that has been specifically developed for the retirement business owner. You will soon discover what is required to market and sell your products and services like a seasoned pro and be privy to secrets that top sales professionals use daily to qualify buyers, control negotiations, close sales, and get a landslide of referral business. I'll also show you how to sell your products and services from home, from a retail storefront, and wholesale or on-consignment. And don't forget about the internet, especially when e-commerce sales are expected to reach $230 billion by 2008! I'll show you how to get online and start doing business.

There are also a great number of excellent selling opportunities in every community—trade shows, consumer shows, flea markets, and craft fairs, and you'll learn what is needed to sell your products and services at these events for maximum profitability. Amazing advertising secrets will show you how to write great copy, create attention-grabbing newspaper ads, get on the radio, and create red-hot fliers to promote your products and services. You will also learn how to use public relations tools such as news releases, talk radio, and community publicity to secure free and valuable publicity in print, on air, and on the web.

Everything Else You Need to Know

Face it. There is a lot you need to know about starting and operating a successful and profitable business, especially if you're a first-time entrepreneur. My goal is to make sure that you know it all, so that you will not only meet your business and income goals but also exceed them. To that end, I have specifically created a chapter covering a few of the more important business issues not covered in other chapters. You will learn about the importance of providing great customer service, being reliable, being flexible when your customers need you to be, and showing your customers that you really appreciate their business. Standing behind your products and services is also important. Inside you'll discover what you need to know about providing ironclad product and service guarantees, and how to develop a return, refund, and cancellation policy.

Of course, to make a profit you need to know how to determine your pricing strategy and calculate pricing formulas. I'll show you how. Because you always want to get paid in full and on time for products and services, I have included information that will teach you how to secure deposits, process payments, and establish credit accounts for commercial customers. You will also discover information about product packaging, product delivery, and inventory management, as well as a host of other helpful information, ideas, and tips that have been specifically developed to put you well on the path to success and profitability.

The Best 202 Ways to Supplement Your Retirement Income

Now get ready to earn big profits. An entire chapter is devoted to informing you about the best 202 ways to supplement your retirement income—selling products, providing services, or manufacturing simple products. This information includes a complete description of each business or moneymaking opportunity, the skill level needed to operate the business, how to effectively market and sell the product or service, and how much income you can expect to earn. You will also find hundreds of valuable resources throughout the book, which have been included to take you to the next level. The resources featured include American, Canadian, and international private corporations, business associations, government agencies, individuals, web sites, publications, products, services, and lots more.

All of the resources featured include web links, telephone numbers, and mailing addresses that were active at the time of writing. Over time, however, some information changes or is no longer available. In an effort to ensure resource information remains beneficial and active for the long term, I have endeavored to find reputable businesses, organizations, publications, and individuals to feature as resources. But featuring a resource in this book is by no means an endorsement of the company, organization, product, or service. It is the responsibility of all entrepreneurs to do their own due diligence to make sure they are doing business with reputable firms and individuals, and purchasing quality products and services.

Resource icons used represent the following:

- ♂ A mouse icon represents an online resource web site address.
- ☎ A telephone icon represents a resource's contact telephone number.
- 📖 A book icon represents a book or other publication that offers further information.
- ☆ A star icon represents a franchise or business opportunity.

■　　■　　■

202 Ways to Supplement Your Retirement Income is the most authoritative and comprehensive book available on its topic. It gives you the ability to identify the best ways for *you* to supplement your retirement income, as well as the information and tools you need to get started right now. Harness the power of this book by putting it to work for you today.

CHAPTER

1

GETTING STARTED

Why might you need or want to supplement your preretirement or postretirement income? There are a host of reasons—necessity, desire, health, or just because. Any reason to start a business is a good one. It's up to you.

Reasons to Supplement Your Retirement Income

The best place to start is to determine why you want to or need to supplement your retirement income. A discussion of the 11 most common reasons follows.

1. **YOU WANT TO KEEP UP WITH INFLATION.** Retirement businesses have become extremely popular these days because the cost of living has dramatically increased, often outpacing retirement wages and savings. The cost of energy is soaring; the cost of housing is soaring; the cost of food is soaring. The result is lots of people heading into retirement who need to supplement their incomes to cover expenses. Starting your own business is a great way to safeguard against present and future inflationary pressures.

2. **YOU WANT TO MAINTAIN YOUR PRERETIREMENT LIFESTYLE.** Having to do without "things" that you are use to can be a tough pill to swallow. A common denominator for most retired people is that they have had to cut back on activities like vacations, meals out, and new clothing to be able to afford to stay retired. Starting a business and earning extra income helps you to supplement your income so that you can maintain your preretirement lifestyle and not have to do without after retirement.

3. **YOU HAVE ALWAYS DREAMED OF OWNING YOUR OWN BUSINESS.** If you are like many people close to or at retirement age, you have probably spent the better part of your adult life putting the needs of others (spouses, children, and parents) ahead of your own dreams and ambitions. Life is not a dress rehearsal, and you only get one kick at the big can. If you have always dreamed of owning your own business, don't let your age deter you. There is never a better time than right now to get started.

4. **YOU HAVE BEEN LAID OFF.** It's no secret that manufacturing, technology, and middle management jobs are disappearing to cheaper labor markets overseas at an alarming rate. It doesn't really matter what you call it—laid-off, downsized, forced retirement, bought out, or flat out fired because of restructuring—thousands of workers are being sent packing every day in North America. And, guess what? The older you are, the harder it is to find new work and rebound financially. Starting a business enables you to take control of your future and gain financial security, without having to worry about the next pink slip.

5. **YOU DIDN'T SAVE IN YOUR YOUNGER YEARS.** If you only knew then what you know now, what changes would you have made? If you didn't save for retirement in your younger years, you're not alone. Millions of people living in the United States and Canada are in the same boat. Perhaps it wasn't a case of not saving money, but rather you couldn't save any extra money because you were too busy raising kids, paying bills, and funding college educations. Don't worry. The purpose of this

book is to show you what you can do to supplement your retirement income and how to get started.

6. You want extra money to pay for travel and recreational pursuits. You have worked hard. Now it's time to travel and pursue other recreational activities, but there is a problem—you do not have enough retirement income to cover the costs of traveling or other activities. Starting a part-time or seasonal business to earn extra income is a fantastic way to fund your pastimes. In fact, many innovative retired entrepreneurs have learned how to combine business with travel and work their way across the country enjoying their retirement the entire time. Stay a while in any RV park, and you will soon discover many people who sell products at flea markets, online, and through community events, as well as provide services as handypersons or instructors. They fund their retirement and travel at their own pace and on their own schedules—while stopping to take in the sights and make new friends along the way.

7. You want to help your children or grandchildren financially. Helping your children and grandchildren is an excellent reason why you might want to earn additional postretirement income—providing you are not supporting a 35-year-old child still living at home with no gumption to work. In that case, it's time for some tough love and a stiff kick in the butt to get him or her out the door. Getting an education, buying a house, and looking after a young family are not cheap pursuits. If you want to help out your children so their lives are easier than yours was at their age, then starting a postretirement business is one way to accomplish that without having to strain your fixed retirement income.

8. You want to pay off debt. Getting rid of debt quickly is always a good idea, but this can be very hard to do if you are trying to pay off debts on a fixed retirement income. Earning extra income from a business is a great way to quickly pay off debt from a mortgage, a car loan, or credit cards. Even if you only earn an additional $200 per week, that adds up to a whopping $10,400 per year that can be used to pay down and pay off debts, and this does not even include the money you'll save in interest charges by ridding yourself of debt before the loan is due.

9. You want to stay active. The days of sitting on a porch in a rocking chair growing old are long gone. People are living longer and are much healthier now than in decades past. Because of this, many are seeking new challenges, and starting and operating a business is a fantastic way to stay active physically and mentally. It's true that you're only as old as you let yourself be. Staying active as you grow older is proven to extend longevity, benefit your physical fitness, benefit your mental fitness, and, more importantly, lead to overall good health, all of which means a better quality of life as the years progress. You can't halt time by staying active, but you sure can slow it down.

10. YOU WANT TO BUILD WEALTH. There is absolutely nothing wrong with being motivated to build wealth. Starting a retirement business is an excellent way to reach your financial goals, especially if you already have sufficient retirement income to pay your personal expenses so that the profits the business earns can be reinvested into expanding the business, building holdings, or adding to real estate investments. Building wealth is good because money can be used to support charities and the arts, passed on to your children, or used to raise your own standard of living.

11. AND FINALLY . . . BECAUSE YOU CAN. One of the biggest benefits and privileges of living in a democratic and free enterprise society is the fact that no one can tell you that you cannot start and operate a business and earn income. It is your right to do so if you please. *Remember, freedom and democracy do not have a mandatory retirement age.* I believe this to be one of the strongest arguments for supplementing your retirement income—because you can!

What Can You Do to Supplement Your Retirement Income?

Obviously, you can get a job working for someone else to add to your income. That's a viable option for many people. But, this book is not about how to land a job or employment options for people 50-plus. It is about being self-employed and generating your own income to supplement your retirement income. Your options here are:

1. Start a business providing services.
2. Start a business buying products wholesale and reselling them for a profit or buying secondhand products at dirt-cheap prices and reselling them for a profit.
3. Start a business manufacturing and selling products.

You also need to decide if you should start a business, buy a currently operating business, or buy a franchise or business opportunity. The advantages and disadvantages of each are discussed later in this chapter.

Provide a Service

The first option is to provide a service(s). The best aspect about providing a service is that everyone is qualified. We all have a skill, knowledge, or experience that other people are willing to pay for as a service or as to teach them. Providing services knows no boundaries—anyone with a need or desire to earn extra income can sell a service, regardless of age, business experience, education, or current financial resources. In Chapter 7, which discusses possible businesses, you will find many services that you can provide to earn extra income, everything from starting a handyperson service to starting a small business support service, and lots of opportunities in between. Selling service is a great option because in many instances the initial investment to get started adds up to little more than printing business cards and doing a bit of advertising. If selling a service appeals to you and you would like even more ideas than are featured in Chapter 7, pick up a copy of 📖 *202 Services You Can Make and Sell for Big Profits* (Entrepreneur Press, 2005).

Sell Products

The second option is to purchase new products, such as sunglasses, clothing, fashion accessories, furniture, or gifts, in bulk and at wholesale prices and resell these for a profit from home, online, at flea markets, from mall kiosks and vending carts, or from a commercial storefront. You might also choose to purchase secondhand products, such as furniture, antiques, collectibles, cars, restaurant equipment, or books, at bargain basement prices by scouring garage sales, flea markets, business closeouts, auction sales, and private seller classified ads and resell these items for a profit utilizing many of the same venues where they were purchased. Like providing a service, selling new or used products knows no boundaries. Everyone is qualified, regardless of age, experience, education, and financial resources. If buying and selling products appeals to you and you would like even more ideas than are featured in Chapter 7, pick up a copy of 📖 *202 Things You Can Buy and Sell for Big Profits* (Entrepreneur Press, 2004)

Manufacture Products

The third option for supplementing your retirement income is to manufacture and sell a product at retail prices directly to consumers or at wholesale prices and in bulk directly to other businesses such as retailers, exporters, wholesalers, and distributors. I know this sounds like a broken record, but once again, everyone is qualified because we all know or can quickly learn how to make something that can be sold for a profit. Ideally, you want to capitalize on your skills and knowledge and turn a hobby such as making woodcrafts or quilting into a profitable business. However, with basic training, there are literally hundreds of products that can easily be made at home and sold for big profits, including candles, soap, toys, clothing, art, jewelry, furniture, garden products, herbs, birdhouses, and picture frames. If manufacturing products appeals to you and you would like more ideas than are featured in Chapter 7, pick up a copy of 📖 *202 Things You Can Make and Sell for Big Profits!* (Entrepreneur Press, 2005).

Advantages of Starting and Operating Your Own Business

There are many advantages associated with starting your own business, regardless of the type of business. Perhaps the biggest advantage is you become your own boss, take control of your future, and in effect become the master of your destiny. With careful planning, you can get started on a minimal investment, work from the comforts of home, and, in many instances, benefit from numerous tax advantages.

Minimal Investment

The majority of moneymaking opportunities featured in this book only require a minimal investment to get started. In fact, there are many income-producing opportunities listed in Chapter 7 that can be started for only a few thousand dollars in total investment, yet have excellent growth and income potential. Because you can start a business with a minimal investment, you only take minimal financial risks should business plans not come to fruition. The old adage "nothing ventured, nothing gained," is as true today as the day it was coined. Remember, too, if you can start a business that you enjoy, with the potential to earn what you want started on a minimal investment, do it. Save the rest of your money, or use it for something you want—travel or a convertible.

Work from Home

Another big benefit of starting your own business is that there are hundreds of ways to supplement your retirement income working right from the comforts of home. Many of these opportunities are listed in Chapter 7. Income earning opportunities exist selling products online, operating a homebased bookkeeping service, teaching computers, cooking, or fitness classes from your home, operating a dog-grooming service, or making and selling soap, candles, and wind chimes, and there are lots more. Other benefits of a homebased business operation include no commute and saving money by making the most out of existing resources. After all, why pay store or office rent along with extra utilities, telephone, and maintenance costs if you don't have to? I have worked mainly from home for many years. I highly recommend it if it suits your plans.

Tax Advantages

Operating a legal small business also has numerous tax advantages, whether it is part time, full time, or operated only seasonally. This is true even if you are earning income from other retirement sources. And it is especially true if you operate the business from home. Ultimately, these tax advantages will leave more money in your pocket at the end of the year and less in Uncles Sam's. For instance, if you operate a business from home, a portion of your utility bill is tax deductible against business revenues, a portion of home maintenance and yearly property tax bill is also tax deductible, and a portion of your transportation costs equal to the percentage that your car is used for business is tax deductible. Likewise, if you were to combine travel and business, such as selling products at flea markets across the country, then many of your RV expenses, such as a portion of your fuel bill, park fees, and insurance and maintenance, would be tax deductible against business revenues. Of course, before you get started, consult with an accountant to find out exactly what expenses are legitimate business deductions. I am sure you will be pleasantly surprised by the long list.

The Amount of Extra Income You Can Earn

You can have as much extra income as you need or want to supplement your postretirement income or replace your preretirement income. Operating your own business, even a small part-time business, gives you the potential to make as much income as you need and as much income as you want. Why? Simple duplication. When you work for someone else, there is only you and only so many hours in the day to work for a wage. When you operate a business, you can duplicate yourself and hire employees to sell more products and services. You also have the ability to duplicate your customers and find more just like them to purchase your products and services, and you can even duplicate your business model and open in new geographical areas to sell more products and services to more customers and earn more profits and income. Without question, there are upper limits to how much money you can earn operating a small business and other factors such as health issues and economic pressures that can affect income potential. But at the same time, your ability to earn an above average income will be determined by your ambition and motivation, and not by punching a time clock trading hours for a wage.

Income Needs and Wants

You must determine very early on how much extra income you need to earn, as well as how much extra income you want to earn. This is important because it will probably have a bearing on the type of business you ultimately start. If you need to earn $50,000 per year to pay your personal expenses, there is little sense in starting a seasonal garden tilling service if that will be your only source of income. Perhaps there are garden tilling services earning this much, but it is not a realistic expectation. Therefore, the business you choose must have the potential to generate the income you need to earn.

How much money do you want to earn, that is, how ambitious are you? Again, you must be realistic and be relatively sure that the products or services you sell have the potential to generate enough income to live on in the short term and also have the potential to match your income goals in the longer term. Income does not have to factor into the business start-up equation for everyone. If you want and need to earn only a little money from a part-time business, income will not factor into your decision equation as heavily as other issues.

Internet Profits

Another topic worth discussing in terms of income potential is the internet, which gives entrepreneurs access to a global audience of buying consumers. The internet has made it easier for the small business owner to market and sell products and services in the global marketplace utilizing online sales venues such as eBay, internet malls, affiliate programs, and e-storefronts, as well as your own web site. Only a decade ago, selling products and services outside of a specific geographic location (close to one's base of operations) was not a option for most small business owners because of the amount of time and the costs associated with penetrating and managing far off markets. Now with the simple click of a mouse, you can promote and sell your products and services to consumers worldwide, offering the opportunity to make more sales and earn more income. As e-commerce continues to expand, it provides entrepreneurs, regardless of age, an excellent opportunity to earn extra income selling products and services online.

Picking a Time Commitment

How many hours, and how often, do you want to work to supplement your postretirement income or replace your preretirement income altogether? Of course, each person's answer will differ, based on his or her needs and wants. However, before you do decide how you will supplement or replace your income, you have to determine what time commitment is right for you—part time, full time, or seasonal.

Part-Time Commitment

The first option is to start off on a part-time basis, which is a good idea because it enables you to eliminate risk by limiting your financial investment. It also allows you to test the waters to make sure that being self-employed is something you enjoy and want to pursue. If all goes well, you may decide to transition from your current job (if you have one), devoting more time to your new enterprise each week while decreasing the time at your current job until you are working at your new business on a part- or full-time basis, depending on your goal. There are many advantages to starting part-time, including keeping income rolling in (if applicable), taking advantage of any current health and employee benefits, and building your business over a longer period of time, which generally gives it a more stable foundation. If it turns out you are not the type of person who is comfortable being the boss, you have risked little and still have the security of your job (if applicable). Of course, if your ambitions are only to generate enough extra money to supplement your post retirement income every month, help pay down debts, travel, or help out the kids financially, a part-time business venture selling products or services is the perfect choice.

Full-Time Commitment

You can also jump in with both feet and start your new business full time. This option would appeal to people without a current job or people who really want to add substantial income. There is nothing wrong with starting off full time, especially if you take the time required to research the business, industry, and marketplace. You must also develop a business and marketing plan and have the necessary financial resources to start the business and pay yourself until the business becomes profitable.

The main downside to starting off full time is risk. If you jump ship and leave your job (if applicable), you risk loss of current employee benefits and have no guarantee of steady income, contributing spouses or partners excluded. The upside to starting off full time is potential rewards, including the opportunity to make more money than you can at your current job and to gain control of your future. Your decision to operate your new business on a full-time basis will largely be determined by your current financial situation, your own risk-reward assessment, and your goals and objectives for the future.

Seasonal Commitment

Another option is to start a seasonal business selling products and services which can be operated with a full- or part-time effort. But most are run full time to maximize income over a normally short season. Seasonal businesses include flea market vending, garden tilling, snow plowing, traveling RV handyperson, and yard maintenance. But just about any business can be run seasonally, although some are obviously better suited than others.

A seasonal venture appeals to people who want the ability to earn enough money during part of the year in order to do as they please with the remainder of the year—travel, pursue an education, or look after the grandkids. The main downside to a seasonal business, especially one that can be operated year around, is that you do not want to spend thousands of dollars and hundreds of hours promoting your business only to shut it down for half the year, sending customers running to your competitors. It may well be very difficult to lure them back when you reopen for business.

Finding a Good Match

You must be well suited to operating the business you are considering. In other words, the business and you must be a good match. You may have an interest and even experience in a specific business selling a product, providing a service, or making and selling a product, but that does not necessarily make it a good match. There are many points to consider about matches, including what you love, your skills and knowledge, the amount of capital you have to invest, your health, and the investment that you need to make in specialized and ongoing training, certificates, and education. All of these topics are discussed below, and many are discussed in greater detail throughout the book.

Do What You Love

What you get out of your business in the form of personal satisfaction, financial gain, stability, and enjoyment will be the direct result of what you put into your business. If you do not enjoy what you are doing, in all likelihood that will be reflected in the success of your business—or subsequent lack of success. All successful business owners share a common trait—they love what they do. For example, if you enjoy working with your hands, consider making a product; if you love dogs, start a pet sitting service; or if you love to cook, start a catering service. The old adage "Do what you love and the money will follow" is great advice, especially when combined with solid research and planning. Ultimately, if you do not think that you would enjoy it, then don't start. You can't stay motivated and rise to new challenges if you do not like what you're doing.

Capitalize on Your Skills and Knowledge

The first thing you should know about capitalizing on your skills and knowledge is not to worry if you lack business skills and experience in areas such as personal-contact selling, bookkeeping, or creating effective advertisements. These are important skills to have, but they are also skills that can be learned and mastered. More important is the question, "What specific skill(s) or specialized knowledge do you have that can be used for your benefit and, ultimately, financial gain?" Skills and knowledge that you possess are your best and by far your most marketable asset. If you know how to plan and throw one heck of a party, that is a skill that people are willing to pay you for as their event and party planner. If you know how to build fine furniture, that is skill needed to make a product that people will pay for. If you have knowledge about the value of antiques, that is a skill that can be used to buy antiques cheap and resell them for a profit.

Every person has one or more skills that other people are prepared to pay for in the form of a service or a product they want. Most people, of course, have a tendency to underestimate the true value of their skill sets, experiences, and knowledge. You have to remember that what comes naturally to you may not come so naturally to others. And although you might think that your particular knowledge or expertise has little value, someone who needs or wants to learn about that knowledge, have that service, or buy that product finds it very valuable.

Investment Capital

A very important issue to consider in terms of finding a good match is the investment capital needed to start. Do you have the financial resources needed to start or purchase the business and enough money to pay the day-to-day operating bills until the business is profitable? If not, it is probably not a good match and you should consider alternatives. Investment capital must be broken into two categories: start-up capital and working capital. Start-up capital is needed to purchase equipment, rent a business premise, buy office furniture, meet legal requirements, and pay for training or purchase a business. Working capital is perhaps even more important because it's the money needed to pay the bills and wages until the business reaches a break-even point. More than a few entrepreneurs have failed in business because lack of operating capital prevented the business from reaching positive cash flow. Thus, the amount of money you have to invest is an important element when finding a good business match. More information about financing your business can be found in Chapter 2.

Health

Your health is also a major consideration to finding a good business match. Are you healthy enough to handle the physical strains of starting and running the business? If not, you may end up having to hire people for the job, which can be problematic if the business revenues are not there to support management and employee wages. Of course, some businesses require a higher degree of good health and physical fitness than others. But if you do not feel well physically and mentally, it is very difficult to be creative, efficient, productive, and stay motivated in any business. I would give great importance to finding a good match in terms of your health because this is a topic many potential entrepreneurs fail to consider.

Invest in You

Successful entrepreneurs, regardless of age, share a common denominator that transcends all types of business ventures and every industry sector—they never stop investing in products, services, information, and education that will make them better, smarter, and more productive businesspeople. Investing in you makes up part of finding a good match. I say this because you should not overlook otherwise good business and moneymaking opportunities just because specialized training or certification is needed to start and operate the business. Every dollar you invest in educational activities and tools that are geared to making you more productive and innovative in business and marketing will pay back tenfold or more. This is a time-tested and proven concept. These types of investments give you an advantage in today's extremely competitive global business environment.

Top entrepreneurs buy and read business and marketing books, magazines, reports, journals, newsletters, and industry publications, knowing that these resources will improve their understanding of business and marketing. They join business associations and clubs and network with other skilled businesspeople to learn their secrets of success and help define their own goals and objectives. Top entrepreneurs attend business and marketing seminars, workshops, and training courses, even if they have already mastered the subject matter. They do this because they know that education is an ongoing process that never ends. There are always ways to do things better, in less time, and with less effort. They also invest in equipment and technology to improve their business and marketing efficiency. In short, top entrepreneurs never stop investing in the most powerful, effective, and best business and marketing tools at their immediate disposal—themselves.

Your Business Options

There are three ways of going into business: starting a business from scratch, buying an operating business, or purchasing a franchise or business opportunity. Each option has advantages and disadvantages. Which works best for you is ultimately determined by factors such as your investment criteria, income needs, and health, as well as by your short-term and long-term business and personal goals.

Starting a Business

The majority of people, regardless of age, choose to start a business from scratch. There are many advantages to choosing this path. Depending on the venture, operating location, and equipment needs, less money is usually needed. In fact, it is possible to start a business that has good growth and profit potential for an intial investment of less than $10,000. Additionally, starting a business from scratch allows you to have full control and independence; most franchises and some business opportunities impose strict management and reporting guidelines. When you start a business, you can choose the time commitment that works best for you—part time, full time, or seasonal. That flexibility can be difficult to achieve when buying a business or franchise.

There are also disadvantages to starting a business from scratch. Unfortunately, positives like low initial investment, little regulation, and quick start-up can also spell big trouble. Why? Because you can literally have a business start-up idea today and be open for business tomorrow, which leaves little, if any, time for two business essentials—research and planning. And unlike an operating business, start-ups have no existing revenues to help pay for or offset fixed operating costs. You have to build the business to profitability from scratch. Finally, unlike purchasing a franchise or existing business, there is also no road map that clearly identifies the steps needed to get the business started, operational, manageable, and profitable.

In addition to the 202 business and moneymaking ideas featured in Chapter 7, you might also want to sign out a copy of 📖 *Entrepreneur's Ultimate Start-Up Directory* (Entrepreneur Press, 2001) from the library. The book contains information about 1,350 business start-up ideas. The U.S. Small Business Administration (SBA), 🖝 www.sba.gov, and the Canadian Business Service Center, 🖝 www.cbsc.org, provide information, products, services, and programs to assist new business start-ups.

Buying a Business

The second option is to purchase an existing business, one that has customers and is generating revenues. Buying a business is perhaps the better choice for people who want instant results and do not want to invest the extra time required to start a business from scratch. Certainly, as people get older, they may be less inclined or able to wait a few years before they see profitability. If you choose this route, planning and research still has to go into finding the right business to buy. Perhaps even more is necessary. Buying an operating business usually means investing a larger amount of money, warranting careful research and planning to minimize financial risk. You still need to research the marketplace, create a target customer profile, identify competitors, and develop business and marketing plans just as you would for any business venture. A big advantage of purchasing an operating business is that you can often negotiate terms, meaning you can pay a portion of the purchase price up front and the balance in installments or balloon payments. This gives you the ability to pay the installments out of business revenues. In effect, you will actually be purchasing the business for no more than your down payment.

Before buying any business, however, make sure to hire a lawyer to go over the purchase agreement and an accountant to review all of the financial statements and conduct a business valuation. These precautions are especially important when larger sums of money are at stake. Also make sure do your own investigative work by talking to current customers, employees, suppliers, and the local Better Business Bureau. Make sure all agreements and contracts with clients, suppliers, and manufacturers are transferable and stay with the business, not the exiting owner. It is also a good idea to have the current owner stay on after the transfer for a reasonable amount of time to train you and help in the transition. Finally, make sure that you have a noncompetition clause built into the sale agreement. Noncompetition clauses prevent the previous owner from starting a similar type of business or selling similar goods and services within a set geographic area, generally within the same state, and for a fixed period of time, which can range from one to ten years.

If you decide to buy an operating business, you can search for suitable candidates in a number of ways, including through real estate agents, by scanning business-for-sale advertisements in newspapers, and by visiting Biz Buy Sell, ♂ www.bizbuysell.com, which is billed as the internet's largest business-for-sale portal, with over 20,000 listings. You can also contact The International Business Brokers Association, ♂ www.ibba.org, which has links to more than 1,100 independent business brokers around the world.

Buying a Franchise

The third option is to purchase a franchise or business opportunity, which can cost anywhere from a low of a few hundred dollars for a basic business opportunity to well into the seven-figure range for an internationally known franchise. A franchise is perhaps a better option for people who want a proven management system, initial and ongoing training and support, and the benefits associated with branding on a large scale. With a franchise operation, you usually have the combined strength of many franchisees as opposed to the possible weaknesses of one independent small business. The combined strengths can help lower costs on goods and services, as well as reach a broader audience through collective advertising. Unfortunately, there are also disadvantages associated with purchasing a franchise. When you own and operate a franchise, you have less control and independence in all areas of your business than you do in an independent business. One of the key doctrines of the franchise model is conformity through consistent brand management. Consequently, if you are the independent type, you might find operating a franchise to be more like managing someone else's business.

If you do decide to purchase a franchise, you have to take the same precautions that you would when starting or purchasing any business. Do your research and plan. Visit and talk to other franchisees to get firsthand feedback about the business, franchisor, and management systems, and become a customer to make sure that you like and believe in the products or services being sold. Conduct your own market research to make sure that the local market will support the franchise and that the franchisor's research, statements, and forecasts are accurate. Finally, always enlist the services of a franchise lawyer to go over the franchisor's Uniform Franchise Offering Circular to decipher the legalese for you and help guide you through the purchase and setup process.

In Chapter 7, I have included many franchise and business opportunity resources. You can also contact the International Franchise Association, ♂ www.franchise.org, or the Canadian Franchise Association, ♂ www.cfa.ca. Both organizations can provide information to help you find a franchise that is right for you.

2

LEGAL AND FINANCIAL ISSUES

When starting or buying a business, there are always lots of legal and financial issues to consider and satisfy: registering a business name, selecting a legal business structure, obtaining a business license and sales tax ID number, shopping for insurance coverage, opening a commercial bank account, and preparing and filing business and income tax returns. Money spent on professional advice when dealing with legal and financial issues is always money well spent, especially if your business plans include a substantial investment of money and time. Lawyers with small-business experience will be able to advise and help make sense of complicated matters, such as which legal business structure best meets your specific needs, insurance and liability issues, drafting of legal documents, supplier agreements, and many other legal issues. Likewise, accountants will decipher the tough financial information you need to know in order to comply with state and federal tax issues, as well as help establish and maintain financial record-keeping. In this chapter, you will learn about legal business structure options, business license and permits, insurance, business financing, banking, and money management.

Legal Business Structure Options

From a legal standpoint, the starting point is to choose and register a business name and to select a business structure—sole proprietorship, partnership, limited liability corporation, or corporation. Budget, business goals, and personal liability issues will be determining factors for most entrepreneurs when selecting a business structure. Many people choose a sole proprietorship if they are on a tight budget and comfortable with liability issues. A partnership is the right choice if you will be running your new business with a spouse, family member, or friend. A limited liability corporation (LLC) or corporation will be the right choice if your plans include expansion and you want to minimize personal liability concerns.

Business Name Registration

Regardless of the legal structure you choose, you need to select and register a business name. You can name the business after your legal name, such as Wendy's Window Fashions, or you can choose a fictitious business name, such as Fabulous Window Fashions. When naming your business, it is important to remember that your business name will promote your business and be used regularly in print and conversation. Therefore, your business name should be descriptive so that it becomes an effective marketing tool. It should also be short, easy to spell, easy to pronounce, and very memorable. You have to think visual impact and word-of-mouth referral; both rely on short, easy-to-spell-and-remember, descriptive names. Keep your business name geographically universal so that you do not limit growth potential. Your business name should also convey the image you want to project. For instance, if you sell high-end window fashions, a name such as Exquisite Window Fashions is suitable. Conversely, if you cater to budget-minded consumers, Low-Cost Window Fashions is suitable.

Business registration costs vary by state and province, but generally, they are less than $200 to register a sole proprietorship, including name search fees. Normally, you have to show proof of business registration in order to establish commercial bank accounts, buy products wholesale, and secure credit card merchant accounts. So there are no shortcuts; you have to register your business. In the United States, you can register your business name through the Small Business Administration (SBA). Log on to ♂ www.sba.org to find an office near you. In Canada you can register your business through a provincial Canadian Business Service Center. Log on to ♂ www.cbsc.org to find an office near you.

Sole Proprietorship

The most common legal business structure is the sole proprietorship, mainly because it is the simplest and least expensive to start and maintain. A sole proprietorship means your business entity and your personal affairs are merged as one—a single tax return, personal liability for all accrued business debts and actions, and control of all revenues and profits. But it is still important to separate your business finances from your personal finances for record-keeping and income tax purposes. The biggest advantage of a sole proprietorship is that it is very simple and inexpensive to form and can be started, altered, bought, sold, or closed at any time, quickly and inexpensively. And, outside of routine business registrations, permits, and licenses, there are few government regulations. The biggest disadvantage of a sole proprietorship is that you are 100 percent liable for any number of business activities gone wrong. This can mean losing any and all personal assets, including investments and real estate, as a result of successful litigation or debts accrued by the business.

Partnership

Another popular type of low-cost legal business structure is a partnership, which allows two or more people to start, operate, and own a business. Even if you choose to start a business with a family member or friend, make sure the partnership is based on a written partnership agreement, not just a verbal agreement. The agreement should address issues such as financial investment, profit distribution, duties of each partner, and exit strategy should one partner want out of the agreement. Like a sole proprietorship, business profits are split amongst partners proportionate to their ownership and are treated as taxable personal income. Perhaps the biggest advantage of a partnership is financial risks and work are shared by more than one person, which allows each partner to specialize within the business for the benefit of the team. Record-keeping requirements are basic and on par with a sole proprietorship. Unfortunately, partnerships also have disadvantages. The most significant is that each partner is legally responsible and personally liable for the other partners' actions in the business; a nonincorporated partnership offers no legal protection from liability issues. All partners are equally responsible for the businesses debts, liabilities, and actions.

Limited Liability Corporation

A limited liability corporation combines many of the characteristics of a corporation with those of a partnership. Like a corporation, it provides protection from personal liabilities, but the tax advantages are those of a partnership. Limited liability corporations can be formed by one or more people, called LLC members, who alone or together organize a legal entity separate and distinct from the owners' personal affairs in most respects. The advantages of a limited liability corporation over a corporation or partnership are that it is less expensive to form and maintain than a corporation, offers protection from personal liability that partnerships do not provide, and has simplified taxation and reporting rules in comparison to a corporation. Because of these advantages, limited liability corporations have become the fastest-growing form of business structure in the United States. In the United States, you can file online using a service such as Corp America, ✆ www.corpamerica.com, or contact the American Bar Association, ☎ (202) 662-1000, ✆ www.abanet.org, to find a lawyer who specializes in corporate filing in your area. In Canada, you can file online using a service such as Canadian Corp, ✆ www.canadiancorp.com, or contact the Canadian Bar Association, ☎ (800) 267-8860, ✆ www.cba.org, to find a lawyer who specializes in corporate filing in your area.

Corporation

The most complicated business structure is the corporation. When you form a corporation, you create a legal entity separate and distinct from the shareholders of the corporation. Because the corporation becomes its own entity, it pays taxes, assumes debt, can legally sue, can be legally sued, and, as a tax-paying entity, must pay taxes on its taxable income (profit) prior to paying any dividends to the shareholders. But the company's finances and financial records are completely separate from those of the shareholders.

The biggest advantage to incorporating your business is that you can greatly reduce your own personal liability. Because a corporation is its own entity, it can legally borrow money and be held legally accountable in a number of matters. In effect, this releases you from personal liability. The major disadvantage is double taxation. Corporation profits are taxed, and then the same profits are taxed again in the form of personal income tax when distributed to the shareholders as a dividend. Unfortunately, the same does not hold true if the corporation loses money.

Financial losses cannot be used as a personal income tax deduction for shareholders. In the United States, you can file online using a service such as Corp America, ✆ www.corpamerica.com, or contact the American Bar Association, ☎ (202) 662-1000, ✆ www.abanet.org, to find a lawyer who specializes in corporate filing in your area. In Canada, you can file online using a service such as Canadian Corp, ✆ www.canadiancorp.com, or contact the Canadian Bar Association, ☎ (800) 267-8860, ✆ www.cba.org, to find a lawyer who specializes in corporate filing in your area.

Licensing and Permits

Whether you are selling antiques from home or operating a nonmedical home care service, you are classified as a business, and all businesses must be licensed. In all probability, you will to need to obtain several licenses and permits, depending on the products and services you sell and how these products and services are sold. At minimum, you will need a business license, a vendor's permit, and if you sell products, a resale certificate or sales tax permit ID number. In addition, you will need professional and trade certificates if your profession or trade is regulated, a health permit if you sell or prepare food, a police clearance certificate if you sell home security services and products, a home occupation permit to work from home in some states, and a building permit if you significantly alter your home to suit your new venture. It should be noted that taking the time to jump through the hoops to obtain the necessary licenses and permits is very important from a legal standpoint, and to buy products wholesale, open commercial bank accounts, open merchant credit card accounts, and to conduct many other business activities.

Business License

To legally operate a business in all municipalities in the United States and Canada, you will need to obtain a business license. Business license costs vary from $50 to $1,000 per year, depending on your geographic location, expected sales, the type of business you are engaged in, and the types of services and products you sell. Because they are issued at the municipal level, contact your city/county clerk's or permits office for the full requirements for a business license. The Small Business Administration (SBA) also provides an online directory indexed by state, outlining where business licenses can be obtained, ✆ www.sba.gov/hotlist/license.html. In the United States and Canada, you can also contact the chamber of commerce to inquire about business license requirements and fees. Contact the chamber in the United States, ✆ www.chamber.com, and in Canada, ✆ www.chamber.ca.

Permits

The name may vary depending on geographic location—resale certificate, sales tax permit, ID number—but whatever you want to call it, you need a permit to collect and remit sales tax if you will be selling any products and even some services. Almost all states and provinces now impose a sales tax on products sold directly to consumers, or end users. It is the business owner's responsibility to collect and remit sales taxes. The same sales tax permits are needed when purchasing goods for resale from manufacturers and wholesalers so the goods can be bought tax-free. (Taxes will be paid by the retail customer when resold.) The SBA provides a directory indexed by state outlining where and how sales tax permits and ID numbers can be obtained, including information on completing and remitting sales tax forms. This directory is located at ♂ www.sba.gov/hotlist/license.html. In Canada, there are two levels of sales tax. One is charged by most provinces on the sale of retail products to consumers and the second is charged by the federal government. The latter is known as the goods and services tax and is charged on the sale of almost all goods and most services. You can obtain a federal Goods and Services Sales/Harmonized Sales Tax (GST/HST) number by contacting the Canada Customs and Revenue Agency at ♂ www.ccra-adrc.gc.ca.

There may be other licenses, permits, certificates, and laws to comply with in terms of starting and operating your business, or selling certain products and services. These might include fire safety inspection permits, hazardous materials handling permits, import/export certificates, police clearance certificates, environmental laws, and laws pertaining to food and drug safety administered through the U.S. Food and Drug Administration (FDA). Keep in mind that the obligation is on the business owner to learn about the laws and regulations that must be followed and the relevant permits and registrations that are required.

Insurance Coverage

Purchasing appropriate insurance is the only way that you can be 100 percent sure that in the event of a catastrophic event, your business, assets, and clients will be protected. Finding the right insurance for your specific needs can be a time-intensive endeavor because of the shear number of insurance companies and coverage types available. Consequently, it makes sense to enlist the services of a licensed insurance agent to do the research and legwork for you. Not only will the agent be able to decipher insurance legalese for you, but she will also be able to find the best coverage for your individual needs and at the lowest cost. To find a suitable insurance agent in the United States, you can contact the Independent Insurance

Agents and Brokers of America at ✆ www.iiaa.org. In Canada, you can contact the Insurance Brokers Association of Canada at ✆ www.ibac.ca. Below a few of the more important types of insurance coverage—property, liability, workers' compensation, and disability are covered.

Property Insurance

Property insurance generally covers buildings and structures on property as well as the contents, regardless of whether you rent or own your business location. Most property insurance policies provide protection in the form of a cash settlement or paid repairs in the event of fire, theft, vandalism, flood, earthquake, wind damage, and other acts of God. Floods and earthquakes generally require a separate insurance rider. Property insurance is the starting point from which business owners should build, branching out to include specialized tools and equipment, office improvements, inventory, and various liability riders depending on what you sell.

As a rule of thumb, property insurance should protect buildings, property, improvements, tools, equipment, furniture, cash on hand, and accounts receivable and payable, as well as restricted liability, discussed in greater detail below. Additionally, special riders will be needed to cover working at your clients' locations as well as tools and equipment in transit to work sites. All insurance companies provide free quotes, but it is wise to obtain at least three so you can compare costs, coverage, deductibles, and reliability. If you are going to run your business from home, make sure to contact your current insurance agent and ask questions specific to the business you will be operating. In most all cases, you will want to increase the value of the contents portion of the policy if you use expensive computer and office equipment in your business, as well as the amount of liability insurance if clients will be visiting your home.

Liability Insurance

No matter how diligent you are in terms of taking all necessary precautions to protect your customers and yourself by removing potential perils from your business and the products and services you sell, you could still be held legally responsible for events beyond your control. Product misuse, third-party damages, and service misunderstandings have all been grounds for successful litigation in the United States and Canada. As the old saying goes, "It's better to be safe than sorry." The best way to protect yourself is to get liability insurance that specifically provides protection for the type of business you operate and the products and services you sell. Extended liability insurance is often referred to as general business liability or umbrella business liability and insures a business against accidents and injury that might occur at the business location, at clients' locations, or other perils related to the products and services sold. General liability insurance provides protection from the costs associated with successful litigation or claims against your business or you and covers such things as medial expenses, recovery expenses, property damage, and other costs typically associated with liability situations.

There are also more specific types of liability insurance protection that some business owners will need in the event of misadventure, especially professional liability insurance. Professional liability insurance, commonly known as errors and omissions insurance, is designed to protect you or your company from the financial losses that might arise if you are sued by a client(s) due to alleged negligence on your part while rendering professional services or advice. In many states and provinces, professional liability insurance is mandatory. Without it, you cannot legally practice. At one time, only practicing professionals such as lawyers, notary publics, certified accountants, and engineers carried professional liability insurance, but it is now commonplace for just about every type of business professional and consultant to carry such insurance. Basically, anyone that charges a fee for advice or professional services should carefully consider obtaining professional liability insurance. American Professional Online, ♂ www.americanprofessional.com, provides visitors with free professional liability quotes.

Workers' Compensation Insurance

In the United States and Canada, workers' compensation insurance is mandatory for all the people your business employs, whether they work full time, part time, or seasonally. Workers' compensation insurance protects employees injured on the job by providing short- or long-term financial benefits as well as covering medical and rehabilitation costs directly resulting from an on-the-job injury. If you have no employees and operate your business as a sole proprietorship or partnership, workers' compensation insurance is not mandatory; unless your business is incorporated, officers and any employees must be covered. Rates are based on industry classification, which generally means the more dangerous the work, the higher your premiums will be. Likewise, the more claims for workers' compensation your business files, the higher your rates will go. Because workers' compensation classifications, forms, and guidelines can be confusing, I would advise you to visit the U.S. Department of Labor Office of Workers' Compensation Programs online at, ♂ www.dol.gov/esa/owcp-org.htm. This web page has links to all states and the District of Columbia, explaining workers' compensation rules and regulations. In Canada, log on to ♂ www.awcbc.org, the Association of

Workers' Compensation Boards of Canada, which provides links to all provincial and territorial offices.

Disability Insurance

Disability insurance is especially important to service providers because often jobs in that area involve physical work. Disability insurance makes payments to you in the event a physical or mental illness or bodily injury prevents you from working. Policy benefits and costs vary, depending on coverage, but regardless of the policy you choose, be sure to have a cost of living clause built into the policy that will increase benefits proportionate to the consumer price index. Also tell your insurance agent that you want your disability coverage to include partial disabilities, which enables you to collect partial benefits while working part time in your business when you cannot return to full-time active duty. And, build in a clause that gives you the right to increase your disability insurance benefits as your business and income grows. This is known as an additional purchase option and can be extended to include key employee disability insurance as well.

Financing Your New Business

How much money do you need to start your business? It depends on the type of business you plan to start, the products and services you will sell, equipment requirements, business location, transportation needs, and marketing. If this is your first foray into business ownership, you should also know there are generally three funding components: start-up, working, and growth capital. All are important and serve a specific function.

Start-up capital is the money used to start a business, buy a business, or buy a franchise. Start-up capital is needed to purchase equipment, rent a business premise, buy office furniture, meet legal requirements, and to pay for training. There are ways of limiting the amount of start-up capital, as you will see later in this section, but you will require some money to start or purchase a business. Working capital is important because it's the money that is needed to pay all the bills and your wages until the business reaches a break-even point. More than a few entrepreneurs have failed because lack of operating capital prevented the business from reaching positive cash flow. Growth capital is the money needed should you decide to expand your business. Even if your plans are not to expand, lack of growth capital can become an issue when forces beyond your control, such as new competition or new government regulations, take effect. You may not want to grow, but forces beyond your control may necessitate growth in your business, if for no other reason just to survive and remain viable. It is not necessary to have growth capital sitting in the bank, but it is a good idea to have a plan in place to access growth capital should the need arise.

Personal Savings

The first way to finance your business venture is by using your own personal cash savings or by cashing in an investment. Self-funding is a good idea for most entre-preneurs because that enables you to stay in control of how, when, and why funds are distributed: You do not have to satisfy a banker's or investor's requirements. You will not feel anxious about whether or not you can get the proper funding. You do not have to worry about debt accumulation; there is no bank or investor loan and interest repayment to make each month. To fund your business start-up personally, the money can come from your bank savings account, investment cer-tificates, retirement funds, mutual funds and stocks, or insurance policies. Keep in mind, though, that in some instances money you remove from fixed certificates or retirement investments may be subject to additional personal income tax or penal-ties for early withdrawal or cancellation. It is always wise to consult with an accountant prior to cashing, selling, or redeeming any personal investment. You can also sell or borrow against other personal assets such as real estate, antiques, or boats to fund your new business. At the end of the day, you will have to decide to what lengths you are prepared to go in personally financing your business ambitions.

Love Loans

Another way to fund your business is to ask family members or friends for a loan. These loans are often referred to as love loans. There is a potential downside to this method of financing: if your business venture were to fail, would you still be able to pay back the loan? If not, the relationship could be damaged beyond repair. That said, many successful business ventures have been built upon love loans. If you decide to borrow from friends or family to fund your business, treat the trans-action as you would if you were borrowing from a bank. Have a promissory note drawn up and signed (see Figure 2.1), noting the details of the agreement.

Bank Loans

Business loans can be secured or unsecured. Secured loans are guaranteed with some other type of investment, such as a guaranteed investment certificate. Unse-cured loans are not backed by any investments or assets, and funds are advanced because of your creditworthiness. The advantage of a secured loan is that the interest rate is generally lower, by as much as 5 percent. The disadvantage of a

FIGURE 2.1: Sample Promissory Note

This loan agreement is by and between:

Borrower Information

Name _____

Address _____

City _____ State _____ Zip Code _____ Tel _____

Lender Information

Name _____

Address _____

City _____ State _____ Zip Code _____ Tel _____

I, (borrower's name here), promise to pay (lender's name here) the sum of $ _____, bearing interest at the rate of _____% per annum, and payable in _____ equal and consecutive monthly installments, commencing on the _____ day of each month until paid, with a final installment of $ _____ on the _____ day of _____, 20_____, upon which the loan shall be repaid in full with no further principal or interest amounts owing.

_____ _____   _____ _____
   Borrower's Signature   Date   Lender's Signature   Date

_____ _____
     Witnessed by   Date

secured loan is that many first-time entrepreneurs do not have investments to secure the loan; otherwise, they would be able to self-finance the start-up. You can also talk to your bank or trust company about setting up a secured or unsecured line of credit. One advantage of a line of credit over a standard business loan is that you only have to repay interest based on the account line balance and not the principal, which is exactly the type of funding flexibility new business start-ups need to get established and grow without the pressure of high-debt repayment. If you decide to seek a business loan or line of credit, go armed with a bulletproof business and marketing plan. Bankers want to know that they are investing in sound and well-researched ideas that have the potential to succeed. Many banks offer entrepreneurs small business loan programs, including Bank of America, ♂ www.bankofamerica.com, and Royal Bank, ♂ www.royalbank.com/sme/.

Government Business Loans

In the United States and Canada, there are government programs in place to assist people starting a new business or to provide growth funding for existing small businesses. In the United States, these programs are administered thought the SBA, ♂ www.sba.gov/financing. In Canada, most small business financial aid and incentive programs are administered through the Business Development Bank of Canada, ♂ www.bdc.ca. Three SBA financial assistance programs are aimed specifically at small business—Business Loans Program, Investment Program, and Bonding Program.

The SBA's Business Loan Program is available to new business enterprises. It provides start-up funds supplied through microlending institutions (participating banks and credit unions) and guaranteed in full or in part by the government. There are various levels of qualification for the Business Loans Program, so check with your local SBA office for more details and to see if you qualify. The SBA's Investment Program supplies new business ventures with funding and existing small- to medium-sized businesses with venture capital that can be used to fuel growth and expansion. There are various programs available and qualifications to meet, so contact your local SBA office for details. Finally, the SBA also offers a Security Bond Guarantee (SBG) program, which provides small and minority contractors with the opportunity to bid on supply and service contracts. Again, contact your local SBA office for details.

United States	*Canada*
U.S. Small Business Administration (SBA)	Business Development Canada
Financial Programs	BDC Building
409 Third Street SW	5 Place Ville Marie, Suite 400
Washington, DC 20416	Montreal, Quebec H3B 5E7
☎ (800) 827-5722	☎ (877) 232-2269
♂ www.sba.gov/financing/	♂ www.bdc.ca

Private Investors

Business start-up funds can also come from private investors, but almost always there are strings attached. Private investors may want an incredibly high rate of interest, an equity interest, or even a controlling interest in the business. They may want to work in the business. Or they may require a combination of these conditions for funding. If you go looking for private investors to help you float your business dream, be prepared to make sacrifices.

If you decide to take in a private investor who wants to remain silent in the business, then a good match between you is of little concern. However, if the investor will be taking a hands-on role in the business, effectively making him or her a partner, there are more issues to consider. You will need a formal partnership agreement, and all parties should share a similar excitement for the business and have similar goals and ambitions. The investor should also have specific experiences and resources that can be utilized in the business.

The most common way that people find investors to help finance a business start-up or expansion is by placing a classified advertisement in their local newspapers or an industry magazine, especially if the deals involve small amounts of money, that is, less than $100,000. There is also a great number of venture capital web sites, such as Venture Directory Online, ♂ www.venturedirectory.com, or V Finance, ♂ www.vfinance.com, listing entrepreneurs or venture capitalists (also known as business angels) who want to invest in new and existing businesses.

Bootstrapping Techniques

There are also bootstrapping techniques that a financially challenged entrepreneur can use to fund a business venture. These include using credit cards, barter, leasing or renting, and supplier terms to help reduce the amount of money initially needed. The obvious drawback to using credit cards is that most have high annual interest rates. But if money is in short supply, and you feel confidant of your business plans, using your credit card may be your only option. If you do, plan early. Try to pay off your credit cards to a zero balance while you are still working so that you are carrying less debt, with lower monthly obligations, and have the opportunity to borrow more money against the cards to start your business. Also, shop for credit cards with the lowest interest charges, no annual fees, and rewards for purchases, such as air miles or redeemable shopping points. I would also suggest that you apply for credit cards that are specifically for small business use, such as the Visa Small Business Card, ♂ www.usa.visa.com/business, or American Express Small Business, ♂ www.americanexpress.com.

Bartering your way into business is yet another option for the more creative entrepreneurial set. Barter clubs for small business owners, such as National Trade Association, ♂ www.ntatrade.com, and First Canadian Barter Exchange, ♂ www.barterfirst.com, have become extremely popular, particularly online barter because all it takes is a click of the mouse. The premise behind barter is basic: You offer the goods or services that you sell in exchange for goods and services that you need to start, operate, or promote your business. Bartering with other businesses will not supply all the money that you need to start and operate your new business, but it can greatly help. Leasing or renting equipment is another strategy that will not completely fund your entire start-up, but can greatly reduce the amount of cash needed upfront. Renting or leasing equipment, tools, or fixtures lets you save your precious money for other business-building activities such as marketing. An additional benefit of renting or leasing equipment is that in most cases rent or lease payments are a 100 percent business expense, as opposed to the sliding scale of depreciation on owned equipment.

The final way to bootstrap your way into business is to ask your suppliers for a revolving credit account that gives you up to 90 days to pay for goods and services you need to start or operate your business, or to resell to customers for a profit. More times than not, however, asking nicely will not work until you have demonstrated to suppliers that you are a worthy credit risk. This is usually accomplished by the supplier conducting a credit check on you or through some sort of security guarantee that you provide. If your credit history is good, in some cases you can establish revolving credit accounts that will give you up to 90 days to pay.

Money Management

Money management can be tricky business because, in addition to customers, cash flow and managing your accounts properly is what keeps you in business. Consequently, money management has to be a priority, even if you elect to hire an accountant or bookkeeper to manage the books. You will still need to familiarize yourself with basic bookkeeping and money management principles and activities such as understanding credit, reading bank statements and tax forms, and making sense of accounts receivable and payable. You also have to give careful consideration to the purchase payment options you offer customers, including cash, checks, debit cards, credit cards, and online payment options, as well as debt collection in the event of nonpayment. All are discussed in further detail below. Information about pricing products and services, as well as establishing pricing policies and terms, can be found in Chapter 6, Everything Else You Need to Know.

Opening a Bank Account

Once you have chosen a name and registered your business, you will need to open a commercial bank account. Setting up a business bank account is easy. Start by selecting the bank you want to work with, think small business friendly, and call to arrange an appointment to open an account. When you go, make sure you take personal identity as well as your business name registration papers and business license because these are usually required to open a commercial bank account. The next step will be to deposit funds into your new account (even $100 is okay). If your credit is sound, also ask the bank to attach a line of credit to your account, which can prove very useful when making purchases for the business or during slow sales periods to cover overheads until business increases. While you are there, also be sure to ask about credit card merchant accounts, debit accounts, and other small business services.

Bookkeeping

When it comes time to set up your financial books, you have two options—do it yourself or hire an accountant or bookkeeper. You might want to do both by keeping your own books and hiring an accountant to prepare year-end financial statements and tax forms. If you opt to keep your own books, make sure you invest in accounting software such as QuickBooks, ♂ www.quickbooks.com, or Quicken, ♂ www.quicken.com, because they are easy to use and make bookkeeping almost enjoyable. Most accounting programs also allow you to create invoices, track bank account balances and merchant account information, and keep track of accounts payable and receivable. If you are unsure about your bookkeeping abilities even with the aid of accounting software, you may wish to hire a bookkeeper to do your books on a monthly basis and a chartered accountant to audit the books quarterly and prepare year-end business statements and tax returns. If you are only pet sitting to earn a few extra dollars, there is little need for accounting software or accountant services. Simply invest in a basic ledger and record all business costs and sales. You have to use a common sense approach when calculating how much to invest in your business versus expected revenues and profits. Also, remember to keep all business and tax records in a dry and secure place for up to seven years. This is the maximum amount of time the IRS and Revenue Canada can request past business revenue and expense information. To find an account or bookkeeper in your area, you can contact the United States Association of Chartered Accountants, ☎ (212) 334-2078, ♂ www.acaus.org, or the American Institute of Professional Bookkeepers, ☎ (800) 622-0121 ♂ www.aipb.com. In Canada, you can contact the Chartered Accountants of Canada, ☎ (416) 977-3222 ♂ www.cica.ca, or the Canadian Bookkeepers Association, ☎ (205) 334-2427 ♂ www.c-b-a.ca.

Accepting Cash, Checks, and Debit Cards

In today's super competitive business environment, you must provide customers with many ways to pay, including cash, debit card, credit card, and electronic cash. There is a cost for providing these payment options—account fees, transaction fees, equipment rental, and merchant fees based on a percentage of the total sales value. These expenses must be viewed as a cost of doing business in the 21st century. Not all banks, merchant accounts, and payment processing services are the same, and fees vary widely. So shop around for service and prices. Also check with small business associations such as the chamber of commerce to see if they offer member discounts. It is not uncommon to save as much as 2 percent on credit card merchant fees, for example. Remember, consumers expect choices when it comes time to pay for their purchases, and if you elect not provide these choices, expect fewer sales.

Cash is the first way to get paid, which is great because it is liquid with no processing time required. As fast as the cash comes in, you can use it to pay bills and invest in business-building activities to increase revenues and profits. The major downside is that cash is risky because you could get robbed or lose it. In such cases, collecting from your insurance company could prove difficult if there is no paper transaction as proof. Even if you prefer not to receive cash, there are people who will pay in cash, so get in the habit of making daily bank deposits during daylight hours. Also invest in a good-quality safe for cash storage when you cannot get to the bank.

Checks are another popular payment method, especially for paying for services. Needless to say, most entrepreneurs selling services will have to become comfortable with being paid with a check. Even so, you still have to take a few precautions to ensure you don't get left holding a rubber check, especially when dealing with new clients. Ask to see picture ID and write the customer's driver's license number on the back. If the amount of the check exceeds a few hundred dollars, ask the buyer to get the check certified or pay with a bank draft instead, especially if the client is new to your business. Also get in the habit of checking dates and dollar amounts to make sure they are correct. I have been caught a few times with wrong dates and dollar amounts, and it can be time-consuming to have to get a new check because of a simple error.

The debit card is another option, but will require you to buy or rent a debit card terminal to accept debit card payments. Most banks and credit unions offer business clients debit card equipment and services. The processing equipment will set you back about $40 per month for a terminal connected to a conventional telephone line and about $100 per month for a cellular terminal, plus the cost of the telephone line or cellular service. There is also a transaction fee charged by the bank and payable by you every time there is a debit card transaction, which ranges from 10 cents to 50 cents per transaction, based on variables such as dollar value and frequency of use.

Opening a Credit Card Merchant Account

Many consumers have replaced paper money all together in favor of plastic when buying products and services. In fact, giving your customers the option to pay for purchases with a credit card is often crucial to success. This is especially true if you plan to do business on the web, because credit cards and electronic cash are used to complete almost all web sales and financial transactions. Therefore, most entrepreneurs will want to offer customers credit card payment options, and to do this you will need to open a credit card merchant account. Visit your bank or credit union, or contact a merchant account broker such as 1st American Card Service, ✆ www.1stamericancardservice.com, Cardservice International, ✆ www.cardservice.com, or Merchant Account Express, ✆ www.merchantexpress.com, to inquire about opening an account. Providing your credit is sound, you will run into few obstacles. If your credit is poor, you may have difficulties opening a merchant account or have to provide a substantial security deposit. If you are still unsuccessful, the next best option is to open an account with an online payment service provider, which is discussed in the next section.

The advantages of opening a credit card merchant account enabling you to accept credit card payments are numerous. In fact, studies have proven that merchants who accept credit cards can increase sales by up to 50 percent. Not to mention that you can accept credit card payments online, over the telephone, by mail, in person, and sell services on an installment basis by obtaining permission to charge your customer's credit card monthly, or as per agreement. All of these benefits come at a cost, especially when you consider you will have to pay a application fee, setup fee, purchase or rent processing equipment and software, pay administration and statement fees, and pay processing and transaction fees ranging from 2 to 8 percent on total sales volumes. Once again, these fees must be viewed as the cost of doing business.

Online Payment Services

Online payment services allow people and businesses to exchange currency over the internet electronically, and these services are very popular with consumers and merchants. PayPal, ✆ www.paypal.com, is one of the more popular online payment services with more than 40 million members in 45 countries, offering personal and business account services. Both types of accounts allow funds to be transferred electronically amongst members, but only the business account enables merchants to accept credit card payments for goods and services. Another popular online payment services is Veri Sign Pay Flow, ✆ www.verisign.com. Online payment services are quick, easy, and cheap to open, regardless of your credit rating or anticipated sales volumes, and you can receive payment from any customer with an e-mail account. You can also have the funds deposited directly into your account, have a check issued and mailed, or leave funds in your account to draw on using your debit card. The only real disadvantage is most services redirect your customers to their web site to complete the transaction. This can confuse people who in some cases will abandon the purchase. Nonetheless, the advantages of online payment services far outweigh the disadvantages.

Debt Collection

No matter how careful you are when it comes to extending credit privileges to customers, once in a while you will not be paid on time, or at all. What can you do to get paid? The first rule of getting paid is to keep the lines of communication open with your delinquent client and keep the pressure on to get paid through the use of nonthreatening telephone calls, letters, and personal visits. You cannot legally intimidate customers into paying you, but you can explain why it is in their best interests to pay you—namely that you can hurt their credit ratings or sue them in court if they do not pay.

Another option is to hire a collection agency to collect the outstanding debt. Collection agencies generally charge a percentage of the total amount owed as their fee, as much as 50 percent. The Association of Credit and Collection Professionals, ♂ www.acainternational.org, is a good starting point in terms of finding a collection agency.

Your final option is to take the delinquent account to small-claims court, but remember small-claims courts have limits on how much you can sue for in your state or province. The limits range from $1,500 to $25,000. Filing fees vary by state and province as well. These must be paid upfront; but if you win, the fees are added to your award. As a rule of thumb, small business owners that use the small-claims court represent themselves because the amount of the potential award usually does not justify lawyers' fees. Even if you win, you will not necessarily be paid the amount that you are awarded. You may win a judgment, but still have to chase the defendant through garnishment of income or seizure of assets to get paid. You can learn more about the small-claims court process and filing fees by contacting your local courthouse.

Small Business Taxation

Operating a small business has numerous tax advantages, but with that comes a big disadvantage—lots of bookkeeping and complicated tax forms to complete, especially if you have employees, are incorporated, or import and export goods.

The constant in terms of business taxation is that there are no constants, other than change. Because small business taxation is complicated, you are always well advised to seek professional help. There are also books specifically developed to help the small business owner understand and prepare tax forms. Perhaps the best information that you can obtain about small business and income taxation comes directly from the source—the Internal Revenue Service and Canada Customs and Revenue Agency.

The Internal Revenue Service provides small business owners with a number of free publications that explain small business taxation issues and can be used as guides for completing small business and self-employed tax forms. You can order IRS small business information, tax forms, and publications in person at your local IRS office, online at ☞ www.irs.gov/business/small, or toll-free for mail delivery by calling ☎ (800) 829-3676.

Canada Customs and Revenue Agency also provides small business owners with a number of free publications that explain small business tax issues and can be used as guides for completing small business tax and self-employed tax forms. You can order Canada Customs and Revenue Agency small business information, tax forms, and publications in person at your provincial business service centers, online at ☞ www.ccra-adrc.gc.ca/formspubs/request-e.html, or toll-free for mail delivery by calling ☎ (800) 959-2221.

3

BUSINESS PLANNING

Business planning are two very scary words to most would-be entrepreneurs, but do not feel intimidated by the business and marketing research and planning process. It is nothing more than collecting, analyzing, and recording the information that you need in order to start, operate, and prosper in business. The purpose of this chapter is to help you build your business and marketing strategies in order to minimize financial risks and maximize the potential for success and profitability. Depending on your venture, your business and marketing plans may not have to be highly sophisticated. Even a few well-researched and documented pages covering the basics are often sufficient to reveal the information you need to describe your business, identify your customers, reveal your product's or service's benefits, develop your sales goals and marketing strategies, and create your action plan. To assist in this endeavor, information is provided here in a workbook format requiring you to answer critical business and marketing questions. Your responses can be used to develop a basic business and marketing plan—a suitable road map to guide new entrepreneurs from business idea, to setup, to marketing, to sales, and ultimately to success.

Information is divided into four sections—company, marketing, financials, and appendices, which will enable you to easily tackle business and marketing planning exercises in a step-by-step format. If you need more specific information than is provided here, there are a multitude of good books available that are dedicated solely to business and marketing planning. Barnes and Noble, ♂ www.barnes andnoble.com, and Amazon, ♂ www.amazon.com, both provide convenient online shopping for business and marketing planning books. There is also business plan software available to assist you in writing a business plan. See Palo Alto, ♂ www.paloalto.com, and Plan Magic, ♂ www.planmagic.com. Most office and word processing software programs also include basic business plan templates and tutorials that can help novice entrepreneurs create and write a business plan.

Company

In the company section, describe your business in detail, including the management team, legal issues, and potential risks your business faces, as well as contingency plans that can be activated in the event that plan A does not come to fruition.

Business Description

Get started by providing an overview of the business that you have started or will be starting. Include business name, legal structure, location, and stage of development (see Figure 3.1).

FIGURE 3.1: Business Description Worksheet

A. What is your business name? _____

_____

FIGURE 3.1: Business Description Worksheet, continued

B. What services and/or products does your business sell? _____

_____

C. What is the legal structure of your business? _____

❑ Sole proprietorship ❑ Partnership ❑ Limited liability corporation ❑ Corporation

D. Is your intention to incorporate a sole proprietorship or partnership in the near future, and
if so, when? _____

_____

E. Where is your business located? _____

City _____ State/Province _____

F When did the business start, or when will the business be started? _____

_____

G. If your business is already operational, list:

1. Current stage of development. _____

_____

_____

2. Successes to date. _____

_____

3. Challenges to date. _____

_____

Management Team

Next, describe the management team (see Figure 3.2), including the owner(s) and
key employees, as well as sales agents, professional service providers, and subcontractors. When describing the management team, think about what type of
people your business needs to hire or be aligned with in order to operate and meet
your business, marketing, and sales objectives.

FIGURE 3.2: Management Team Worksheet

A. List the owners of the business, and describe their experience, training, and the duties each will perform.

1. _____

_____

2. _____

_____

3. _____

_____

B. List key employees, and describe their experience, training, remuneration, and the duties each will perform.

1. _____

_____

2. _____

_____

3. _____

_____

C. List professional service providers (lawyers, consultants, accountants, etc.), and describe the services each will provide.

1. _____

_____

2. _____

_____

3. _____

_____

FIGURE 3.2: Management Team Worksheet, continued

D. Will you contract with independent sales agents to sell your services? If so, describe their experience, the duties they will perform, and how they will be remunerated. _____

_____

_____

E. Will you hire subcontractors to provide a portion or all of the services you sell? If so, describe their experience, the services they will provide, the guarantees they provide, and how they will be remunerated. _____

_____

_____

Legal Issues

In this section, describe key legal issues in terms of setting up and operating your business. Break this information down into what registrations, permits, licenses, and other legal documents have been obtained to date, and what must still be obtained. Also, describe all insurance coverage needs as well as any intellectual property information (see Figure 3.3).

FIGURE 3.3: Legal Issues Worksheet

A. Describe any legal issues specific to your business, in terms of regulations governing start-up and operations. _____

_____

B. Record the important licenses, permits, or registrations that are needed or have been obtained, as well as the cost of each.

Needed	Obtained	Cost	Item
❏	❏	$ _____	Business license

FIGURE 3.3: Legal Issues Worksheet, continued

Needed	Obtained	Cost	Item
❏	❏	$ _____	Employer identification number
❏	❏	$ _____	Vendor permit
❏	❏	$ _____	Sales tax permits
❏	❏	$ _____	Import/export certificates
❏	❏	$ _____	Professional certificates
❏	❏	$ _____	Police clearance
❏	❏	$ _____	Zoning/building permits
❏	❏	$ _____	Fire safety/hazardous materials permits
❏	❏	$ _____	Food safety permits
❏	❏	$ _____	Internet domain name registration

C. Describe your insurance requirements, such as fire, general liability, automotive, health, or business interruption insurance.

Type of Insurance	Date Needed	Cost
1. _____	_____	$ _____
2. _____	_____	$ _____
3. _____	_____	$ _____

D. List and describe any intellectual properties, trademarks, patents, or copyrights that the business owns, has applied for, or will be using under license from the property owner. Include the nature of these intellectual properties and the advantages associated with ownership or right of use. _____

_____

_____

_____

_____

Risks and Contingencies

It is also important to assess and discuss the risks associated with your business, products and services, marketing environment, and other aspects, as well as a contingency or backup plan that will be implemented to overcome risks that materialize (see Figure 3.4). For instance, a risk might be a supplier going out of business. A contingency would be to identify additional supply sources that could be called upon if needed.

FIGURE 3.4: Risks and Contingenices Worksheet

Potential risk: _____

Contingency plan: _____

Potential risk: _____

Contingency plan: _____

Potential risk: _____

Contingency plan: _____

Marketing

For small businesses, marketing is of key importance. Based on your research, you will be able to prove that there is sufficient demand for your product or service, that you can compete in the marketplace, and that the market is large enough to support your sales and marketing goals. In this section you want to describe the marketplace, target customers, competition, sales goals, the four Ps, marketing budget, and your action plan. This information can then be used to market your products and services and guide your marketing decisions from where you are now to where you want to be in the future.

Marketplace

Describe the marketplace where you will be doing business (see Figure 3.5). The biggest benefit of conducting and recording marketplace information is that it enables you to greatly reduce your exposure to financial risk, increases your chances of capitalizing on marketplace opportunities, and proves that there is a big enough marketplace to support your anticipated sales.

FIGURE 3.5: Marketplace Worksheet

A. Describe the geographic trading area that your business will serve. _____

_____

_____

B. How big is the current market? _____

_____

_____

C. How big is the potential market? _____

_____

_____

D. What is the current economic status of the market area? _____

_____

_____

Target Customer

Describe your target customers (see Figure 3.6), including information such as where they live, their ages, their genders, what they do for a living, what they like to read, and what is important to them when they make buying decisions. This information enables you to aim your advertising, marketing, and sales activities directly at your target customers, saving you money and time by not using ineffective advertising and marketing activities.

FIGURE 3.6: Target Customer Worksheet

A. Where are your target customers geographically located? _____

_____

_____

B. What percentage of your target customers are male, and what is their age range? ____

_____

_____

C. What percentage of your target customers are female, and what is their age range?

_____

_____

D. What is the marital status of your target customers?

  ❏ Single   ❏ Married   ❏ Divorced

E. What is the average level of education of your target customers?

  ❏ High school   ❏ Trade school   ❏ College diploma   ❏ University degree

F. What do your target customers do for a living?

  ❏ Student   ❏ Homemaker   ❏ Laborer   ❏ Trade person   ❏ Management

  ❏ Executive   ❏ Business owner   ❏ Professional   ❏ Retired

G. What is most important to your target customers when making purchasing decisions?

  ❏ Price   ❏ Value   ❏ Service   ❏ Warranty   ❏ Quality

H. What publications do your target customers like to read, and what radio stations and pro-grams do they listen to, what web sites do they visit, and what clubs or associations do they belong to?

1. Publications: _____

FIGURE 3.6: Target Customer Worksheet, continued

2. Radio: _____

3. Web sites: _____

4. Clubs and associations: _____

Competition

You also need to know what other businesses are selling the same or similar services as you, in the same area, and to the same target audience. You can use this information to develop strategies to turn competitors' weaknesses into your strengths, as well as to capitalize on marketplace opportunities (see Figure 3.7).

FIGURE 3.7: Competition Worksheet

A. List and describe your competitors.

1. _____

2. _____

3. _____

B. What are your competitors' strengths?

1. _____

2. _____

3. _____

C. What are your competitors' weaknesses?

1. _____

2. _____

3. _____

FIGURE 3.7: Competition Worksheet, continued

D. What do your competitors do well that you should also be doing?

1. _____

2. _____

3. _____

E. Strengths are the skills and resources you have that can be capitalized upon and used to your advantage to help you reach business and marketing objectives. Describe the strengths and resources of your business. _____

_____

_____

F. Describe how your company will be positioned in the marketplace relative to competitors. Will you be known as the low-price leader, providing quality and service above all, or will you cater to the high-end segment of the market? _____

_____

_____

Sales Goals

Your sales goals should be given in easily measured and quantifiable financial terms. If you are planning on utilizing more than one sales method such as the internet, wholesale sales, or trade shows, you will want to separate and list sales goals for each method individually (see Figure 3.8).

FIGURE 3.8: Sales Goals Worksheet

A. What are your first-month sales goals? _____

_____

_____

FIGURE 3.8: Sales Goals Worksheet, continued

B. What are your six-month sales goals? _____

_____

_____

C. What are your first-year sales goals? _____

_____

_____

D. What are your five-year sales goals? _____

_____

_____

Product, Price, Place (Distribution), and Promotion

Developing your marketing strategy revolves around the four marketing Ps—product, price, place (distribution), and promotion. It is the combination of the four Ps that creates your marketing mix, which is, in effect, the entire marketing process. Essentially, the four Ps are about finding the right portions of each, enabling you to create the perfect mix of the marketing strategies that will allow you to meet and exceed your objectives (see Figure 3.9). Information about pricing products and services can be found in Chapter 6, Everything Else You Need to Know.

FIGURE 3.9: Product, Price, Place, and Promotion Worksheet

Product

A. In detail, describe the product(s) you sell and the service(s) you provide. _____

_____

_____

FIGURE 3.9: Product, Price, Place, and Promotion Worksheet, continued

B. What special features do your products and service have, and how do customers benefit by purchasing and using your product or service? _____

_____

_____

C. What advantages do your products or services provide over competitors' products or services?

_____

_____

D. Describe your product warranties and customer service guarantees. _____

_____

_____

E. Describe any key product or service research and development initiatives underway or planned. _____

_____

_____

Price

A. How much will you charge for your products and services; how did you arrive at your selling price, and what is your pricing strategy? _____

_____

_____

B. How sensitive are your target customers to pricing issues, and why? _____

_____

_____

C. How much do competitors charge for their products or services? _____

_____

_____

FIGURE 3.9: Product, Price, Place, and Promotion Worksheet, continued

D. List the purchase payment options that you will provide to your customers—e.g., credit cards, debit cards, electronic transfers—and the benefits of providing customers with these options, as well as the costs of providing each. _____

_____

_____

Place (Distribution)

A. Describe the primary method you will use to sell your products and services (e.g., from a retail storefront, office, homebased, trade shows, internet, etc.). _____

_____

_____

B. Describe any secondary methods you will utilize to sell your products and services in addition to your primary sales method. For example, if you plan to sell your products and services from home, secondary sales methods might include seasonal trade shows._____

_____

_____

C. Describe any unique or proprietary systems that will be used in the delivery of services or in the manufacturing of products. _____

_____

_____

D. Describe the operations system you will use to manage sales from initial order to delivery of the product or completion of service(s) to post-completion/sale follow-up. _____

_____

_____

Promotion

A. Describe what advertising media you will employ in the promotion of your products and services (newspaper, radio, television, Yellow Pages), and your marketing materials (fliers, signs, and business cards). _____

_____

_____

FIGURE 3.9: Product, Price, Place, and Promotion Worksheet, continued

B. Describe any direct sales tactics you will employ, including personal-contact selling, mail, telephone, and electronic approaches. _____

_____

_____

C. Describe how you will utilize public relations tools and media in promoting your business, products, and services. _____

_____

_____

D. Describe how you will use the internet to promote your products and services; include your web site and online marketing strategies. _____

_____

_____

Marketing Budget

Use a ground-up approach as in Figure 3.10 to calculate the cost of each marketing strategy and activity you intend to use to advertise, market, and sell your products and services. Break down each activity by individual cost, and add them together to estimate your overall marketing budget.

FIGURE 3.10: Marketing Budget Worksheet

List your main marketing activities, the time period covered, and the cost to implement each.

Marketing Activity	Time Period	Cost
1. _____	_____	$ _____
2. _____	_____	$ _____
3. _____	_____	$ _____

FIGURE 3.10: Marketing Budget Worksheet, continued

Marketing Activity	Time Period	Cost
4. _____	_____	$ _____
5. _____	_____	$ _____
6. _____	_____	$ _____

Action Plan

The action plan section is really a big to-do list broken into categories and timetables (as shown in Figure 3.11), outlining when each promotional activity will be implemented and managed and how and when you will measure the progress, success, or failure of each activity implemented. By measuring results incrementally, you can make sure that the promotional activity is working, and that you are on track to meet your marketing and sales objectives.

FIGURE 3.11: Action Plan Worksheet

A. Describe how each marketing strategy will be implemented. _____

_____

_____

B. Outline the timetable for implementation of each marketing strategy. _____

_____

_____

C. Describe how you intend to manage each implemented marketing strategy. _____

_____

_____

FIGURE 3.11: Action Plan Worksheet, continued

D. Describe how you will track and measure the effectiveness of each marketing strategy.

_____

_____

E. Describe any contingency plans that you will use if any of these marketing strategies fail to meet sales goals and objectives. _____

_____

_____

Financials

Many new entrepreneurs feel intimidated by financial planning because of a lack of experience. But remember, it only has to be as simple or as difficult as you want to make it. For a small business venture, you have to cover the basics— funding requirements, sources of funding, balance sheet, equipment and inventory lists, break-even analysis, start-up costs worksheet, and fixed monthly overhead worksheet, all of which are discussed in greater detail in Figures 3.12 through 3.17.

Business plan software, such as Plan Magic, ♂ www.planmagic.com, and Palo Alto, ♂ www.paloalto.com, and accounting software, such as QuickBooks, ♂ www.quickbooks.com, include customizable templates for financial forecasting and statements.

Funding Requirements

The first information to include are the funding requirements for your new business. Specifically, you want to describe how much money is needed to start or grow the business, what it will be used for, and any future funding requirements (see Figure 3.12). Later in this section you will find a handy start-up costs worksheet to help calculate the total costs of starting your business.

FIGURE 3.12: Funding Requirement Worksheet

A. Describe your current funding requirements. _____

_____

_____

B. Describe what the money will be used for (e.g., purchasing tools and equipment, leasing a business location, obtaining business permits, etc.). _____

_____

_____

C. Describe any future funding requirements and what the money will be used for (e.g., business expansion, equipment upgrades, etc.). _____

_____

_____

Funding Sources

The next step is to identify and describe the source of your funding requirements (see Figure 3.13). In other words, this is the section where you describe where the money will come from to get started or grow the business—bank loan, private investors, or partnerships; how the money will be repaid (cash or equity); and where the money will come from to meet a repayment schedule (generally through the business revenues).

FIGURE 3.13: Funding Sources Worksheet

A. Describe how will you fund your business start-up investment. If you are going to fund the investment from more than one source, describe each. _____

_____

_____

_____

FIGURE 3.13: Funding Sources Worksheet, continued

B. If you are borrowing money to start your business, describe the terms and conditions, including rate of interest and how the money will be repaid, with a repayment schedule.

_____

_____

_____

_____

Balance Sheet

If your business is already operational, you will also want to create a balance sheet, which lists your business assets and liabilities, thus allowing you to determine your net equity position. Assets are items of value that your business owns, while liabilities are debts that your business owes—net equity is the difference between the two. Completing Figure 3.14 will enable you to generate a basic balance sheet. However, consult with your accountant to create a legal and audited balance sheet, which takes into account short- and long-term assets and liabilities, as well as depreciation on physical assets for tax or business valuation purposes.

FIGURE 3.14: Balance Sheet Worksheet

A. Calculate the value of current and fixed business assets.

Item	$ Value
Cash on hand	$ _____
Inventory	$ _____
Accounts receivable	$ _____
Loans receivable	$ _____
Investments	$ _____
Buildings and land	$ _____
Leasehold improvements	$ _____
Equipment and tools	$ _____

FIGURE 3.14: Balance Sheet Worksheet, continued

Item	$ Value
Transportation	$ _____
Deposits	$ _____
Miscellaneous assets	$ _____
Total assets	$ _____

B. Calculate liabilities.

Accounts payable	$ _____
Mortgages	$ _____
Accrued expenses	$ _____
Loans	$ _____
Total liabilities	$ _____

C. Subtract your total liabilities from your total assets to calculate your net equity

Total assets	$ _____
Total liabilities	$ _____
Net equity	$ _____

Capital Equipment and Inventory Lists

Equipment and inventory lists should include what you currently have, what is needed in the short term (less than 12 months), and what is needed in the long term (more than 12 months). Additionally, you should include the number of units that are required, the cost of the items, and the date when the required items will be purchased (see Figure 3.15).

FIGURE 3.15: Capital Equipment and Inventory Lists Worksheet

Current Equipment

Equipment Description	# of Units	$ Unit Cost	Total Cost
_____	_____	$ _____	$ _____
_____	_____	$ _____	$ _____

FIGURE 3.15: Capital Equipment and Inventory Lists Worksheet, continued

Equipment Description	# of Units	$ Unit Cost	Total Cost
_____	_____	$ _____	$ _____
_____	_____	$ _____	$ _____
_____	_____	$ _____	$ _____

Needed Equipment

Equipment Description	# of Units	$ Unit Cost	Total Cost	Date Required
_____	_____	$ _____	$ _____	_____
_____	_____	$ _____	$ _____	_____
_____	_____	$ _____	$ _____	_____
_____	_____	$ _____	$ _____	_____
_____	_____	$ _____	$ _____	_____

Current Inventory

Inventory Description	# of Units	$ Unit Cost	Total Cost
_____	_____	$ _____	$ _____
_____	_____	$ _____	$ _____
_____	_____	$ _____	$ _____
_____	_____	$ _____	$ _____
_____	_____	$ _____	$ _____

Needed Inventory

Inventory Description	# of Units	$ Unit Cost	Total Cost	Date Required
_____	_____	$ _____	$ _____	_____
_____	_____	$ _____	$ _____	_____
_____	_____	$ _____	$ _____	_____
_____	_____	$ _____	$ _____	_____
_____	_____	$ _____	$ _____	_____

Break-Even Analysis

The break-even analysis is used to determine how much product or service must be sold for the business to break even, for the total amount of incoming revenues to match the total amount of outgoing expenses. To calculate your break-even point, you will need to estimate your fixed expenses (overhead). (See Figure 3.17, Monthly Overhead Costs Worksheet) You will also need to know how much the variable costs are for purchasing products or delivering of services, as well as the gross margin for each sale. For example, if you sold watches online and at flea markets, your fixed costs were $10,000 per annum, and you sold each watch for $10, which included variable costs and a gross margin of 25 percent, you would have $2.50 gross profit per unit sale. You would need to sell 4,000 watches per year to break even, $10,000 in fixed costs divided by $2.50 gross margin per unit sale equals 4,000 unit sales per year or 333 unit sales per month.

Start-Up Costs Worksheet

Use this handy worksheet shown in Figure 3.16 to calculate how much money you will need to start your new business. Ignore items not relevant to your specific business start-up, and add items as required.

FIGURE 3.16: Start-Up Costs Worksheet

A. Business Setup

Business registration	$ _____
Business license	$ _____
Vendor permits	$ _____
Other permits	$ _____
Insurance	$ _____
Professional fees	$ _____
Training and education	$ _____
Bank account	$ _____
Merchant accounts	$ _____
Payment processing equipment	$ _____
Association fees	$ _____
Deposits	$ _____
Other _____	$ _____
Subtotal A	$ _____

FIGURE 3.16: Start-Up Costs Worksheet, continued

B. Business Identity

Business cards	$ _____
Logo design	$ _____
Letterhead	$ _____
Envelopes	$ _____
Other _____	$ _____
Subtotal B	$ _____

C. Office/Storefront/Workshop

Rent deposit	$ _____
Damage deposit	$ _____
Communication equipment/devices	$ _____
Computer hardware	$ _____
Software	$ _____
Furniture	$ _____
Other office equipment	$ _____
Office supplies	$ _____
Renovations and improvements	$ _____
Fixed tools and equipment	$ _____
Portable tools and equipment	$ _____
Other _____	$ _____
Subtotal C	$ _____

D. Transportation

Upfront cost to buy/lease transportation	$ _____
Registration	$ _____
Insurance	$ _____
Special accessories	$ _____
Other _____	$ _____
Subtotal D	$ _____

FIGURE 3.16: Start-Up Costs Worksheet, continued

E. Web Site

Domain registration $ _____

Site development fees $ _____

Search engine and directory $ _____

Equipment $ _____

Software $ _____

Content and web tools $ _____

Hosting $ _____

Other _____ $ _____

Subtotal E $ _____

F. Marketing

Research and planning costs $ _____

Signs $ _____

Brochures and fliers $ _____

Catalogs $ _____

Initial advertising budget $ _____

Initial online promotion budget $ _____

Product samples $ _____

Other _____ $ _____

Subtotal F $ _____

G. Product Inventory (if applicable)

1 _____ $ _____

2 _____ $ _____

3 _____ $ _____

4 _____ $ _____

5 _____ $ _____

Subtotal G $ _____

FIGURE 3.16: Start-Up Costs Worksheet, continued

H. Adding Up the Costs	
Business setup	$ _____
Business identity	$ _____
Office	$ _____
Transportation	$ _____
Web site	$ _____
Marketing	$ _____
Inventory	$ _____
Total start-up costs	$ _____
Working capital	$ _____
Total investment needed	$ _____

Monthly Overhead Costs Worksheet

Use Figure 3.17 to calculate your businesses fixed costs overhead expenses. Complete only the items that are relevant to your particular business and leave the rest blank.

FIGURE 3.17: Monthly Overhead Costs Worksheet

A. General Office	
Rent or mortgage	$_____
Utilities	$_____
Loan and interest repayment	$_____
Bank and merchant account fees	$_____
Business taxes	$_____
Business permits	$_____
Insurance	$_____

FIGURE 3.17: Monthly Overhead Costs Worksheet, continued

Workers' compensation $_____

Equipment leases, loans, and rentals $_____

Equipment maintenance $_____

Alarm monitoring $_____

Office supplies $_____

Postage $_____

Courier and delivery $_____

Cleaning and maintenance $_____

Other _____ $_____

Subtotal A $_____

B. Communications

Telephone and fax lines $_____

Toll-free line $_____

Internet connection $_____

Cellular telephone $_____

Answering service $_____

Pager $_____

Two-way radio $_____

Communications equipment lease $_____

Other _____ $_____

Subtotal B $_____

C. Wages and Fees

Personal wages $_____

Employee wages $_____

Employee and management benefits $_____

Accounting fees $_____

Legal fees $_____

Consultant fees $_____

Business association fees $_____

Other _____ $_____

Subtotal C $_____

FIGURE 3.17: Monthly Overhead Costs Worksheet, continued

D. Marketing

Yellow Pages	$_____
Print advertising	$_____
Broadcast advertising	$_____
Outdoor advertising	$_____
Fliers	$_____
Direct mail and telemarketing	$_____
Trade shows and seminars	$_____
Public relations	$_____
Contests	$_____
Product samples	$_____
Sponsorships	$_____
Surveys, polls, and research	$_____
Customer appreciation and gifts	$_____
Graphic design and copy fees	$_____
Other _____	$_____
Subtotal D	$_____

E. Web Site and E-Commerce

Hosting	$_____
Maintenance	$_____
Content and web-tool fees	$_____
Internet advertising	$_____
Search engine fees	$_____
Paid placement fees	$_____
Online payment system fees	$_____
Other _____	$_____
Subtotal E	$_____

F. Transportation

Lease or loan payment	$_____
Fuel	$_____
Insurance	$_____
Repairs	$_____

FIGURE 3.17: Monthly Overhead Costs Worksheet, continued

Licensing		$_____
Parking		$_____
Cleaning		$_____
Other _____		$_____
	Subtotal F	$_____

G. Miscellaneous

Travel		$_____
Entertainment		$_____
Uniforms and dry cleaning		$_____
Subscriptions		$_____
Charitable donations		$_____
Other _____		$_____
	Subtotal G	$_____

H. Adding Up the Costs

General office	$_____
Communications	$_____
Wages and fees	$_____
Marketing	$_____
Web site and e-commerce	$_____
Transportation	$_____
Miscellaneous	$_____
Fixed monthly overhead total	$_____

Appendices

The appendices section of the business plan is reserved for supporting documents such as resumes for the principals, research surveys, market studies, financial forecasts, supplier and/or vendor agreements, and if your business is already established, things such as client testimonials. Think in terms of all the documents that support your plans—activities, statistics, and forecasts, divided into three categories: personal documents, legal and financial documents, and marketing documents.

Supporting documents can be especially helpful if you are going to use your business plan as a tool to secure funds to start or grow your business. If your business and marketing plans are going to be used strictly as a road map to guide your business, you will not need to create and include these documents. Nonetheless, it is still a good idea to create appendices, if for no other reason than to keep all important and relevant business documents together in one binding. If your intentions are to use your business plan to secure funds, make sure to only include copies of supporting documents, not originals.

Personal Documents

The personal support documents should include resumes of the business owner(s), managers, key employees, sales agents, and subcontractors, even if they are only a simple one page list of highlighted experiences in a bullet list format. Copies of training certificates or specialized licenses held by the owner(s), managers, or key employees should also be included. If the purpose of the business plan is to secure funding, you will need to include a personal assets statement for each person applying for the loan. The asset statement should list all assets, such as real estate, automobiles, equities, and savings plans, and all personal liabilities, including property mortgages, personal loans, and credit card balances.

Legal and Financial Documents

There are also legal and financial documents to include with your business plan, and depending on the purpose of your business plan, these documents, statements, and forecasts might include any or all of the following:

- Business registrations, incorporations papers, permits, and licenses
- Business insurance coverage documents
- Warranties and guarantees you provide
- Vendor, supplier, and/or subcontractor agreements in force
- Domain name registrations
- If applicable, patents, trademarks, and copyright documents
- Start-up cost estimates and fixed operating cost projections
- Break-even analysis, and short-term and long-term sales projections
- Equipment and inventory projections, estimates, and lists

Marketing Documents

Documents supporting your marketing research and statements within your business and marketing plan should be included. Any or all of the following would qualify as marketing support documents:

- Research documents, including surveys, questionnaires, and focus group results
- Target customer profile
- PEST (Political, Economic, Social, and Technical) and SWOT (Strengths, Weaknesses, Opportunities, and Threats) analysis
- Business marketing materials, such as brochures, product photographs, catalogs, price lists, and print advertisements
- Press clippings, client testimonials, and company, individual, or organizational endorsements
- Competitor brochures, price lists, warranties, and print advertisements, and Better Business Bureau report, if available
- Marketing budgets and projections

4

SETTING UP SHOP

Now it's time to set up your business. In order to sell products and services, you need a base of operations; you need to set up shop. Setting up shop goes far beyond a business location and includes equipping your business with furniture, technology, communication devices, and tools, and sometimes it means taking your business online with a web site so that you can sell products and services to a worldwide audience. Setting up shop also means building a team to help operate your business to maximize the potential for success and profitability. Your business team can include family members, employees, professional services, sales agents, suppliers, subcontractors, and business alliances. You also have to create a business image, one that over time and with consistent use, will cause people to visually identify your image with your business and the products and services you sell (referred to as branding). This chapter covers some of the more important guidelines when it comes time to physically set up your business.

Business Location

Choosing a location for your business will depend on a number of factors, such as the types of products or services you plan to sell, your budget, and your office, retail, or workshop space requirements. Many businesses, such as a boat detailing service, flea market vending, or a holiday decoration service, can also be operated on a mobile basis. For entrepreneurs operating mobile businesses, suitable and reliable transportation will be of greater importance than a physical business location. But you will still need to establish some base of operation, probably in your home. This section covers information on three basic operating locations—homebased, office, and storefront. Setting up shop on the internet is also discussed in this chapter.

Homebased

If you plan on operating your business from home, the first issue to tackle is whether you can legally operate a business from your home. Chances are you can, although probably with some restrictions. Every community in the United States and Canada has its own home business zoning regulations and specific usage guidelines. The majority of municipalities do allow businesses to operate from a residence, providing the business activities do not negatively impact neighbors and the neighborhood in general. From a zoning standpoint, the potential issues include exterior signage, parking, noise, fire, storage of hazardous substances, deliveries and shipping, nonfamily employees working from your home, and customers visiting your home. Long before you decide to start and operate your business from home, you need to check zoning rules, regulations, and restrictions at your city or municipal planning department or bylaws office for further information.

The second issue is determining what space in your home will best suit your business needs. Homebased workspace options range from any room of the home, such as a den, living room, spare bedroom, or basement, to a separate outside structure such as a garage. Careful consideration must be given to the needs of your family and how space in the home is currently being utilized for day-to-day living, special occasions, seasonal activities, and guests. Because setting up a home workspace requires balancing the needs of your business with the needs of your family, compromises will probably have to be made on both fronts.

If you will have no (or few) clients coming to your home, workspace issues are not as important, but there are still a few things to consider. If money is tight, select a room that will require the fewest alterations and preferably one with a door that shuts to keep business in and family, friends, and pets out when necessary. At the same time make sure your workspace is large enough to operate your business. Working out of two or three separate areas of the home is far less productive than working from one. If you will be having many customers visiting your home, some workspace issues are much more important—separate entrance, washroom facilities, and parking. Another consideration is the appearance of your home. Peeling paint, threadbare carpets, and broken porch boards send customers the wrong signals about your business. If your home needs a spruce up, then do it before you open for business.

Whether you have customers coming to your home or not, you will also need storage space for equipment, inventory, and business records. Provided you have enough storage space to meet your needs, the space you use will also need to be easily accessible, dry, and free of critters. It must also be secure so there is no risk that valuable business equipment, inventory, and records will be stolen. If you do not have suitable storage space, is there suitable storage for rent close by with good access, and how much does it cost?

There is lots to know about operating a business at home, more than space here permits. Consequently, you might want to sign out a copy of 📖 *Entrepreneur Magazine's Ultimate Homebased Business Handbook* (Entrepreneur Press, 2004) from your local library or to purchase one from retail booksellers nationwide and online. The book is an A to Z explanation about everything you need to know about starting and operating a homebased business. Small Office Home Office (SOHO) is an organization comprised of small business owners that mainly operate their businesses from a homebased location. In the United States, click on to, 🖱 www.soho.org for more information, and in Canada click on, 🖱 www.soho.ca. In Chapter 5, Sales and Marketing, you will find information about selling products and services from home, including interior showrooms and exterior displays.

Office
Depending on the products or services you sell, you may need to rent commercial office space in a strip plaza, mall, office tower, or low-rise building. The space you rent could be on a month-to-month basis, but the majority of landlords prefer to

lease space for a set amount of time, generally no fewer than 12 months and commonly as long as ten years. An alternative to a long-term lease agreement is to rent office space in a shared office space environment, also known as an executive office suite. There are many benefits to shared office facilities, where you have your own individual office along with access to traditional extended office facilities and services for the use of all tenants. An executive office suite can give you everything you need at a fraction of what you would normally pay to rent, equip, and staff a traditional office space. These facilities and services can be included in your rent or charged on a user basis, depending on your rental agreement, and cover things such as boardroom space, centralized reception, answering service and toll-free options, fax service, internet and e-mail accounts, web site hosting and maintenance, shipping and receiving options, mailboxes, word processing, database management, centralized client waiting rooms, and notary and paralegal services. Executive office space is a great choice for small businesses just getting off the ground because most come fully furnished, there are no long-term lease agreements, and as a rule, rents are very reasonable.

If you need your own traditional office space, issues that should be addressed before signing the lease agreement include:

- Is the rent within your budget?
- Are the lease terms and conditions favorable?
- Does the office require substantial renovations or improvement, and what are the costs?
- Is there adequate parking and access to transit?
- If necessary, does the location provide good visibility to passing motorists and pedestrians?
- Is the location in close proximity to your primary target audience or current customers?
- Are there adequate washroom, kitchen, and boardroom facilities?
- Is the office located in a safe and secure area?

Storefront

Renting a retail storefront will be necessary if your business depends on walk-in traffic to generate new sales. Potential retail storefront locations include a shopping center, a freestanding commercial building, the downtown core, or a strip plaza. For any business that relies on walk-in traffic to generate the bulk of sales, location is the critical factor. You have to choose your real estate wisely; without the right location, the chance of failure and financial loss increases exponentially. Consequently, your storefront location needs to be in proximity to the largest population of your primary target audience, and it must also have excellent visibility to your target audience. Choosing a less visible space to save $1,000 a month on rent is actually a waste of money because you will spend an additional $2,000 to reach your target audience through advertising and promotion, just to inform them of your location. When selecting the right retail location, there are also many additional points to consider:

- The rent must be within your budget, and the lease terms must be favorable.
- The location must meet your size requirements.
- The location must meet zoning, fire, and handicap-accessibility regulations.
- Mechanicals, such as electricity, heating, plumbing, and communications must meet your requirements.
- Renovations are costly. Look for a location that requires the least amount of alterations possible while still meeting your needs.
- The location should have adequate customer parking, preferably free, and also have good access to public transit.
- The store should have excellent visibility and meet your pedestrian foot and passing motorist traffic count requirements.
- Regardless of location—mall, strip plaza, or freestanding building—the store should have great "curb appeal" and be consistent with the type of business image you want to project.

Additionally, make sure that there are no restrictive covenants in place that would prevent you from making your specific product, or rules that would prevent you from marketing and promoting your business in the style that you want. Restrictive covenants cover areas such as sign size, style, and placement, as well as store operating hours. The following are a few helpful retailing business resources: The National Association of Store Fixture Manufacturers, ☎ (954) 893-7300, ✆ www.nasfm.org; National Retail Federation, ☎ (202) 783-7971, ✆ www.nrf.com; Retail Merchandiser Magazine Online, ✆ www.retail-merchandiser.com; and Retail Source, ✆ www.retailsource.com

Business Equipment

The need for business equipment such as office furniture, technology, communication devices, store fixtures, and tools varies depending on your business location and the types of products and services you sell. But every business will need to establish a basic office. Budget comes into play when you are equipping your business. For the financially challenged entrepreneur, here are a few hints on how to do this on a shoestring budget and substantially reduce the amount of money you need up front. Reduce business equipment costs by bartering or trading for what you need. For instance, if you operate a cleaning service, barter with a local print shop to trade cleaning services for printed materials such as business cards, fliers, and estimate forms. Alternately, you can join a local barter club and trade the products or services you sell with members who have the products and services you need. You can also visit *Barter News*, ♂ www.barternews.com, an online magazine dedicated to the world of business barter clubs, organizations, and industry information, to track down a barter club in your area.

Purchase secondhand, factory seconds, or floor models. Scan classified ads and auction listings in your local newspaper for secondhand furniture and equipment. Generally, you'll save as much as 75 percent off new costs by buying used. Also, call around to your local office outfitters and inquire about factory seconds and the floor models they have available. Purchasing seconds or floor models with slight blemishes will often save you as much as 25 percent off the retail price. You can also take the no-money-down route and lease or rent business equipment. Granted, you will have to pay for these items monthly, but you will not be tying up precious cash, cash that can be used for marketing. Another benefit is that lease and rent payments are 100 percent deductible business expenses.

Furniture

If clients will be visiting your office, your furniture and décor will need to reflect this, both in appearance and function. If clients are not visiting your office, you will have much more leeway because it won't really matter if furniture colors and styles are mismatched, or if the desk is purchased secondhand.

What are the basics that every office needs? It needs a desk large enough for a computer monitor with tower storage underneath, a printer, and a telephone/fax machine. If you can only splurge on one piece of office furniture, a comfortable and ergonomically correct chair should be that item, especially if your business keeps you in front of the computer or on the telephone for long periods of time. Key features to look for are distance from the seat to floor, adjustable armrests, and adjustable seating positions.

Business and client records are important, so an investment on a good-quality file storage system is money well spent. Purchase a file cabinet with a locking mechanism and with hangers and folders large enough to suit your business at the present and for future growth. Bookshelves and worktables are also indispensable items. Bookshelves can be used to organize and store not only books, but also product catalogs, office supplies, and computer software and disks. Worktables separate from your desk are also big time-savers because they can be used for working on lower-priority jobs, opening and sorting mail, bookkeeping and record-keeping duties, and much more. Ikea, ♂ www.ikea.com, Staples, ♂ www.staples.com, Office Depot, ♂ www.officedepot.com, and Office Max, ♂ www.officemax.com, all sell office furniture and supplies.

Technology

There is also basic technology that every business needs, including a computer, operating system, software, monitor, modem, and printer. Again, depending on the products and services you sell, you may not need the latest technology. But your equipment must be reliable and your software suitable so you can be efficient and productive.

The first piece of technology you need is, of course, a computer. When purchasing a computer for business, the main considerations are processing speed and data storage capabilities. Both change on a daily basis, so the best advice is to get as much speed and memory as you can afford. Desktop computers range in price from $600 to as much as $3,000 for a top-of-the-line computer used by web developers and designers. The majority of computers come with a standard 56K modem, which is needed to connect to the internet. You can also opt for a more expensive modem, giving you the ability to connect to high-speed broadband or cable internet (if available in your area). The latter allows you to download files up to 20 times faster than a standard dial-up internet connection. You will also need a computer monitor. If desk space is limited, consider purchasing a LCD flat panel monitor, which costs in the range of $250 to $1,000 depending on features and size. Traditional monitors can be purchased for about $150. Basic keyboard and mouse sets are very inexpensive, only about $50. But if you dislike wires cluttering your desktop, consider spending an extra $100 to upgrade to a wireless keyboard and mouse set. If your business takes you on the road, a notebook computer will be a better choice than a desktop computer. Again, purchase as much speed and memory as you can afford. Expect to pay in the range of $1,000 to $4,000 for a good-quality notebook computer.

To complete your business computer system, a printer and perhaps a digital camera will be needed. Inkjet printers start at about $50, while a laser printer costs in the range of $200 to $1,000 depending on features, color option, and print speed. I suggest that you buy a laser printer if you are going to be doing a lot of printing because on average each printed page will cost half as much as it costs to print with an inkjet printer, saving considerable money over the long term. A digital camera is also an indispensable piece of equipment for business owners. You can take pictures of products, clients, and completed jobs, and because the images (photographs) use digital technology, they are easily transferred to your web site, e-mails, or desktop publishing programs. It enables you to easily create brochures, presentations, catalogs, and fliers inhouse and for a fraction of what it costs to have these items created at a printer. Dell Computers, ♂ www.dell.com, IBM Computers, ♂ www.ibm.com, and Apple Computers, ♂ www.apple.com, all offer affordable small business computer packages.

Communications

The proliferation of high-tech communication devices in the last few years makes it very easy to spend a whole lot of money here in a very short time. But if you can get by with basic communication devices at first, you have the potential to upgrade to new and better equipment using future profits. One of the first communication devices you should purchase and install is the good old desktop telephone. Ideally, this telephone will have business features and functions such as on-hold, conferencing, redial, speakerphone, broadcast, and message storage capabilities. If your business keeps you working at a computer all day or in your car, a headset is a definite need. It leaves your hands free to work on the computer as you talk on the phone or to drive your car in relative safety. Count on spending in the range of $25 to $75 for a desktop or cellular telephone hands-free headset. Although fax transmissions have greatly declined in the last few years because of the increased use of e-mail, a fax machine is still needed in business. Most contracts and agreements that need to be signed are legal when faxed if both parties agree in the contract. If you do not want to purchase a separate fax machine, you might consider purchasing an all-in-one office document center, which generally includes a telephone, fax, scanner, and copier in one machine, and costs in the range of $200 to $400.

Cellular telephones are now a must for all business people. Not only do they enable you to take incoming calls from almost anywhere, but they also enable you to stay in constant contact with your best customers and hottest prospects. Cellular telephone service plans are now very inexpensive. For less than $50 per month, you can have nearly unlimited access to as many minutes as you want. Consider purchasing a cell phone with internet features so as to have the ability to check e-mail when you are away from your computer. You will also need an internet connection that enables you to access the web, and send and receive e-mails. Unlimited dial-up access generally costs in the range of $15 per month; high-speed access generally runs in the range of $20 to $50 per month, but you will also need to upgrade your modem if you choose high speed.

Tools

Tool and equipment requirements will be determined by the types of products you manufacture or install, or by the types of services you provide. There are options in terms of how you acquire tools and equipment for your business. You can purchase new, purchase secondhand, lease, or rent tools and equipment on an as-needed basis if you are on a shoestring budget.

The advantage of purchasing new tools and equipment is obvious—no need to worry about equipment breakdowns—but buying new can be a very costly endeavor. Purchasing tools and equipment secondhand is a viable option because with a bit of legwork (scanning classified ads, business closeouts, and auctions), it is possible to buy good quality items in excellent working condition at a fraction of the cost of new. The benefit of leasing or renting tools and equipment is lease and rent payments are 100 percent tax deductible, unlike a sliding scale of depreciation used to calculate the tax benefits associated with purchasing new or used equipment.

Building a Business Team

Building a business team is just as important as any other piece of the business puzzle. Depending on your business structure and the products and services you sell, your business team might include family members, employees, sales agents, subcontractors, suppliers, business associations, and cross-promotional partners. So your business team has the potential to be very comprehensive. Consequently, a plan must be developed to build your business team for present and future growth.

Family

Family members make up the first part of your business team, especially the ones who will also be working in the business. Even family members who do not work in the business will be affected by the business and often by the business decisions you make: The business will have an affect on your family, and your family will have an affect on your business. It is inevitable. Consequently, an important goal of the business owner should be to gain the support of the family for the venture, especially the support of spouses. Don't be upset if your family members do not share your level of enthusiasm for your new business. Remember, in most cases the new business will be your dream, not theirs. As in any new business venture, there are inherent financial risks, which may make some family members nervous, especially when the business is started later in life and retirement funds are used to finance it.

Employees

Depending on the products or services you sell and your business goals, you may or may not need to hire employees. Employing people adds additional administrative and management work, but if your plans are to grow your business, at some point you will need to hire employees. The trick is, of course, to hire the right people the first time around. Poor customer service practices will alienate customers, and salespeople that prefer to talk when they should be listening can drive business to the competition faster than a speeding bullet. Unfortunately, discovering that you have hired the wrong person for the job generally comes too late, long after the damage has occurred. So, what are the characteristics of a good employee? Good employees are productive, professional, honest, loyal, confidant, and punctual and can work with minimal supervision. Hiring good employees is only part of the equation. To attract and retain good employees, you need to be able to offer them a fair salary, opportunities for advancement, job security, new challenges, and above all, recognition. Additional benefits such as heath care and dental plans, profit-sharing plans, and flexible work schedules also go a long way to attracting and retaining top talent.

There are alternatives to employing people—hiring temporary workers on an as-needed basis, hiring sales agents, and using subcontractors. Sales agents and subcontractors are discussed below. Employing temp workers to meet your short-term labor requirements is one of the better alternatives when you need help. The cost is more expensive per hour on average than you would have to pay if you hired an employee, but when you factor in the time saved by not having to run help wanted ads, interview candidates, and check work references, the difference may be negligible.

If you decide that hiring employees is the best option, you will have to comply with laws and regulations governing employment practices, including, but not limited to, labor laws, minimum wages, health and safety workplace issues, work hours, and workers' compensation insurance coverage. As an employer, you will need to obtain an Employer Identification Number (EIN), and you are also required to withhold and remit employee income tax and Social Security Insurance. Labor laws may be researched in the United States by contacting the Department of Labor, ☎ (877) 889-5627, ✆ www.dol.gov; in Canada, you can contact Human Resources Development Canada, ☎ (800) 567-6866, ✆ www.hrdc-drhc.gc.ca. To obtain an Employer Identification Number in the United States, visit your local Internal Revenue Service office or visit the IRS web site, ✆ www.irs.gov, to download the EIN form. In Canada, you can visit your local

Canada Customs and Revenue Agency office or visit the CCRA web site, ☞ www.ccra-adrc.gc.ca, to download the EIN form.

Sales Agents

An alternative to hiring salespeople to sell your products and services is to contract with a freelance sales agent. This is often an excellent alternative for small business owners operating sales-driven businesses, such as home improvement services, consulting services, internet technology services, and product manufacturers. First, the majority of sales agents (also known as freelance sales consultants) prefer to work on a contract basis for tax reasons and to maintain the ability to represent more than one client at a time. This saves you extra paperwork, and you do not have to worry about employee benefits because, in effect, freelance sales agents are self-employed. Second, sales agents generally are armed with the tools they need to sell—transportation, computer hardware and software, cellular telephones, and other tools of the trade, saving you from having to purchase these items. Third, and perhaps the biggest benefit of contracting with sales agents, there's the fact that they bring two big assets to the table—the ability to prospect effectively for new business and, in most cases, an existing customer and contact base that can be capitalized on immediately. Almost all sales agents prefer to work on a performance-based fee system, retaining a portion of their total sales as a commission. Depending on what is being sold and the costs associated with selling the service, gross commissions can range from 5 to 30 percent of total sales value.

Subcontractors

It is also common practice for small business owners to subcontract all or some of their work to other qualified individuals and businesses, especially service providers. For instance, general contractors will subcontract various segments of a renovation contract to different subtrades—framing crews, roofers, painters, and electricians. A dog-walking service might hire subcontract walkers. Or, a desktop publishing service might subcontract various tasks such as printing, proofreading, and graphic design to qualified businesses when fulfilling a client's contract. Depending on how you structure your business and fulfill contracts, you might also find that you need to hire subcontractors to complete all the work for some clients. When hiring or contracting subcontractors, you do have to take some precautions because your subcontractor's work or performance is viewed as your work or performance in the eyes of your customers. After all, your client contracted with you for the job, not your subcontractors. Likewise, you will need to make sure your subcontractors are reliable and fully insured. You will also need to know how they warranty or guarantee their work. Additionally, always work from a written and binding contract that spells out all of the details, including payment, performance, and liability issues between the two parties.

Suppliers

Suppliers from whom you purchase products and services for the operation of your business are also important members of your business team. Suppliers can play a major role in your ultimate success or failure. Consequently, these relationships need to be carefully developed and managed. Decisions to select and work with one supplier over another cannot be based solely on who offers the lowest price; you also have to factor many other influences, such as payment terms, warranties and guarantees, and reliability. Remember, your supplier's promises to you are your promises to your customers. If your supplier lets you down, you let your customers down. Also, when selecting suppliers find out what tools, equipment, or marketing materials they offer free or at greatly reduced costs to their vendors. Many have programs in place in which they offer their trade accounts valuable equipment, marketing materials, and cooperative advertising opportunities that will help businesses to be more efficient, productive, and profitable. Items that you might be able to tap your suppliers for range from ongoing specialized training, to advertising specialties, to customer service support.

Business, Industry, and Professional Associations

Joining business, industry, or professional associations relevant to your business and the products and services you sell, or the community where you do business, can be a goldmine for valuable information, assistance, and business-building opportunities. Joining means that you can have access to member discounts on products and services used to operate your business, as well as networking opportunities, new business alliances, advertising opportunities, and educational opportunities through seminars and workshops. Business, industry, and professional associations can have a larger and more positive benefit on business than most entrepreneurs think. The largest small business association in North America is the Chamber of Commerce. To find a chapter near you in the United States visit, ♂ www.uschamber.com, and in Canada visit, ♂ www.chamber.ca.

Cross-Promotional Partners

Building cross-promotional partnerships with other businesses in your community can also prove to be very beneficial and profitable, mainly because you can capitalize on each partner's experiences, resources, and customer base. Cross-promotional activities should be developed so they increase brand awareness, reach a broader audience, and attract new business to you, while driving down the costs for each partner to market and promote his respective businesses, goods, and services. Basically, cross-promotional activities enable entrepreneurs who share similar goals and objectives to band together to minimize financial risk and maximize potential profits.

Professional Service Providers

Professional service providers such as lawyers, bankers, accountants, and consultants also play an important role in helping small business owners reach their business and marketing objectives. When selecting professional service providers, it is imperative to keep in mind that often it is the professional's experience, knowledge, and advice that you will be leveraging to help you start your business, keep you in business, grow your business, and keep you out of trouble. Of course, a commonsense approach must be taken when hiring professional service providers. For example, if you plan to operate a part-time pet-sitting business, there will be no need to enlist the services of a professional to get started. On the other hand, if you are going to purchase a franchise and hire employees, professional advice and services will certainly be needed to help guide you through the process.

Lawyer

Competent lawyers with small business experience can advise you on which legal business structure best meets your needs, insurance and liability issues, drafting of legal documents, money collection and small-claims courts matters, estate planning and continuation of your business, and other contracts. Anyone who has ever been in business knows that operating a business and having access to good legal advice go hand-in-hand, especially if your business plans include a substantial investment and aggressive growth strategies. To find a lawyer in the United States, contact the American Bar Association, ☎ (202) 662-1000, ✆ www.aba net.org, and in Canada, the Canadian Bar Association, ☎ (800) 267-8860, ✆ www .cba.org. These associations will help you locate a lawyer in your area who specializes in small business legal matters.

Banker

Establishing a business relationship with a banker means also developing a relationship with all of the bank's key employees—managers, loan officers, and tellers—at the bank or credit union where you open your business accounts. Having a good working relationship with a bank or credit union is often a critical success factor for small businesses. Access to cash is one of the most vital business tools at your disposal. You never know when you will need to borrow working capital, growth capital, or obtain just a quick loan to get you through the next 60 days until a client contract is completed, billed, and collected.

Accountant

Accountants pride themselves on the fact that they do not cost you money, but rather make you money by discovering items overlooked on tax returns, by identifying business deductions you never knew existed, and by creating financial plans that can help you reach your business objectives. Even with the proliferation of accounting and bookkeeping software, hiring an accountant to take care of more complicated money matters is wise. Contact the Association of Chartered Accountants in the United States, ☎ (212) 334-2078, ♂ www.acaus.org, to find a small business CPA in your area; in Canada, you can contact the Chartered Accountants of Canada, ☎ (416) 977-3222, ♂ www.cica.ca.

Consultants

Professional consultants have long played a role in helping small business owners to meet and exceed their business and marketing objectives through coaching, planning, new business development, and training strategies. Consulting experts are available in just about every business discipline imaginable, including small business, logistics, marketing, sales, employee and management training, computer, internet technologies, franchising, advertising, and public relations. The first step in hiring a business consultant is to define your objective. What do you want to fix, improve, or venture into? Once you know your objective(s), you can select and interview a few potential candidates for the job. There are a number of online consultant directories such as The Training Registry, ♂ www.trainingregistry.com, which lists consultants by specialty and indexed geographically. Elance Online, ♂ www.elanceonline.com, is also a great place to find expert consulting services.

Developing a Business Image

When setting up your business, you will also need to create a business image to help brand your business, products, and services, as well as to project a positive image. Developing an appropriate business image is important for all businesses, but it is especially important for service providers because most do not have the advantage of elaborate offices or elegant storefronts to impress prospects and customers. Instead, they must rely on imagination, creativity, and attention to the smallest detail when creating and maintaining a professional business image.

Logos and Slogans

Attention-grabbing logos and memorable slogans help build consumer awareness of your business, products, and services and help project a positive business image. Business logos and promotional slogans play a major role in branding, especially logos because of their visual recognition qualities—consumers see instantly that it is a brand they know, like, and trust. To develop a slogan, think about the biggest benefit people receive from buying your products or services, and create a brief, yet powerful slogan around that benefit.

Logos can be a little trickier to create unless you have design experience and a creative flair. Don't worry if these are skills you lack; there are many logo design services, such as The Logo Company, ♂ www.thelogocompany.com, and Logo Bee, ♂ www.logobee.com, that can help create a professional logo for your business. Prices for basic design services start at less than $100. Once you have decided on a logo design and a promotional slogan, you must consistently incorporate these into every area of your business, including stationery, signage, promotional materials, uniforms, and advertising. The more often consumers are exposed to your brand through the consistent use of logos and slogans, the more they will remember it, giving your business, products, and services brand recognition.

Print Identity Package

An identity package is comprised of the various print elements that you use daily in the course of operating your business—business cards, stationery, receipts, envelopes, estimate forms, and the like. Key to a great print identity package is consistency throughout the entire package, just as in your entire marketing program. To get the most out of your print identity package, you want to develop a standard color scheme and font, combine these with your logo and slogan, and use it consistently so that customers and prospects begin to visually link your business with your identity program. Always get three quotes for all of your printing needs, and do not necessarily buy based only on price. Instead, base your purchasing decision on quality, value, reputation, and turnaround time. In addition to your community printer, there are also many printers doing business online, for example, Print USA, ♂ www.printusa.com, which offers free quotes on a wide variety of products.

Uniforms

Top businesspeople have long understood the benefits associated with staff and management wearing uniforms emblazoned with a business name and logo. These benefits include branding the business name, products, and services, as well as projecting a professional image and helping identify employees. Uniforms also happen to be terrific advertising and promotional tools, especially T-shirts, which only cost about $10 each and can also be given to customers through special promotions. In fact, great-looking uniforms do not have to be expensive; for as little as $20 each you can purchase smart casual golf shirts silk-screened or embroidered with your business name and logo. Hats start at $10 each, and jackets for about $50, all of which is money wisely spent to project a professional image and advertise your business.

Taking Your Business Online

If you are excited about the idea of selling your products and services online, you should be. American consumers spent more than $95 billion on online purchases in 2003; that total is expected to reach $230 billion by 2008! Granted, products do account for the larger portion of online sales, but many entrepreneurs also sell services online. There is a lot to know and learn about taking your business online and selling your products and services to consumers around the globe. Needless to say, space restrictions do not allow for an in-depth explanation of everything you need to know about doing business online here, but the following covers the basics—building a web site, choosing a domain name, and search engine registration.

Building a Web Site

Your first decision is to determine if you need a web site. Even if you are not planning to sell your products or services online, a site can still be a very effective communication tool and be used to gather information captured from visitors for research and planning purposes. Ultimately, you have to decide if the time and money spent to develop, maintain, and market a web site is a wise investment that may help you to meet your business objectives. If you do decide to sell your products and services online, the advantages are apparent—the ability to sell 24 hours a day, communicate with prospects and customers quickly and cheaply, update your marketing message and special promotions almost instantly, and sell to consumers around the globe.

Once you have made the decision to build a web site, there are many decisions to be made: How much will it cost to create it? Who will build it? Who will maintain it? Who will host it? What purchase payment options will you provide customers? And how will the site be promoted?

Your first option is to design, build, and maintain your own web site. Fortunately, there are numerous good web site building programs available to enable novice webmasters to build and maintain their own sites, but you will still need to be familiar with computers and the internet if you go this route. Hosting and maintenance costs will vary depending on the services you select—e-commerce shopping carts, payments systems, order tracking, content, web tools, site statistics, and database storage options. Expect to pay a minimum of $50 per month for basic business web site hosting and about $250 per month for premium services.

Your second option is to hire a professional to design and build your web site. Costs here have dramatically decreased in the past few years. In fact, for less than $1,000 you can have a complete, fully functional web site built with e-commerce, visitor interaction, and database marketing options. Click onto the Web Design Developers Association, ♂ www.wdda.org, to locate a web designer in your area, or consult your local Yellow Pages for web developers in your community.

Choosing a Domain Name

Selecting a domain name for your new web site or web business requires careful consideration because the domain name you select must be suited to the products and services you sell. That's often easier said than done. There are various extensions that can be used, such as .com, .biz, and .tv, or country extensions, such as .ca in Canada and .us in the United States, but .com is still king in terms of online business. Good dotcom designations are becoming increasingly difficult to acquire. The domain name that you choose should also be short, easily remembered, and easily spelled. Start the process of choosing a domain name right away, and register a few variations as soon as you have compiled a short list. Domain name registration fees vary depending on the designation and the registration service you choose, but expect to pay from a low of $10 per year for a budget registrar to as much as $75 per year with a full-service registration company. Most registrars also offer discounts if you register a name for a longer period—up to ten years. The majority of domain registration services also provide various additional internet and e-commerce services and packages, web site design, shopping carts, hosting and maintenance, and web site promotional services. A few of the more popular domain name registration services include Domain Direct, ♂ www.domaindirect.com;

Register, ♂ www.register.com; Go Daddy, ♂ www.godaddy.com; and Network Solutions, ♂ www.networksolutions.com.

Search Engine Registration

Because you don't know which search engine or directory people will use when looking for products and services online, you will need to register your web site and pages with numerous engines and directories to ensure maximum exposure. But before you start registering, you should know the basics. Search engines are indexed by bots or spiders, which extract specific information and keywords from web site pages and are then used for indexing. Search directories use people, directory editors, who compile information by hand, generally indexed and grouped based on relevancy to the submitted search. However, the line between search engine and search directory is increasingly blurred. Most major search engines and directories use both mechanical and human power to build and index information or supplement each other's services, so you need to register with both.

Registering with engines and directories can be very frustrating and time consuming because there are no standard guidelines, as most searches engines and directories have individual submission policies. There are search engine and directory submission services that will automatically submit to or register your web site on all major search engines and directories. That is a wise choice for entrepreneurs on a tight time schedule. Most of these services require only that you complete one relatively basic form; they will do the rest. Some submission services are free, but the majority charge fees if you want quick listings, regular maintenance, and other premium listing services. These services offer small business owners with limited time to optimize their web sites for the best search rank results great value for a relatively small fee. The more popular submission services include Add Me, ♂ www.addme.com, Submit It, ♂ www.submit-it.com, and Submit Express, ♂ www.submitexpress.com. Google, ♂ www.google.com, remains the most widely known search engine, and Yahoo!, ♂ www.yahoo.com, is the most widely known search directory.

5

SALES AND MARKETING

In this entire chapter on sales and marketing, you will learn basic personal contact selling techniques as well as how to sell your products and services from home, a retail location, online, and at community events such as flea markets. If you manufacture products, you will also learn how to sell wholesale and via consignment placements with retailers. As you read through the information, keep in mind that many of the sales and marketing ideas in this chapter are portable. This means most merchandising and selling techniques that work for homebased showrooms will also produce sales results at trade and consumer shows. You will also learn about advertising via radio, newspapers, and Yellow Pages, and public relations tips that can be employed to secure valuable media exposure for your business, products, and services.

Personal Contact Selling

Don't feel intimidated if "selling" is not your strongest business skill. The vast majority of people who start a business selling products or services are not professional salespeople. They don't have to be. Personal contact selling success is a combination of education, practice, persistence, building on your strengths, and duplicating what gets the best results in terms of location, promotion, price, and selling technique. So what are the basic personal contact selling skills that you should learn? You need to get ready to sell, learn how to qualify buyers, brush up on your negotiating skills, get in the habit of asking for the sale, and always ask for referrals. All of these selling topics are discuss below.

Getting Ready to Sell

Preparation is the starting point for all personal contact selling. You have to know what you are selling inside out and upside down, and how customers benefit by purchasing and using your products or services. Product and service knowledge can be acquired through research, specialized training, your suppliers, and published information, but the two of the most important methods are probably feedback from customers and hands-on experience. You must also know your target audience well: Which are the people who need and want to buy the products and services you sell? Where does your target audience live? How can you gain access to them? How often do they buy? And, what do they base buying decisions on—price, quality, convenience, or guarantees? Being prepared to sell means you also know your competition thoroughly—what people like and dislike about their products, services, prices, and warranties.

The final aspect of getting ready to sell is to have a toolbox packed with great sales tools. Think of your sales tools as the instruments you will use to grab your prospects' attention, create buying desire, and most importantly, motivate them to take action and buy. Depending on the products and services you sell, sales tools can include specialized training and certifications, promotional literature, product samples, attention-grabbing signage, customer testimonials, ironclad guarantees, value-added promotions, and numerous purchase payment options such as credit cards, debit cards, and consumer financing for big-ticket items.

Qualifying Buyers

Qualifying buyers is the process of asking potential customers questions and using their responses to determine if they really want to buy the products or services that you are selling. The importance of qualifying your buyers is apparent—the better qualified a prospect is, the greater the chance you will close the sale. Qualifying buyers basically revolves around three issues—need, decision maker, and money. You have to determine right away through questioning if the person needs or wants what you have to sell. It makes no sense to waste your time by trying to sell RV detailing services to someone who doesn't own an RV.

You must also make sure you are dealing with the person who has the authority to make the buying decision. The best way to find out is to simply ask, "Who will be making the purchasing decision? Will you be making the decision on your own, or will there be other people involved in the purchasing decision?" Again, you do not want to waste time trying to sell to people who do not have the authority to make the buying decision.

Finally, you also have to be able to determine if the person has the money or access to the money needed to make the purchase. Ask, "What is your budget?" "Can you afford it?" Regardless of how you phrase the question, you have to know if they can afford to buy what you are selling. This is not to say all hope is lost if they cannot afford to buy, but you will have to explore other options, such as a cheaper model or creative financing.

Become a Power Negotiator

It pays to become a power negotiator because when you are in business you never stop negotiating. You negotiate with customers to buy more and at higher prices. You negotiate with suppliers for lower prices and better terms. You negotiate with your bank for lower merchant account fees. Needless to say, learning how to become a power negotiator results in selling your products and services at higher prices and in greater quantities, while paying less for the products and services needed to operate your business.

In negotiations, the more information you have about your prospects in terms of their wants, needs, and budget, the stronger your position for getting what you want out of the selling and negotiating process. This means you have to find out as much as you can about what your potential customer wants and needs, and how these are prioritized—by benefits, budget, quality, or schedule. Having this information lets you know what they want to achieve through negotiations—lower price, longer warranty, fast delivery, or more features.

Also remember, if someone really needs the product or service you are selling, price often becomes a secondary issue to user benefits, such as an improved lifestyle or solving a problem. So it makes sense that before negotiations start you must first position the value of your product or service in relationship to the benefits the person will receive by buying. This is a critical step. If what you have to sell is properly positioned in terms of customer perceived value, it gives you increased leverage and power to get what you want in the negotiating process without having to accept less money or other unfavorable conditions.

Asking for the Sale

Why should you always ask for the sale? The answer is simple: Few people will take it upon themselves to offer you the sale unless they are asked to do so. Asking for the sale is the golden rule of closing. If you do not ask for the sale every time you present your products or services, all you will have accomplished is to educate your prospect, making them a very easy closing target for competitors that do ask for the sale. In fact, if you do not ask every prospect to buy, you are, in effect, telling them that they can purchase better products and services elsewhere, so they best keep shopping. Forget that. You have the best products and services, otherwise you wouldn't be selling them, right?

Closing is an essential selling skill, but at the same time, it is nothing more than the natural progression in the sales cycle. You qualify, present, overcome objections, and close. Therefore, asking for the sale should be nothing more than a formality. You can even go one step further and assume that all prospects will buy. Do this by making statements like, "We can deliver this for you next week." "I just need your signature on this agreement so we can get started." "How would you like to pay for this?" Or you can phrase the closing question in the form of an alternate choice question such as, "So which one do you prefer, the basic dog-grooming package, or the premium package?" The alternate choice pulls your prospect into making a buying decision and selecting one of the options you present. Not buying is no longer an available option with the alternate choice closing question.

At the end of the day, volumes can, and have, been written about closing sales. The most successful salespeople, however, are the ones that take the time to qualify buyers, identify and understand their customers' needs, meet these needs, and always ask for the sale.

Asking for Referrals

One of the fastest and most effective ways to increase sales and profits, while reducing sales cycle time and the advertising and marketing costs associated with finding new customers, is to get more referrals. Referrals are often the defining line between business success or failure for many small business owners. This is especially true when you consider that it is much easier to sell a warm prospect, that is, someone familiar with your business, products, or services, than a cold prospect who doesn't know anything about them.

How do you get more referrals? There are a number of ways, but the easiest is to simply ask for them. Securing more referrals often requires nothing more than asking for one. People seldom offer you referrals unless asked to do so. Just as you must always ask for the sale, so must you always ask for referrals. Wording the question doesn't have to be difficult, or particularly clever. "Mrs. Jones, do you know anyone who would benefit from the products we sell"? Or, "We take pride in providing the highest quality services at fair prices. Do you know any one, like you, who needs our service and who wants to be treated fairly"? But don't stop with your customers. Also enlist your family, friends, suppliers, and business associates to refer your business, products, and services to their friends, family, co-workers, and customers. The idea is to build an army of people that can refer your business to others. You will quickly discover that when other people believe in your business and your products or services, they will be more than happy to spread the word by telling others.

Selling Products and Services from Home

One of the advantages of selling products or services from home is that it can be combined with many other sales methods—online sales, trade or consumer shows, or flea markets, depending on the products you sell or the services you provide. There are also a great number of benefits to selling from home, including no commute, tax advantages, and saving money by making the most out of existing resources. Not every home is suitable for product and service sales, and some communities do not allow or have restrictions in place for homebased businesses. But for entrepreneurs who have suitable homes, products, or services, selling from home is a great option. The information below focuses on selling products and services from home utilizing interior showrooms, exterior display, and in-home sales parties. Additional information about equipping a homebased business can be found in Chapter 4. Because there is a lot to know about operating a home-based business, you might want to sign out a copy of *Entrepreneur Magazine's Ultimate Homebased Business Handbook* (Entrepreneur Press, 2004) from your local library or purchase a copy from retail booksellers nationwide and online. The book is an A to Z explanation of everything you need to know about starting and operating a homebased business. Small Office Home Office (SOHO), an organization comprised of small business owners that mainly operate their businesses from a homebased location, can also be helpful. In the United States click on to ♂ www.soho.org for more information, and in Canada click on to ♂ www.soho.ca.

Interior Showrooms

Homebased entrepreneurs have lots of options in terms of establishing an interior showroom to showcase and sell products such as clothing, antiques, or craft items and services such as dog-grooming, wedding planning, and photography. You can convert your garage, basement, den, or just about any room of your home into a well-stocked showroom to peddle your products or an office to meet with clients to discuss or provide services. Ideally, the space you choose will have a separate entrance to provide privacy for your family and customers alike. You will need to decide if your showroom/office will be open every day, weekends only, or by appointment only.

What are the best products to sell from a homebased interior showroom? Just about any product can be sold from home, but some are better suited than others. Some of the better-suited products are jewelry, antiques, pottery, clothing, furniture, craft products, food products, art, fashion accessories, and toys. Regardless of the products, be sure to display and merchandise them just like a traditional storefront retailer. Take advantage of proper display cases, racks, lighting, mirrors, and signage, and renovate and decorate the showroom to project the appropriate image for your business and products.

What are the best services to sell from a homebased office or workspace? Just like products, almost any service can be sold from home, but again, some are better suited than others. A few of the better ones are desktop publishing, bookkeeping, engraving, consulting service, appliance repair, and instruction classes. Just like a traditional office or workspace, renovate, equip, and decorate to project the appropriate image for your business and services.

Exterior Display

Exterior display is also a good option for product sellers because of increased interest from passing motorists and pedestrians that get to see the products you sell. Perfect products to display outdoors include outdoor items such as patio furniture, greenhouses, sheds, and whirligigs. Ultimately, the products you sell will determine the best places around the home to display items—patio furniture right on your own sundeck, greenhouses in the garden, and weathervanes adorning your roof line.

Theft can become a problem when displaying products outdoor, so be sure to install motion lights, fencing, and gates as required. Like an interior showroom, you also have to consider the image you want to project for your business. Peeling paint, overgrown gardens, and broken windows will all have a negative impact on a business. Consequently, before displaying products for sale, make sure you spruce up the exterior of your home and property, make repairs as necessary, and keep on top of ongoing maintenance.

In-Home Sales Parties

In-home sales parties are also an excellent option for selling products that you manufacture, import, or purchase in bulk at wholesale prices. The biggest advantage of home party sales is zero competition. That is to say, you have the undivided attention of party guests. The best items to sell at in-home sales parties are personal products (lingerie, specialty foods, cosmetics, bath and body products), gift items, and craft products.

To expand sales is as easy as enlisting other people interested in making extra money to organize and host parties in their own homes to sell your products. Your new sales force can be paid in three ways: commissions based on total sales, profits after buying from you wholesale, or free products based on their total sales. Perfect candidates to recruit to your sales team include stay-at-home parents, students, retired folks, and anyone else looking to make extra money working from their homes. Your sales agents can take orders for products, which you can later ship from your central location. Or, they can have product on hand for customers to take home. You will need to supply each with product samples, sales brochures, and a sales and operations manual that includes how they can organize and host the event.

To boost sales and profits at in-home sales parties, offer free gift wrapping for smaller items because it motivates people to buy extra product as gifts for people not in attendance. Also design and print $10 gift certificates and distribute one to each guest in attendance. But mark void if not used that night. People will feel compelled to buy rather than risk losing the $10. Other ways to increase sales include offering additional savings at various purchase levels. For example, buy $50 worth of product and receive a $5 credit, $100 receives a $12 credit, and $200 receives a $30 credit toward the purchase of more product. Or in advance of the party, tell each guest that if they bring a friend, both will receive a 10 percent discount on all purchases. Also be sure to stage a contest and give away a prize at each party. Have guests complete an entry form, including full contact information and draw for the prize. The entry forms can be later used to build a database of potential customers, who can be routinely contacted with special product offers via e-mail, mail, and telephone.

Selling Products and Services from a Retail Location

If selling products or services from home is not an option, you may decide to rent retail space, such as a storefront, mall kiosk, or vending cart to enable you to sell directly to consumers. Selling products and services from a retail location rather than selling from home has advantages. First, customers may perceive your business as more professional. Second, retail locations generally have much better visibility than a residential district, thereby greatly increasing the potential for walk-in business. There are also disadvantages, namely the additional cost of rent, utilities, and building maintenance. And you may face the cost of hiring employees to keep the store staffed during normal retail business hours. Whether you sell from a retail storefront, kiosk, or carts, many of the merchandising ideas featured in this section are portable, that is, they can be employed to sell products and services regardless of the location.

Storefront

Retailing is a very broad subject and continually evolving. The information featured here covers only the tip of the retailing iceberg. What worked ten years ago may not work in today's highly competitive retail environment. You need to carefully research and plan every aspect of a retail venture in order to maximize the potential for success. You have to invest the time and financial resources needed to educate yourself about retailing—buy and read books on retail business, hire retail sales consultants, join retailers' associations, and talk to a whole bunch of retailers before taking the leap of faith and opening up shop.

The objective when designing a retail store and merchandising products is to appeal to the largest segment of your target audience so that they feel comfortable in the store and want to return and shop often. This is an area where it pays to hire a professional retail store designer. When arranging product displays think profit zones—the areas around the sales checkout, around the entrance, and areas on a direct path to the sales counter. These areas account for the largest percentage of impulse buying. Consumers also go shopping for pure entertainment value, and you have to keep this in mind when creating in-store merchandise displays. Make product displays exciting, attention grabbing, and memorable by using props, signage, and demonstrations. Also group products that complement each and make a logical sales package. Designer clothing should be displayed with fashion accessories such as handbags, costume jewelry, and shoes, for instance. Complementary product grouping helps to increase sales and the value of each sale.

Window space is one of the best and least expensive marketing tools available to most retailers; think of your window space as a 24-hour silent salesperson that never sleeps. Windows can be used to display new products, demonstrate products and services, and motivate impulse buying. In short, well-planned, well-executed window displays can increase revenues and profits. If you are new to designing window displays, get out with a camera and look at what other retailers are doing with their windows. Take pictures and make notes about window displays that work so you can get your creative juices flowing. The best window displays are lean and mean with one central focal point; you do not need your entire inventory on display. You might occasionally want to create window displays around popular entertainment, sports, or musical events and use props and movement to make your displays come alive and exciting. Remember the goal is to grab attention and pull people into your shop to buy.

The following are a few helpful retailing business resources: The National Association of Store Fixture Manufacturers, ☎ (954) 893-7300, ✆ www.nasfm.org, National Retail Federation, ☎ (202) 783-7971, ✆ www.nrf.com, Retail Merchandiser Magazine Online, ✆ www.retail-merchandiser.com, and Retail Source, ✆ www.retailsource.com.

Kiosks and Carts

Kiosks and pushcarts also represent great selling opportunities for vendors with the right products, small products like sunglasses and craft items, as well as some services, like a nail business. Kiosks and pushcarts are available in both interior and exterior styles, though the focus here is on interior kiosks and pushcarts that you find in malls, office buildings, and transportation facilities. Many of these carts and kiosks are available to rent on a short- or long-term basis: from one day to an entire year. Generally speaking, it is the building or property management company that rents vending space, so these are the people that you want to contact. In addition to a vendor's permit, most locations also require you to have liability insurance. Many locations can be lucrative, but vendors who specialize in selling from mall kiosks tend to fare the best and produce the highest sales, especially during the Christmas shopping season. Carriage Works manufactures custom kiosks and pushcarts, and can be contacted at ☎ (541) 882-9661 or online at ✆ www.carraigeworks.com. The Cart Owners Association of America is a good source of pushcart vending information. The association can be contacted at ☎ (559) 332-2229 or online at ✆ www.cartowners.org.

Selling Products Wholesale

If you manufacture products, you can sell directly to consumers or go after the big market opportunities by wholesaling your products in mass quantities to independent retailers and chain retailers or to wholesalers and distributors. If you choose the second route, there are basically three avenues available to you—grassroots wholesaling, established wholesalers, and the business-to-business trade shows. All three have advantages and disadvantages. Depending on your products, price point, and business and sales objectives, you may elect to combine one or more of these approaches to wholesale the products you make.

Grassroots Wholesaling

Grassroots wholesaling means setting appointments with independent and chain retailers. Armed with product samples and catalogs, you present and pitch your products. Of course, this is often easier said than done. Securing appointments with independent retailers is not difficult, generally only requiring a telephone call or introduction letter to get the ball rolling. Chain retailers, however, are an entirely different ball game because all buying decisions are made at the head office level, even if the retailer is a franchise operation. It can be very difficult to get past the gatekeepers and to the people who make buying decisions. If you do get five minutes of their time, you better have something very impressive to pitch or get use to rejection. Chain retailers want to know why they should buy your products, what the competitive advantages and special features are, and how their customers benefit by purchasing it. They also want to know how you are going to promote the product to motivate consumers to go to the retailers' stores and buy. It is possible to land vendor accounts with major chain retailers, but be prepared to work hard and smart to accomplish this goal.

Established Wholesalers

This approach is much like the grassroots approach, but instead of setting appointments with retailers, you set appointments with businesses that already have established channels of distribution in place, that is wholesalers and distributors. You sell your product to the wholesaler, who in turns sells it to the retailer, who in turn sells it to the consumer. The major downside with this sales option is price point. You have to have the ability to sell your product for drastically less than retail, often by as much as 60 percent off retail, in order for the wholesaler to be able to sell to retailers at a profitable price point. But having said that, you can make up lower profits per unit by selling in larger quantities. A good starting point is to contact the National Association of Wholesale-Distributors, ☎ (202)

872-0885, ✆ www.naw.org, to find wholesalers selling the types of products you manufacture.

Business-to-Business Trade Shows

In terms of landing retailer accounts for the products you make, arguably the best approach is to exhibit your products at business-to-business trade shows. These are basically the same as consumer trade shows with one big exception: Wholesale buyers representing national and international retailers of all sizes attend, and they are there to find new products to buy in quantity. There are industry trade shows for just about every type of product imaginable—from craft items to furniture to recreational products. Best of all, unlike consumer shows, buyers do not want to purchase products and take immediate delivery; they are there to scout products, negotiate prices, and place orders for future delivery. Therefore, all you have to bring are product samples and a catalog listing your products, accompanied by order forms indicating unit pricing, bulk pricing, payment terms and methods, delivery schedules, minimum order amounts, warranty information, and return policy. The National Mail Order Association, ☎ (612) 788-4197, ✆ www .nmoa.org, publishes an annual *Industry Trade Show, Importer, and Wholesale Marketplace Directory*, which includes listing information on more than 150 product trade shows, as well as wholesale publications, trade magazines, and manufacturer directories.

Consignment Sales

If you manufacture products, should you place your products on consignment with retailers? Yes and no. Yes, consigning products with retailers can be a viable way to get your products into stores and ultimately purchased by consumers. No, consignment is not suited to all products, and there are additional drawbacks such as high sales commission fees, loss of control over merchandising, and having to wait weeks, sometimes months, before being paid on sales. Suitable products for consignment include art, gift products, designer fashions, and handcrafted products. If you decide to go the consignment route, there are four main points to consider: the types of retailers and location, the consignment agreement, merchandising and pricing, and inventory management and product delivery.

Picking Retailers

Not all retailers accept consignment products, but many do, especially those selling gift and craft products. You have to choose wisely and make sure your products are compatible with the types of products the retailer sells. You also have to decide if you will consign with local retailers and/or out of town retailers. Both have advantages and disadvantages. Consigning locally is very convenient with easy delivery and inventory monitoring. Out of town consignments add travel time and shipping costs. On the other hand, consigning out of your local area opens the possibility of selling more products to a broader audience of consumers. Overall, when selecting retailers to consign with, consider the types of products they sell, their current sales, their reputation, and the existance of an established consignment program.

Consignment Agreement

The devil is always in the details. Closely scrutinize any retailer's consignment agreement before signing on the dotted line and stocking products. How much is the retailer's sales commission on products sold? Depending on the value of the product, expect the retailer to retain a commission in the range of 25 to 50 percent. Does the retailer generate a consignment sales report, and how often do you get paid on products sold? How are the payments made—check, direct deposit, or cash? Ideally, you want a formal sales report and to be paid by check every 30 days for the previous month's sales. What are the retailer's policies in terms of consignment product returns, refunds, and theft? Does the retailer's insurance cover your products in the event of fire, flood, or other causes of damage? Returns and refunds are inevitable, so you will need to come to a mutually agreeable policy. In terms of theft or damage to stock while in the retailers' possession, it is their liability, not yours. Therefore, make sure that this is included in the consignment agreement.

Merchandising and Pricing

Ideally, you want the ability to merchandise and price your products in each consignment location. Unfortunately, this is not always an option because many retailers reserve the right to decide how consigned products will be merchandised inside the store, as well as the retail price. The right to merchandise and price your products is the key to successful and profitable consigning. Fight for this right. Go armed with the tools needed to persuade retailers to your way of thinking. These tools include a high-quality, in-demand product with a strong warranty, competitive pricing, and attention-grabbing packaging and merchandise displays. Fight for the best real estate inside the store—close to the checkout, around the entrance, and with good window visibility. Ultimately, the retailer is in the business of selling goods, not simply displaying goods. You must develop products and merchandising strategies that will motivate consumers to buy.

Inventory Management and Product Delivery

You also need to develop a standardized inventory management system, especially if you consign products with multiple retailers. The simplest way of doing this is to create a consignment form listing initial inventory stocked in each location, remove items as they are sold or removed from the store, and list new products each time they are stocked. It is crucial to keep a very accurate record of all inventory and to obtain signatures every time products are restocked or removed from the store. Not only will this protect against inventory shrinkage, but also over time you will be able to determine what products sell best at each of the retailers and at what times of year, enabling you to develop marketing strategies to maximize sales at each location. Additionally, you need to think about product delivery. Will you hand deliver to all consignment accounts or have product shipped? If your accounts are close, you can deliver to each; if not, it will likely be cheaper to have products shipped. In the latter case you must determine how much this adds to the unit cost of each product.

Selling Products and Services Online

There are numerous ways to promote and sell products and services online, but this section focuses on three—eBay, e-auctions, and internet malls. You should also develop your own e-commerce web site, so you can sell your products to an audience of worldwide consumers. (Information about building a web site is found in Chapter 4.) The advantages of internet e-tailing are obvious—open 24-hours a day, information to customers in minutes, and quickly, conveniently, and inexpensively updating of marketing messages and strategies. However, it is best not to use a web site as your sole means of selling products online. Instead, use your site in combination with other online sales methods such as eBay as well as offline venues such as homebased sales and trade and consumer shows.

eBay

Online auction and retail marketplace giant eBay, ♂ www.ebay.com, with more than 100 million registered users around the globe, has set up camp in more than 20 countries worldwide, and, even more amazing, has 450,000 registered users claiming that selling products through eBay as their sole source of income! Volumes can, have, and will continue to be written on the subject of profiting by doing business on eBay, but space here does not permit a detailed explanation. eBay is as wide as it is deep. If you're really interested; spend lots of time on its sites, take advantage of its sponsored workshops, and read books about eBay selling before you get started.

The most popular and common type of eBay auction is the traditional, or classic, auction: There is no set reserve price, and at the end of the 1-, 3-, 5-, 7-, or 10-day auction, the highest bid wins. The theory of a short auction is it enables you to generate more heat and bidding excitement, whereas a longer auction might eventually lead to diminished interest as time passes. On the other hand, a longer auction means your product(s) is exposed to more potential buyers and might fetch a higher price. You will have to play around with auction lengths a bit to find what works best for what you sell. eBay also offers a *Buy it Now* option, which means you can set a price for your product, and a buyer can purchase it for the set price without having to wait for the auction to end. But, once you receive a bid, the *Buy It Now* icon disappears and the sale reverts back to a traditional auction.

Sellers also have the option of setting a reserve price, the lowest possible price a seller is prepared to take for the item. Buyers do not know what the reserve price is, only that there is one. Once a bid exceeds the reserve price, the item sells to the highest bidder. If the reserve price is not met before the auction expires, the item does not sell. A seller can choose to relist the product for sale or not. Many sellers like to set a reserve price matching their product cost to protect against selling for less than cost.

A third option is a Dutch auction, which is a good choice for sellers that have multiple units of the same products for sale, such as 500 pairs of sunglasses, 1,000 die cast toys, or 50 designer handbags. There is no upper limit to how many of the same products you can list using a Dutch auction. Ten or 10,000, it's up to you. Bidders have the option of selecting how many they want to purchase: one, some, or all. Sellers start by listing the number of items for sale along with a starting bid. Bidders enter the amount they are willing to pay, usually lower than the starting bid, along with the number of units they want to purchase. The winning price is determined by the lowest successful bid at the time the auction closes, and all winning bidders receive this price whether or not their bid was higher. The concept is that if you receive bids for more items than you have for sale, then the lowest bids drop off, raising the price. Bidders can rebid a higher amount to stay in the game if they choose. A Dutch auction is a great way to move large quantities of products quickly and efficiently, especially high-demand products.

Some useful eBay information sites are:

- eBay Stores, ✍ http://pages.ebay.com/storefronts/start.html
- eBay Learning Center, ✍ http://pages.ebay.com/education/index.html
- eBay Seller's Guide, ✍ http://pages.ebay.com/help/sell/index.html
- eBay Promotional Tools, ✍ http://pages.ebay.com/sellercentral/tools.html

- eBay Shipping Center, ♂ http://pages.ebay.com/services/buyandsell/shipping.html
- eBay Selling Internationally, ♂ http://pages.ebay.com/help/sell/ia/selling_internationally.html

Additional e-Auctions

eBay is the undisputed king of online auctions, but it is not the only game in town. You do not want to limit your selling options to a single venue, especially if you can combine other online auction options to compliment eBay sales. There are hundreds of online auction sites—Yahoo! Auctions, ♂ www.auctions.yahoo.com, and Auction Fire, ♂ www.auctionfire.com, and lots more—but spend some time researching and selecting those best suited to your products and marketing objectives. Some are general auction sites with numerous categories ranging from clothing to furniture, whereas others are more product or industry specific, focusing on fine art, books, antiques, or sports memorabilia. Some operate on a highest bid, reserve bid, and/or Dutch auction format.

Many of the same marketing and promotional techniques used on eBay to attract and secure top bids can be applied to other online auction sites. People making and selling very specific items are encouraged to explore alternate auction services because they do attract targeted buyers searching for specific products. To find more specific online auction sites, visit online auction directories such as Net Auctions, ♂ www.net-auctions.com, and The Internet Auction List, ♂ www.internetauctionlist.com. Both list hundreds of online auction web sites.

Internet Malls

Just like brick and mortar shopping malls, internet malls and e-storefronts offer consumers a one-stop shopping opportunity for a wide range of products and services. There are a number of companies and services offering internet malls and e-storefront programs. The big players are eBay, ♂ www.ebay.com, Amazon, ♂ www.amazon.com, and the Internet Mall, ♂ www.internetmall.com. There are also hundreds of smaller outfits also offering online selling opportunities: American Internet Mall, ♂ www.aimone.com; Canadian Internet Mall, ♂ www.cdn-mall.com; and Mall Park, ♂ www.mallpark.com.

Most internet malls or e-storefront programs offer two basic services. They operate as a directory service listing product and/or service categories; for a fee, your business can be listed under one or more appropriate categories. To take advantage of this option, you need a web site so you can link to the mall's directory. Internet malls and e-storefront services also offer a more complete package, which can include: domain name registration, web site building, hosting, e-commerce tools, back-end administration tools, and promotion. Some programs blend the two types according to your needs and budget. Fees vary widely depending on your level of participation and the services you need, but generally start at a few hundred dollars in development fees along with ongoing monthly fees ranging from $20 to $500. Before signing on the dotted line, do your homework to ensure the mall has a good reputation with vendors and shoppers, offers the services you need, attracts your target audience, and has a strong marketing campaign in place to promote the mall and participating vendors.

Selling Products and Services at Events

In addition to selling products and services from home, retail locations, and online, there are also many special events that provide fantastic selling opportunities: consumer shows, arts and crafts shows, flea markets, and community events.

Consumer Shows

Consumer shows are for the general public to attend, browse, gain information, and shop. For small business owners, few marketing activities in the bricks and mortar world can match the effectiveness of consumer shows as a way to showcase and sell your products or services to a large audience at one time, in one place, and in a very cost-effective manner. Depending on the show and duration, you have the potential to come in contact with hundreds, if not thousands, of qualified prospects. There are consumer shows for every imaginable type of product or service—home and garden shows, food shows, sports and recreation shows, and on and on. Online directories, such as Trade Shows Online, ♂ www.tradeshows.com, makes it very easy to research shows and to gain insight into location, costs, attendance statistics, and competition. You should attend shows in person to get a feel for the vendors, management, and audience before making the commitment to exhibit, especially for more expensive or out-of-town shows.

The consumer show pace can be fast and furious, and time is a commodity always in short supply. So it is important to have a well-rehearsed sales plan ready to put into action. If you sell products, you are probably there to sell these products or take orders for later delivery. Therefore, your sales plan should revolve around four key elements—engage prospects, qualify prospects, present your products, and close the sale. If you sell services, you are probably exhibiting to collect sales leads. Therefore, your sales plan should also revolve around four key elements—engage prospects, qualify prospects, briefly explain the benefits of your service, and generate a sales lead. When designing your booth and displays, keep in mind that booths alive with exciting product and service demonstrations draw considerably more interest and larger crowds then static booths. That generally means more sales and/or more sales leads.

Arts and Crafts Shows

Arts and crafts shows are an excellent forum for selling high-quality handmade products. Shows range in size from small church-organized shows with a handful of vendors to international fine arts and crafts shows lasting for a week and drawing hundreds of vendors and thousands of consumers from around the globe. Most, however, are small weekend events and take place in community centers, exhibition buildings, hotels, convention centers, and school gymnasiums. Booth rent varies widely from $5 to $500 per day, depending on the size of the show and expected audience. It is always a good idea to visit larger and more expensive shows before signing on to vend to make sure the show and audience meet your exhibiting criteria. That also allows you to talk to other vendors to get firsthand feedback about the show and to check out the competition. Additional points to consider include admission fees, parking, competition, rent, operating history, and attendance statistics. Crafts Shows USA, ♂ www.craftshowsusa.com, provides a free online directory service listing information on hundreds of craft shows.

Once you have decided on a show(s), be sure to create a checklist before the event. Check off each item or task as completed so you are 100 percent ready to sell come show time. In terms of your booth, displays, and products, keep them clean, be organized, and use mirrors and lighting to brighten your sales space. Because shows can be very busy, price all items to save time repeating prices to everyone who asks. Also, create a couple of worthwhile show specials to pull shoppers into your booth. A 50-percent-off show special may seem excessive, but revenues and profits can be made up in volume sales and through up-selling opportunities. Likewise, in-booth demonstrations of your art or craft always draw crowds and grab more attention than exhibits without demonstrations. A busy booth equals more selling opportunities.

Ideally, you want to accept credit cards and debit cards because it increases impulse buying by as much as 50 percent. You will also need a receipt book, credit card slips, calculator, pens, price gun or blank price tags, and a cash lockbox. Also bring along a basic toolbox stocked with a hammer, screwdrivers, flashlight, wrench, extra light bulbs, cleaner, rags, stapler, and garbage bags. And bring lots of packing materials such as newspaper, plastic bags, boxes, tape, string, and scissors, as well as offering free gift-wrapping. Associations such as the Arts and Crafts Association of America, ☎ (616) 874-1721, ♂ www.artsandcraftsassoc.com, and the Canadian Crafts & Hobby Association, ☎ (403) 291-0559, ♂ www.cdn craft.org, also provide lots of information about selling handmade products at arts and crafts shows.

Flea Markets

Did you know that many flea market vendors earn as much as $50,000 a year working only a two days a week! Did you also know that here are an estimated 750,000 flea market vendors peddling products in the United States and Canada at more than 10,000 flea markets, bazaars, and swap meets, some of which draw crowds in excess of 25,000 people a day. Needless to say, if you choose to sell your products at flea markets, you'll be in good company and have the potential to earn excellent profits.

Flea markets are everywhere, but before selecting one to set up shop at, visit a few to get a feel for the venue, vendors, and visitors. Check out the venue—do they charge admission, is there adequate parking, and do they heavily promote the event? Check out the vendors—what do they sell, how much are they charging, how much are they selling, and how many are selling the same things as you? Check out the visitors—are they buying or browsing, how many are there, and do they meet your target customer profile?

There are many types of flea markets—weekends only, everyday, summer only, outside under tent, open air, and inside events—each with particular advantages and disadvantages. Booth rents vary widely, from a low of $5 per day to as much as $100 for single-day events. When selecting a flea market, also look for adequate customer and vendor parking, electricity, phone lines for credit card and debit card terminals, on-site ATM machine, washrooms, food services, and excellent overall organization. You will need to supply your own transportation and equipment such as dollies to load and unload merchandise and displays. Some flea markets provide merchandising tables, canopies, and displays, others rent these items separately, and still others do not supply anything except for the booth. So be sure to find out what you get for your money up front.

Here are more great tips to get you started on your way to earning huge profits selling products at flea markets.

- Get a merchant account and wireless terminal for debit cards and credit cards. Many people bring cash to flea markets, but it is proven that accepting plastic can increase impulse buying by as much as 50 percent.

- Invest in professional displays and sales aids to help boost revenues and profits. Have bold and colorful professional signs and banners made, purchase high quality and attractive displays on wheels for easy loading and transportation, keep your merchandise clean and organized, and even consider uniforms, such as T-shirts, hats, or golf shirts with an identifier like Brian's Birdhouses emblazoned across them.
- Stand out by using colorful banners, balloons, lights, music, and flags—basically any and all types of attention-grabbing devices. Large markets have hundreds, sometimes thousands of vendors all vying for the attention of shoppers, so you need to be creative to stand out in the crowd.
- Develop a system for capturing names and addresses so you can utilize this information for direct marketing purposes—mail, e-mail, and telemarketing. Also hand out promotional fliers describing your products and contact information: web site, telephone number, and business address.
- Everyone shopping at flea markets expects to bargain and wants to flex negotiation muscle, so be ready to haggle. Price items 10 to 20 percent higher so you have room to negotiate, yet still get your price.
- Take a box stocked with items like tape, receipt books, pens, business cards—anything small—and packing supplies like newspaper, plastic bags, and cardboard boxes.

To find accessible flea markets, use online directories like Flea USA, ♂ www.fleamarkets.com, Flea Market Guide, ♂ www.fleamarketguide.com, and Keys Flea Market, ♂ www.keysfleamarket.com. All list hundreds of flea markets indexed geographically.

Community Events

Every community in North America has numerous events and celebrations throughout the year, from parades to farmers' markets to music festivals. Many provide excellent opportunities to sell all sorts of products: art, jewelry, soaps, craft items, and specialty foods, to just mention a few. Local associations, such as the chamber of commerce, charities, sport groups, social clubs, churches, or schools, usually organize community events. So you will need to contact event organizers to inquire about available vending opportunities. Booth fees and permit costs vary depending on the type of event, anticipated crowd, and duration of the event. Some are free, but most charge. The most expensive are usually fairs and exhibitions, which can cost as much as $500 a day.

Selling at community events is like any other retailing opportunity—think booth location within the event, signage, professional displays, quality merchandise, fair pricing, quick service, and a smile. Combine these with an outgoing personality, and you cannot help but sell your products. Also, be sure to print fliers describing your products and how you can be contacted after the event. Include web address, e-mail address, telephone numbers, and showroom address if applicable. The fliers should be given to people who purchased products and to people just looking. The latter have the potential to become customers at a later date.

Advertising Basics

The wonderful world of advertising is out there somewhere but where do you start? First off, know that advertising is a tool that when used correctly can drive a multitude of well-qualified prospects to your business to buy. Conversely, advertising can be a complete waste of time and money, reaping few, if any, sales. Consequently, you have to make well-researched and informed decisions when allocating your precious advertising money. Remember to follow the golden rule of advertising for small business owners: You do not need to spend a bundle advertising your business, products, and services. Just make sure the money you do spend reaches your target audience. You will also need to create a system for tracking your advertising activities so you can determine the effectiveness of each. Tracking allows you to allocate your advertising dollars where they have the greatest impact in reaching your target audience and generating the most revenue.

Creating Great Advertising

Great advertising is composed of numerous elements—an attention-grabbing headline, powerful images, an incredible offer, and a clear call to action. It is the combination of these that goes into creating a great advertisement, one that will get the results you want. This is the AIDA advertising formula—attention, interest, desire, and action. Even if you plan on doing little in the way of traditional advertising in newspapers or magazine, for instance, you still need the ability to create great advertising and copy for use in packaging, sales letters, catalogs, fliers, newsletters, signage, or web site content.

You only have a brief moment to grab the attention of your target audience and pull it into your message, so start with a powerful headline. For example, a dog walker might use, "Who's walking your dog while you work?" Clever advertising also appeals to people on an emotional level, utilizing emotional triggers to spark basic human feelings such as the need for friendship, the need for security, and the desire to achieve. The best way to appeal to emotional triggers is through the use of powerful images in your ads. When used properly, emotional triggers can double and even triple ad response rates.

To stand out in a sea of advertising, you also have to provide an incredible offer, something that your target audience cannot get elsewhere. Your incredible offer can be a deeply discounted price, a value-added bonus, limited product quantity, or some other offer to motivate your target audience to take action and buy. Always remember, your advertising must ask people to buy and give them compelling reasons to do so, as well as the contact information they need to take action. Unlike multinational corporations with a bottomless money pit for brand-building advertising, small business owners have to ask for the sale every time, regardless of the advertising or communication medium.

Newspaper Advertising

There are a great variety of newspapers—national, regional, daily, commuter, alternative or underground, community weeklies, penny-saver, school, association, clubs, and electronic—offering small businesses countless advertising options and packages. But the number-one rule of newspaper advertising is to always buy ads based on your marketing plan, advertising budget, and the publication's ability to reach your primary target audience. Never get lured in by huge circulation numbers, critical placement promises, and frequency discounts; if your ads are not reaching your target audience, you will be wasting your money.

There are basically two types of newspaper advertising options—displays ads and classified ads. For the majority of small business owners, display advertising in national and regional newspapers is not effective because small businesses tend to serve a specific geographical area. Community newspapers can be effective for major sales or events, but must be approached with caution. Large display ads tend to be very expensive, and placing ads occasionally because of a limited budget does not work. Generally, outside of special sales or promotional events, you need repetition in order to build long-term beneficial awareness of your business, products, and services. Also, most newspapers, regardless of size, are crammed with display advertisements. That leaves the advertiser fighting with hundreds of other ads to capture the readers' attention. Display advertising can work, but there are certain steps to follow, starting with getting the media kit or card for newspapers you are considering. The media kit will tell you all about the newspaper's readership base—who they are, where they come from, what they do for a living, their level of education, and how much money they make. That information can then be used to determine if the newspaper's target audience is your target audience.

Classified advertising, on the other hand, is unquestionably one of the small business owners' best friends. Not only are these ads easy to create and cheap to run, but they almost always have a higher response rate than display advertisements because people generally read the classifieds looking for a specific product or service to buy, not for entertainment like in other sections of the newspaper. This is especially true of businesses that provide services such as home repair, home maintenance, automobile maintenance, and computer specialties. Because classified advertisements are cheap and quick to post, continually look for ways to improve your results by testing new ads in various publications. Test your headline, your main sales message, and your special offers on a regular basis. Classified advertising costs vary by publication, number of words, number of insertions, and other factors such as the use of icons and photographs. Icons and photographs, by the way, almost always increase response rates, making the few extra dollars they cost a very worthwhile investment.

One way to research newspapers outside of your area is to visit online directories such as News Link, ♂ www.newslink.org, and News Directory, ♂ www .newsdirectory.com. Both list thousands of publications indexed geographically.

Magazine Advertising

Magazines are one of the best advertising mediums for reaching a specific audience because magazines generally cater to one specific portion of the population, based on geographic, demographic, and psychographic profiling, or a combination of market segmenting. The first place to find out more about a magazine's particular target audience is through the publisher's media kit or fact sheet, which like a newspaper media kit, provides information about who reads the magazine. Carefully research this information to determine if the magazine's reader base meets your target audience requirements.

Magazines ads also have a definite edge over many other types of advertising because they have a tendency to be around for a while—on a desk, in the waiting room, in the lunchroom, or on the coffee table. Because magazines have a longer user shelf life than newspapers, newsletters, coupons, and fliers, the advertisements also tend to be seen by the same reader more than once. Most advertising gurus agree that next to radio, magazines offer small business owners the best opportunity to reach a very select target audience in a relativity cost-efficient manner. But, unlike classified advertisements and coupons, you cannot expect immediate results. It takes continuous and consistent exposure to your target audience before you will get results.

There is also much debate about which size advertisement is the best—a full-page, half-page, third-page, quarter-page, and so forth. Full-page advertisements can be costly, but you get great exposure. Quarter-page ads are much cheaper, but they are often featured near the back of the magazine with one or more other advertisements on the same page. You also have to consider frequency, which refers to the number of times that your target audience is exposed to your advertisement in the same magazine. Most advertising experts agree there should be a minimum of three times but preferably six to twelve times consecutively for an ad to have real impact for your business.

To locate magazines and other publications that cater to a specific audience, click on Pub List, ♂ www.publist.com, which lists more than 150,000 domestic and international print and electronic publications.

Yellow Pages Advertising

Not all product sellers and service providers need to advertise in the Yellow Pages, especially when you consider full-page ads can easily cost $1,000 per month or more. Businesses that should purchase Yellow Pages advertising are those that provide emergency or high-demand services, such as home repair and maintenance or computer repair and training, for example. If you decide that Yellow Pages advertising is right for your business, then be sure to design your advertisement from your customers' perspective, so that it will appeal to the majority of your target audience. Ask questions, such as: "Why do they do business with me? What do they like best about my products and services? What competitive advantages do I offer? Is it best quality? Is it convenient 24-hour service? Is it lowest prices, guaranteed? Am I the most qualified to handle the job in the area? Your responses should be featured in your ads. Research has also shown that ads with photographs or illustrations greatly outperform ads without them.

Statistically speaking, size matters. The larger your ad, the more people you can expect to call. Buy the biggest, boldest advertisement you can afford. It positions you closer to the beginning of each new alphabetical heading and ahead of competitors with smaller advertisements. Yellow Pages display advertising is also one of the rare advertising occasions when you want to list as much information as possible. List all of the products you sell or the services you provide, including specialized services or authorized services; all the ways that people can pay, including credit cards and financing options; credentials and special training that you have; and special information such as liability insurance coverage, bonding, special certificates or permits, and professional association memberships. Finally, you also have to motivate people to call by using phrases like, call now for a free estimate. Give them lots of ways to contact you—telephone number, toll-free number, fax number, cellular number, e-mail and web site addresses, and after-hours contact information.

Radio Advertising

Radio speaks to your target audience on a more intimate one-on-one basis in their cars, at the office, or at home. For that reason, radio has long been a favorite advertising medium for small business owners because you can single your target audience out as individuals. The key to successful radio advertising is repetition, which in radio advertising terms is referred to as frequency, the number of times the audience is exposed to your broadcasted message. The more they hear your ad, the more they will recall your business, products, and services when it comes time to buy. Also keep in mind that you are buying the audience, never the station. You need to match the image you want to project for your business to the appropriate radio station. For example, if your target audience is people over 50, try talk radio and easy-listening formats. If you are not effectively reaching your target audience, your ads will simply not be productive, regardless of how frequently they are broadcast.

When writing copy for your radio ads, you have to think and create visually. You must paint an exact visual portrait of how your product or service works and how users benefit. Also, purchase 30-second commercial spots rather than 15-second spots. The latter seldom allow enough time to create a lasting and memorable impression. Thirty seconds will enable you to get across about 50 to 75 words comfortably, along with a simple jingle or memorable audio hook, such as a ringing bell or a lion's roar. Ideally, you will want to have the same time slot day in, day out. Most marketers find the morning 6 A.M. to 10 A.M. or afternoon 3 P.M. to 7 P.M. drive slots are the best. Radio audiences are extremely loyal to their favorite stations, on-air personalities, and on-air programs. Once you have identified your target audience and the station and programs they listen to, stick with them. You want these listeners to feel the same loyalty to your brand. Radio Tower, ♂ www.radiotower.com, and Virtual Tuner, ♂ www.virtualtuner.com, are two online directories that list more than 10,000 radio stations.

Promotional Fliers

Two big benefits of printed promotional fliers are they can be used everywhere, and for everything, even as a replacement for your business card. Hand them out at seminars, trade shows, flea markets, and networking meetings. Hire students to canvas busy parking lots, tucking fliers underneath windshield wipers, and leave them in public transit areas such as buses, subway cars, and train stations for riders to read and take home. You can also stock a supply of promotional fliers and thumbtacks in your car so you can make a weekly run posting your new fliers on every community bulletin board in your area—at supermarkets, libraries, schools, and the like. In fact, promotional fliers represent one of the best advertising vehicles and values available to small business owners because they are a fast and frugal, yet highly effective, way to promote your products and services.

Commercial printers charge $50 to $80 per hour to design marketing materials like fliers, brochures, and newsletters, so you can save a lot of money if you take the time needed to learn basic design skills so that you can create high-impact printed promotional fliers inhouse on your own computer. In addition to computer hardware, you will also need design software. The most popular desktop publishing software comes from Adobe, ♂ www.adobe.com, and Corel, ♂ www.corel.com. In addition to saving money by creating your own fliers, you will also be able to save time because you can create promotional materials and be ready to use them within a day, instead of waiting days or weeks working around a printer's schedule. Once your fliers been have created and printed, they can be copied in bulk for as little as two cents each at your local copy center, or you can invest in a high-speed laser printer for about $350 and also keep the printing inhouse.

Signs

Signs represent incredible advertising value because they're cheap to buy and work to promote your business 24 hours a day, 365 days a year. Depending on the products and services you sell, how these are sold, and your business location, there is a wide range of signs available to help advertise your business and events, including store or office signs, homebased business signs, job site signs, and vehicle signs. Regardless of the type of sign and its use, all signs must be professionally designed, built, installed, and in keeping with the image that you want to project. Use attention-grabbing design elements, colors, graphics, and pictures in your signs to lend visual description. Because you want to always make a positive first impression, keep all of your signage in tip-top condition. Faded signs, peeling paint, torn banners, or signs that require any maintenance send out negative messages about your business.

In terms of store and office signs, with a glance they need to tell people your business name, what you sell, and why they should buy from you, such as, "The Best Sandwiches in Town!" There are a wide variety of store and office signs available, from simple stick-on vinyl letters used on door glass to highly elaborate neon signs that can cost as much as $100,000. Budget, as well as local sign ordinances, will have to be taken into account when deciding what types of signs best suit your business.

Local bylaws also govern homebased business signs, and they are often much more stringent that commercial zoning signs. These bylaws stipulate if signage is allowed at your home as well as the size of the sign, placement, and style. Each municipality has its own sign regulations. So a call to the planning department or city hall will be required to find out the local bylaws. Even if signage is allowed, you want to consult your immediate neighbors to find out their feelings on the issue and get their input on the signs. The last thing that you want to do is alienate neighbors over business signs. Like you, their home is probably their biggest investment, and they do not want that investment to be devalued in any way. In fact, if clients are not coming to your home, you are better off not having signs at all. If you will be having clients coming to your home, keep your signs in open view, make them tasteful to match your home and streetscape—perhaps carved wood or brass on stone—and keep lighting to a minimum unless you can incorporate your sign into your exterior house light or motion lighting.

If you install products or provide services at your customers' homes and offices, you should definitely invest in professional, attention-grabbing job site signage, especially if jobs last more than a few days. Job site signs come in all sizes and price points. They can be metal with metal stands, Coroplast®, or even simple plastic sleeves, similar to political yard signs, but emblazoned with your business name, logo, and promotional message. The plastic sleeve style fits over preformed wire stands, which push easily into the ground, making for very fast installation and pickup. Purchased in bulk, these are very inexpensive, less than $5 each, and can be reused many times. Business Signs Online, ♂ www.businesssigns.com, sells metal and Coroplast made-to-order job site signs in various sizes, whereas Political Lawn Signs, ♂ www.politicallawnsigns.com, manufactures lightweight plastic job site and lawn signs.

Finally, if you are going to use your vehicle for business, sign it; even if you only use it for business occasionally, you can still use magnetic signs that can be quickly installed or removed and stored in the trunk when using your car for personal activities. I would also be sure to park in highly visible and high-traffic locations, even if this means feeding parking meters. Always think about maximizing the marketing value of these rolling billboards. Like store signs, vehicle signs quickly tell people your business name, with a brief promotional message and contact information, including telephone numbers and web site.

Advertising Online

There are many ways to promote your business and advertise your products and services online, but space limits us to discussing the basics—banners, e-publications, and pay-per-click programs. Advertising banners are a popular way to promote your products and services and drive traffic to your web site. Costs range from a few dollars per thousand impressions to a few hundred dollars per thousand impressions, depending on the target audience you want to reach. The idea of cheap banner advertising might be alluring, but your results can suffer dramatically if you don't present your advertising message to your primary target audience. Bigger is not always better. Mega web sites may attract untold numbers of visitors, but that does not necessarily mean they are comprised of your target audience.

Many product sellers and service providers have also found advertising in electronic publications to be a highly effective way to reach their target audience at a very modest cost. With an estimated 100,000 electronic publications distributed monthly to choose from, you can definitely find one that reaches your target audience. Before committing to advertising, though, find out audience size, demographics, and advertising costs. Ezine Listings, ♂ www.ezinelistings.com, list thousands of electronic publications indexed by subject.

Pay-per-click programs are another highly effective form of online advertising. They focus on bidding on priority keywords that you believe your target audience will use to search for the products and services you sell. The big players in this arena are Google's AdWords, ♂ www.adwords.google.com, and Overture's Pay-For-Performance, ♂ www.overture.com. Although each pay-per-click program has different requirements and rules for keyword selection, both programs are similar in the way you bid for keywords. For instance, you can bid one dollar for a specific keyword. If yours is the highest bid, you win and get top search results rankings. On the other hand, if you bid 20 cents and someone else has bid more for the same keywords, your ranking will be greatly reduced.

Public Relations

Publicity offers small business owners the potential to reach thousands or even millions of people for free, yet few take advantage of this fantastic promotional tool. Why? The answer is simple. Most don't realize they could easily create some publicity buzz around the products or services they sell. Start by examining your products or services for unique user benefits, interesting facts or statistics, success stories, or competitive advantage so that you can build PR buzz around it. Sometimes coming up with the right angle just takes a bit of imagination. To help get your creative ideas flowing, below are four simple yet highly effective publicity tools: press releases, articles, talk radio, and community publicity.

Press Releases

One of the easiest way is to let the media know about your business, products, services, and special events is to create a press release outlining relevant details to send to appropriate media outlets. Few forms of advertising or other marketing activities can match the effectiveness and credibility of the media; our daily lives revolve around the news distributed in all formats—broadcast, print, and internet. We read newspapers, watch television, surf the net, and listen to the radio, and we do so because we want to be entertained and informed. A great review in the newspaper about a new music CD is more likely to pull you into the store to buy it than any advertisement every will. Publicity works because it grabs attention, spells out basic details, creates interest, and often forces people to take the desired action. If you are new to writing press releases, read a few to get ideas. A good place to read actual press releases is PR Web, ♂ www.prweb.com. There you can surf through thousands of press releases for free and learn how to write your own.

Articles

One of the best ways to secure valuable publicity is to write informative articles on your area of expertise. Share your wealth of information. Its value increases as more people are exposed to it and benefit because of it. One little-known fact is that every small business owner has important information that can be offered to the media in exchange for free publicity. For example, if you operate a home inspection service, offer to write a weekly article for your community paper on what homebuyers should look out for in property maintenance and repairs. The key to successfully securing exposure in print is to develop a news or story angle that will appeal to a large segment of the newspaper's target audience. Depending on the products you sell or the services you provide and the audience you want to reach, newspapers can be local or national papers, community newsletters, trade journals, association newspapers, e-newspapers, magazines, and school papers. The media loves to get informative articles because they do not pay for them and they appeal to and benefit their target audiences. All media outlets need good news, information, and activities to fill their publications.

Talk Radio

Talk radio represents a potential publicity windfall for small business owners who take the time to develop a strategy for being featured on these programs. Get started by conducting research on the show you would like to be featured on; learn about the show's format, style, and target audience. Next, develop a story idea revolving around something that's relevant to the program and interesting to the show's audience. For instance, if you train dogs, develop a show idea around dog-training tips. Once you have developed your idea, send the program producer a professional business letter detailing your story, how it benefits his audience, and why you should be invited to discuss the topic on air. Also send a background sheet highlighting your qualifications and expertise on the topic. If you have written books or articles on the subject matter, be sure to include this information in your letter. To find suitable talk radio programs, click on Radio Locator, ♂ www.radio-locator.com, which has links to more than 10,000 radio stations.

Community Publicity

Getting involved in the community where you live and do business is also a great way to inform and keep the public up-to-date about your business and the products and services you sell. It's proven that people like to do business with other people they know and like, as well as to refer friends, family, and associates to these businesses. So it makes sense to get active in your community; clubs, churches, charities, and business and social functions are all great places to meet new people, help out, hand out business cards, and talk about your business. Sponsorships are also a fantastic way to help out the community and publicize your business at the same time. You can sponsor a little league team, a charity event, or any number of community events. Or if you are really ambitious, you could develop, sponsor, and manage your own special event for the benefit of the community at large, for example, "(your business name here) 10K Run for Cancer" sponsored by and named after your business.

6

EVERYTHING ELSE YOU NEED TO KNOW

In this chapter you get a brief rundown of some important business issues not discussed thus far, hence "everything else you need to know." You will learn about the importance of providing great customer service and how to stand behind your products and services with ironclad warranties and guarantees. You'll also learn how to pick a pricing strategy and price your products and services for profitability, as well as how to establish payment terms. And if you manufacture or sell products, you will also discover information about product packaging, product delivery, and inventory management, as well as a host of additional helpful information, ideas, and tips that have been specifically developed to put you well on the path to long-term business success.

Providing Great Customer Service

Your ability to survive in business and be financially viable is based on many factors, but one of the biggest is your ability to retain customers and foster long-term, profitable selling relationships. According to the U.S. Small Business Administration, 65 percent of people stop buying from a business because of poor customer service. This is a startling statistic, especially when you consider that it costs ten times as much to find a new customer as it does to keep one customer you already have. The moral of the story is simple: Keep your customers happy by providing great customer service.

One of the easiest customer service concepts to grasp is the simple fact that people like to do business with people they like. It stands to reason that you should go out of your way to be likeable—smile, take an interest in your customers, treat them fairly, and thank them for their continued support. That's about all it takes. The second easiest customer service concept to master is to always fix the customer first. When you have an unhappy customer, regardless of the source of the complaint or problem, always look for ways to fix your customer first, quickly, and without hesitation. Once this has been achieved, turn your attention to the source of the problem or complaint. At the end of the day, the best way to provide great customer service is to treat your customers the way that you like to be treated when you trade your hard-earned money for goods and services at other businesses.

Overcome Mismatched Expectations

Most customer service complaints arise from mismatched expectations, usually caused by a breakdown in communications between seller and buyer or by the way a product or service was described and understood. The cost of mismatched expectations is enormous, especially when you factor in the potential for lost customers and the time spent fixing problems. It makes sense to reduce the potential for mismatched expectations by reviewing all details of the sale prior to delivery or installation of any product or service. Create a checklist so that you can review the product and features, the price, the scope of work, the start and completion dates or delivery date, the payment method, and the guarantees, as well as asking specific questions about what the customer expects the service to do for her or her business. Yes, reviewing the details of the sale does take time, but remember that it costs ten times more to find a new customer than it does to keep the customers you have happy.

Reliability

Another customer service practice that all small business owners must employ is reliability, especially for those providing services. If you say you'll be there at ten, arrive five minutes early. If you guarantee your work, then fix it if something goes wrong, no questions asked. And, if you say you will deliver 100 red widgets, then deliver 100 red widgets on time. Reliability is one of the common denominators that all successful businesses share. Your track record of happy clients is one of your most important marketing tools, and in the case of service providers, often the only one that carries any weight. Customers want products and services they have paid for to live up to promises in terms of reliability. They want to know that when they purchase a product or service, the company that sells it is reliable and will be there for them in the future should something go haywire.

Flexibility

Small business owners must also recognize that customers are not all the same. Customers want and need different things. Each must be viewed as an individual, not merely as part of a group. Be flexible and willing to bend the rules once in a while when your customers need you to, even if it is an inconvenience to you and your business. Ask customers what they want, and develop solutions to meet each individual's needs. Going the extra mile for customers almost always means price will be less of a factor in buying decisions. When you are flexible and go out of your way to treat people especially well, you no longer have to work as hard to persuade them to your way of thinking. When was the last time that you stopped shopping at a particular business because you received exceptional treatment by an owner or employee that went the extra mile for you?

Customer Appreciation

It is no secret that when your customers feel as though you truly appreciate their business, they will go out of their way to refer your business to others. So how can you show your customers your gratitude for their continued support? In addition to sending your customers greeting cards on holidays, birthdays, and other milestones, you could also host an annual customer appreciation party and invite your best customers and hottest prospects. The party can be held at local restaurant or, if your budget is tight, host the party right at your home, perhaps as a backyard barbecue if weather permits.

Another option is to find out what newspapers or magazines your customers like to read and purchase a subscription for them. Every time they read it, they will instantly think of your business, products, or services. This concept can be extended to hobbies and special interests. Find out what hobbies your customers like, and armed with this information, you can purchase gifts for them that are relevant to their hobbies or interests—sports or theater tickets, artwork, or gourmet foods are examples. Giving customers promotional specialties such as key chains, pens, notepads, calendars, coffee mugs, travel mugs, clocks, mouse pads, or T-shirts emblazoned with you business name and logo also shows you appreciate their business. And you receive the additional benefit of your customers thinking about your business every time they use these products. Finally, if your customers are business owners, professionals, or salespeople, work hard to send them a new referral every day, week, or month.

Standing Behind Your Products and Services

Standing behind your products and services means that you will strive to provide customers with the best guarantees and warranties on the products you make and sell, the products you resell, or the services you provide. This is another important element of providing great customer service and building an excellent business reputation. There are many benefits to providing ironclad warranties and guarantees; they can be used to support marketing activities and distinguish your business from competitors with weaker warranty programs. Depending on the products and services you sell, you will need to create service guarantees, product warranties, and develop a return and refund policy.

Service Guarantees

Whether you want to call it a service guarantee or a workmanship warranty, you need to provide clients with some sort of guarantee in terms of the work you perform. It is rare for service providers not to guarantee their work, unless there are circumstances that call for the work to be completed on an as-is basis, which would have to be confirmed with the client in writing before the work is done. For the most part, all service providers guarantee their work in writing. Of course, the stronger your guarantee is, the easier it becomes to use this as an effective marketing tool. Customers want to know that should problems arise after the sale, or after the service has been performed and paid for, they will have an ironclad workmanship or other type of warranty from your business. A warranty should clearly state that you will stand behind your work for the duration period, and will correct any deficiencies within a reasonable time and at no cost. Yes, depending on the services you sell, there must be terms and conditions for workmanship warranties that will protect your business. But every business that sells services should develop the best workmanship warranty possible. For instance, if your competitor's workmanship warranty is one year, make your warranty two; if his is five years, make yours seven. If the competition's workmanship warranty is loaded with small print, then be sure to zap the small print from your warranty. And, if your competitor's warranty is nontransferable, then make yours fully transferable without cost. After all, you know the quality of the service you provide best, and if you are not prepared to back it up with an ironclad warranty, then in all probability you are not providing a quality service.

Product Warranties

If you manufacture products, you will also need to develop a strong product warranty program. Consumers have become very savvy and want to know that if product malfunctions or breaks down for any reason during the warranty period, they can get the problem fixed. Like a guarantee on services, there must be warranty terms and conditions to protect you. At the same time, every business making and selling products should strive to develop the strongest warranty possible. In fact, you should become known as the industry leader. To achieve this will require you to zap the small print, keep your warranty as comprehensive as possible, and extend the standard time frame for the type of product you make and sell. Again, you know the quality of the product you make, and if you are not prepared to back it up with an ironclad warranty, then don't be surprised if consumers are skeptical when it comes time to buy it.

If you are simply reselling products manufactured by other businesses, you will need to know these warranties inside out and upside down. It is not good enough to tell a customer that purchased a defective product from you that it's the manufacturer's problem. They are your customers. Therefore, it's your problem. You need to go out of your way to help your customer get the problem resolved.

Returns and Refunds

It's inevitable. At some point, all business will have customers that want to return products, request a refund, or want to cancel a product order or service contract. Consequently, it is in your best interests to establish your return, refund, and order cancellation policies before opening for business. Doing so enables you to include your policies on invoices, sales receipts, account statements, estimate forms, and contracts, which can prove very valuable, should disputes arise.

You need to consider if you will allow customers to return products or if all sales are final. In what condition will you allow products to be returned? How long will your product return or refund policy be—7, 14, 30 days, or longer? Will you offer customers the option of exchanging products for similar products, a credit against future purchases, or a cash refund? If you are going to provide refunds, make sure your policy corresponds with the payment method. If the customer paid in cash, offer a cash refund. If the customer paid with a credit card, you will need to credit her charge account. And, if a customer paid by check, make sure the check has cleared your bank before refunding any money.

The final consideration is product order or service contract cancellations. Most U.S. states and Canadian provinces have consumer protection mechanisms in place that enable consumers to cancel orders within a prescribed time frame, generally referred to as a cooling-off period. However, there is no single standard time limit. You will need to contact the SBA or your lawyer to determine how the law is applied in your specific area. At the same time, when customers buy made-to-order or special order products from your business, make sure that you get a deposit before making or ordering the product(s). The deposit should at least be equal to the costs of materials that will be needed to make the product or your cost to buy the product.

Picking a Pricing Strategy

Picking a pricing strategy means positioning your business and the products and services you sell in the marketplace. It answers two vital questions: "Where do your products or services fit into the market?" "How does your primary target audience view your products or services in relationship to your competitors?" You can position your business and become known for low prices, moderate prices, or prestige prices, depending on the strategy you select. Once you have chosen a strategy, you should stick with it so as not to confuse or alienate customers.

Low Pricing Strategy

A low-price strategy means that you strive to sell your products and services at the lowest or near lowest price in the marketplace. Businesses that use slogans such as, "We will not be undersold" or "We'll beat any competitors' price," use a low-price strategy in marketing their goods and services. If you select this strategy, you have to sell a greater volume of products or services than you would at higher prices to produce an equivalent profit margin. The majority of small business owners wisely choose not to compete or position their business in the marketplace based on low prices. Many national corporations and franchise operations have already adopted a low-price strategy, making it almost impossible for small independent businesses to compete on this level.

Moderate Pricing Strategy

A moderate pricing strategy means a good quality product or service sold to consumers at a fair price. This is the pricing strategy that the majority of independent small business owners, as well as multinational corporations and franchise operation, wisely choose. A moderate pricing strategy leaves you enough financial leeway for competitive advantages to be developed and introduced to separate your products and services from competitors, such as a 24-hour service or a stronger warranty program. This can be accomplished because there is a greater gross profit margin on each sale, thus generating the capital required to develop and implement creative marketing strategies, and product and service research and development initiatives to improve quality, features, and delivery. The moderate pricing strategy gives small business owners the most flexibility in terms of combining a quality product, value, and good service at a fair price, which is difficult to achieve if you adopt a low price strategy.

Prestige Pricing Strategy

A prestige pricing strategy is generally used to deliver a high-quality product or service in an upscale or exclusive environment, although the quality of the product or delivery of the service is not necessarily always superior, sometimes it is only perceived to be better by consumers. Prestige pricing can be a deliberate pricing tactic in which you set your prices higher to separate your products and services from competitors' by projecting an image of quality and exclusivity. If you are selling a niche product or service to a very small target audience, a prestige pricing strategy can work extremely well. But if you are selling common products or services with no distinguishable advantages over competitors, it becomes more difficult to create a persuasive argument to justify higher prices.

Pricing Products and Services

If your prices are too high, you will probably meet with resistance selling your products or services. If your prices are too low, you may also meet resistance selling your products and services because of perceived quality issues, and even worse, you may lose money on each sale. Factors influencing pricing formulas include costs associated with the delivery of services, costs associated with the manufacturing of a product, or wholesale product costs, as well as fixed operating overheads, marketplace economic conditions, primary and secondary competition in the marketplace, consumer demand, seasonal pressures, political pressures, psychological factors, and how you want to position your services in the marketplace. There are lots of factors that can affect the prices you charge for your goods and services.

A significant pricing concept to keep in mind when determining your prices is that consumers see prices in very clearly defined terms—the price that you charge for your product or service vs. how the product or service will fill their needs and give value. When your pricing is correct, consumers don't think twice because they feel the price is fair in comparison to the value and benefits derived from the product or service. However, as soon as your price goes below or above the threshold of what consumers feel is in the fair range, you will meet resistance to the purchase. At this point, consumers must begin to justify why they will make the purchase, and you never want your target audience to have to convince themselves to buy.

Competitive Pricing

A competitive pricing formula means that you find out how much your competitors are charging for their products and services, and charge more or less depending on how you want to position your business, products, and services in the marketplace. The downside to a competitive pricing formula is it is not scientific. Your variable and fixed costs may be more or less than your competitors' costs, and what may be a profitable price point for one business may not be for another charging the same price. You can find out how much your competition is charging by mystery shopping their businesses, becoming a customer, asking pricing questions, checking advertisements and price lists, and reading the information on their web sites. If you use competitors' prices to determine your own prices, it is in your best interests to create unique competitive advantages to distinguish your products and services from theirs.

Cost Plus Pricing

The best way to determine the prices you will charge for your products or services is to use a cost plus pricing formula and combine this with your overall pricing strategy. To accomplish this, you have to figure out your fixed operating costs, your variable costs associated with the delivery of services, the manufacturing of products, or the wholesale costs of products, and add a profit. The formula therefore is:

Variable costs + Fixed costs + Profit = Selling price.

Assume you sell services. Just remember that the following information can also be used to determine cost plus pricing for products. As a rule of thumb, labor costs generally represent the largest share of expenses for service providers. So the first step is to figure out how much you want to earn per hour. You should base your decision on three factors: How much money you need to earn to pay your personal expenses? What is the industry average for the job? Do you have a premium if the service you provide is highly specialized or risky? Once you have determined how much per hour you want to earn, the next step is to calculate your fixed costs, which are business expenses that do not fluctuate regardless of the number of sales you make, such as the telephone, rent, and insurance. In Chapter 3, you will find a handy monthly overhead costs worksheet that you can use to determine your fixed operating costs.

The next step is to determine the costs incurred in the delivery of the service, which is referred to as variable costs. For instance, if you operated a dog grooming service, the costs to purchase shampoo and grooming supplies for each dog groomed would be the variable costs. The next step is to calculate and add a profit. Every business needs to generate a profit in order to stay in business and stay competitive in the market place. Most small business owners use a percentage to calculate a profit on each job, such as total costs plus 20 percent.

The final step is to tie it all together. The formula used to arrive at a selling price is to:

1. Multiple your labor rate by the number of hours to complete the job.
2. Add fixed expenses.
3. Add variable expenses.
4. Multiple the total of the three by your desired profit margin.
5. The total is your selling price.

For the example below, we will assume that fixed business expenses are $1,000 per month, and there are 160 billable work hours each month; $1,000 divided by 160 hours equals $6.25 per hour fixed expenses, and that the total job required 25 hours to complete.

Labor rate, $20 per hour x 25 hours	= $500.00
Fixed expenses, $6.25 per hour x 25 hours	= $156.25
Variable expenses for the job	= $150.00
Total	= $806.25
Profit 20%	= $161.25
Selling price	= $967.50

Pricing Antiques and Collectibles

Pricing antiques and collectibles for resale is another game entirely, mainly because antiques, collectibles, and memorabilia items are seldom *needed* like food, shelter, and clothing. Instead, theses are things people want, and the target audience can be very narrow, especially for uncommon collectibles and highly-valued antiques. Let's face it, few consumers have an extra $10,000 lying around to buy an antique dining room sideboard. Therefore, pricing antiques and collectibles is largely reflective of what the marketplace will bear.

There are price, value, and condition guides available for every imaginable type of antique and collectible, and these guides are unquestionably a good starting point for pricing and in most instances invaluable, but only to a point. Antiques and collectible values go up and down daily, influenced by many factors. For instance, the value of nautical collectibles, especially cruise line memorabilia, skyrocketed after the release of the movie *Titanic*, as does the value of first edition Hemingway novels for a few weeks a year around the anniversary of his birthday.

Pricing antiques and collectibles is as much about choosing the right sales venues and target audience as it is about the actual item, probably more so. Therefore, success comes to antiques and collectible sellers who pay close attention to what's going on in the marketplace at all times. Professional appraisals and authentications also help to substantiate and support asking prices. Indeed, in many situations, having antiques, collectible, and memorabilia items appraised and authenticated will greatly increase the value.

Establishing Payment Terms

Every small business owner needs to establish a payment-terms policy, which is especially important for service providers, as jobs tend to be spread out over longer periods or billed after the work has been performed. Although you want to standardize the way you get paid, at the same time you also have to be flexible enough to meet client needs on an individual basis. Setting payment terms covers deposits, progress payments, and extending credit. It is important to remember that you want to establish clear, written payment terms with clients prior to providing services or delivering product. Your payment terms should be printed on your estimate forms, included in formal contracts and work orders, and printed on your final invoices and monthly account statements.

Securing Deposits

The first order of business in establishing payment terms is to get in the habit of asking clients for a deposit prior to providing services involving products, especially specialty products. In these cases, the deposit should be equal to the value of the materials. If you are supplying labor only, try to secure a deposit of one-third to one-half of the total value of the contract in advance of doing work. Your order form or contract should have the deposit information clearly stated. Information about canceled product orders or service contracts and the amount of the deposit that will be refunded in these scenarios should also be included in contracts and on order forms. Securing a deposit is your best way of ensuring that basic out-of-pocket costs are covered should the customer cancel the job, contract, or product order.

Progress Payments

Progress payments are also a way to ensure that you do not leave yourself open to great financial risk. The key to successfully securing progress payments is to prearrange your contract and payment terms. Agree on the amount that will be due at various stages of the project. You can use percentages to calculate the progress payments, such as 25 percent deposit, 25 percent upon delivery of any materials, 25 percent upon substantial completion, and the balance at completion or within 30 days of substantial completion. Or you may use more concrete progress payment terms based on indicators that are relevant to the specific scope of work. Regardless of the system you use, progress payments on larger jobs can dramatically lessen your exposure to financial risk.

Extending Credit

In most cases, there is no need to extend credit to consumers buying products, but if you deliver a service such as lawn maintenance that is billed on a monthly schedule or a major contract that is completed in stages, you will probably need to extend credit to clients. As a general rule, when the job is complete, you should be paid in full. However, in the case of business-to-business sales, commercial clients generally want some type of credit on a revolving-account basis, 30, 60, 90, or sometimes 120 days after delivery of the product or completion of the service. Ideally, you want to be paid as quickly as possible, so you might want to offer a 2 percent discount if invoices are paid within one week. And if you do extend credit, make sure to conduct a credit check first, especially when larger sums of money are at stake. There are three major credit reporting agencies serving the United States and Canada: Trans Union, ♂ www.tuc.com; Equifax, ♂ www.equifax.com; and Experian, ♂ www.experian.com. All three compile and maintain credit files on just about every person, business, and organization that has ever applied for credit.

Product Packaging, Delivery, and Inventory Management

Product manufacturers and product resellers have to give thought to developing effective product packaging, as well as to product delivery options and an inventory management system. Service providers are generally off the hook on the first two, but companies that install products do need to create an inventory management system. These are important issues that can negatively effect profits if they are not properly planned for, implemented, and managed.

Product Packaging

If you are going to manufacture a product or purchase products in bulk for resale, you need to design and make product packaging, or have it professionally designed and made. You have to think of your product packaging as a silent salesperson. It doesn't talk, but it speaks volumes about your product and, more importantly, why people should buy it. Great packaging is like a great advertisement; it grabs attention, builds interest, creates desire, and motivates consumers to buy. Mediocre packaging can kill a great product. Incredible packaging will sell a mediocre product. What would you tell people face-to-face if you were trying to persuade them to buy your product? Your answer should be on your packaging. The importance of product packaging cannot be overlooked. Indeed, if you can afford to hire a packaging expert, you should. Someone who can design and create a package that will get the desired results can cause an avalanche of sales. If you intend to wholesale, consign, or sell your products through an online retailer or from a retail storefront, you also need to obtain a Universal Product Code, otherwise widely known as a bar code, and have it printed on your packaging or accompanying price tag. Subdivisions Inc, ☎ (310) 927-1644, ✍ www.buyabarcode.com, sells and registers bar codes. At time of writing, each bar code cost $35, plus a one-time registration fee of $75.

Product Delivery

Whether you're selling direct to consumers or direct to business, product delivery issues must be considered and plans developed. There are numerous options available for getting your products from point A to point B. You can deliver products, hire a delivery service, contract with a courier, use airfreight services, or, if your products are small, rely on the postal system. Decisions are typically based on factors such as quantity, cost, schedule, and the type of product(s) being delivered. Regardless of the delivery method, costs vary depending on product weight, overall dimensions, schedule, geography, and insurable value.

You will need to consider how you will pack items for transportation and the costs of packing and shipping materials such as boxes, wooden containers or pallets, bubble wrap, envelopes, tape, plastic pellets, and plastic bags. Most courier and freight companies sell packing and shipping materials, but shop around. In small quantities these items are very expensive. Office supply stores like Office Depot, ♂ www.officedepot.com, generally have lower costs on packing and shipping supplies, but the lowest costs are found at packaging wholesalers.

Delivery costs and related supplies have to be calculated and added to product pricing. All of the major courier and freight companies such as Fed Ex, ♂ www.fedex.com, and UPS, ♂ www.ups.com, the U.S. Postal Service, ♂ www.usps.com, and Canada Post, ♂ www.canadapost.ca, have software that automatically calculates shipping charges based on the information you enter. A few other benefits of this software are that it allows you to print customer labels, track packages, and automatically arrange for pick-ups and deliveries.

Inventory Management

If you are manufacturing products or buying products for resale, you also have to give thought to how you will manage your inventory. This is not a big concern if you are manufacturing and selling products one at a time or in small quantities, or if you are buying individual products and selling these one at a time. Simply invest in a spiral notebook, create a few columns for product description and units, and you are pretty much set. You can also create your own basic inventory management system using your computer and a spreadsheet program such as Excel.

However, if you are a mid- to large-volume product manufacturer or seller with numerous distribution channels, you will need a much more sophisticated inventory management system. Chances are you will need to invest in inventory management software with features such as customer database options, invoice creation, label making, inventory tracking, bar code scanning, tax codes, and automatic inventory reordering. Prices for inventory management software vary depending on features and peripherals, such as fixed and wireless scanners. You can search online business software directories like Soft Scout, ♂ www.soft scout.com, and The Software Network, ♂ www.thesoftwarenetwork.com, to find appropriate inventory management software.

Another aspect of inventory management is physical: You need a place to put your inventory, one that is easily accessed, dry, and secure, as well as apparatus such as shelving or bins to hold both raw materials and products. If you do not have space at home, you will need to rent space. Security, cost, size, and proximity to your home will all need to be considered for off-site storage. Public mini storage services are one of the best storage alternatives because you are not tied to long-term leases, and you don't have to worry about utilities and maintenance because that is included in the rent.

7

202 WAYS TO SUPPLEMENT YOUR RETIREMENT INCOME

Now the real fun begins! In this chapter you will learn about the best 202 ways to supplement your retirement income by starting a business selling products or services, or by pursuing one of the many moneymaking opportunities listed.

The criteria used to select these opportunities was based on a number of factors, including a minimal to moderate investment level, excellent income and profit potential, a broad range of opportunities appealing to a wide range of people with different skills and experiences, and businesses and opportunities with proven track records. Of course, age also factored in. You won't find any super labor-intensive business opportunities discussed here. Some do require good overall health and a high level of physically activeness, but nothing that will have you rubbing your aching muscles and dreaming of a nice hot bath after ten minutes.

Keep in mind that not every person has the resources, knowledge, or finances to start each business listed here. Some people will be better equipped than others. But don't worry, there is a moneymaking opportunity suitable for everyone, as you will soon discover. Once you have considered the important issues, such as your special skills and experiences, investment criteria, health, level of commitment, and interest, you will ultimately be the best judge of what opportunity is best for you.

The information presented in this chapter is in a brief synopsis format. The opportunity is explained, along with marketing information, and often equipment and training requirements. Franchise and business opportunity resources are also listed, and flagged with a star ☆ icon. This is for people who would prefer to own and operate a franchise instead of starting their own business from scratch

At a Glance

At the end of each listing is a section called *At a Glance*, which covers capsulated information about amount of investment needed to start the business, income earnings, skill level requirements, and helpful resources. This information has been included to provide a quick overview of the opportunity featured, so that at a glance, you will have general information that answers the most frequently asked questions: How much money is needed to get started? How much money can I make? What are the skills needed to run the business? And, what do I do next?

Investment

Every business or moneymaking opportunity listed in this chapter includes information about how much the business or opportunity will cost to start. The information provided should only be used as a general guideline; actual start-up costs may be higher or lower than indicated. Additionally, the investment figures shown are for businesses started from scratch and do not reflect the costs associated with purchasing a franchise or existing business. Investment figures do not take into account the need to purchase transportation, specialized tools and equipment, and working capital reserves, or to buy, rent, and substantially renovate a business location. But it does cover the basics, such as business registration, simple tools and equipment, computer, business cards, fliers, and small initial advertising and marketing budget.

BUSINESS START-UP INVESTMENT CATEGORIES
    Investment: Under $2K = Start-up investment less than $2,000
    Investment: Under $10K = Start-up investment $2,001 to $10,000
    Investment: Under $25K = Start-up investment $10,001 to $25,000
    Investment: Over $25K = Start-up investment greater than $25,000

$ Income

You will also find information about potential income earnings, which is based on industry averages and in most instances shown as an hourly figure. In some cases, income information varies widely and is not indicated. Income information should only be used as a guideline; actual earnings per hour may be higher or lower than indicated. Likewise, income can vary between the United States and Canada, between states and/or provinces, and even from city to city. As a rule of thumb, however, businesses requiring a higher skill level to start and operate generally produce higher incomes.

INCOME CATEGORIES
    Income: $15+ = $15 to $25 per hour
    Income: $25+ = $25 to $50 per hour
    Income: $50+ = $50 per hour and greater

Skill Level

Information is also provided about the skills needed or, in many instances, not needed to start and operate the business or opportunity. This information is based on a scale. Level 1 represents the lowest skill requirement, with no qualifications, previous experience, training, or certifications needed. Skill level 2 means previous experience is recommended. Skill level 3 means previous experience and training is recommended. Skill level 4 is the highest; training is required along with certification.

Like rates, skill level requirements can vary from country to country, state to state, and province to province. Therefore, this information should only be used for general purposes. It is the responsibility of all entrepreneurs to check into legal, training, and licensing requirements prior to starting any business or selling any product or service.

SKILL LEVEL CATEGORIES

Skill Level: 1 = No qualifications
Skill Level: 2 = Experience recommended
Skill Level: 3 = Training required or recommended
Skill Level: 4 = Certification or license required

🗄 *Resources*

Each business or moneymaking opportunity featured includes helpful resources such as associations, equipment suppliers, products, publications, and franchise or business opportunities. None of the resources presented in this chapter is an endorsement of any company, association, product, or service. All resources are included simply as helpful tools to get you to the next level should you decide to pursue any of these business ideas. You may elect to use these resources, or you may choose not to. The decision is entirely up to you. However, every effort was made to select only reputable companies, associations, products, and services to list as resources.

At the end of the day, you must be comfortable in the knowledge that you are doing business with reliable and honest sources. The only way this can be accomplished is through research. Learn everything you can about any company or organization you intend to do business with. All should be happy to answer questions and supply references. If not, look for companies that will. It is your time, money, and energy, all very valuable assets. Do your homework to ensure that you protect these assets!

RESOURCE ICONS

☎ Contact telephone number
ᔌ Web address
📖 Book, magazine, or publication
★ Franchise or business opportunity

202 Ways to Supplement Your Retirement Income

RV Traveling Handyperson

How can you travel the country, have fun, meet lots of people, and earn an excellent part-time income, all at the same time? The answer is to start a traveling handyperson service and cash in on the multibillion-dollar building repair industry. Providing you are handy with tools and a jack-of-all-trades—painting, carpentry, flooring, and plumbing—then you are good to go. The service is the same as a regular handyperson service, but with one exception—your base of operation is your RV and the business is totally mobile, wherever you happen to be traveling at the time. Finding customers should not prove difficult because just about everyone who owns property is in need of handyperson services or knows people who are. Talk to RV park owners and deliver fliers to homes and businesses in close proximity to the park where you are staying to get the ball rolling. It shouldn't take long for your cell phone to start ringing with people calling about having repair work done, especially if you happen to be traveling in areas just hit by storms, tornados, or hurricanes. Handyperson rates are in the range of $25 to $40 per hour, plus materials.

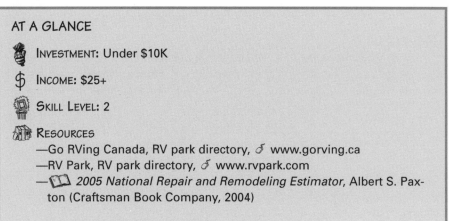

AT A GLANCE

INVESTMENT: Under $10K

INCOME: $25+

SKILL LEVEL: 2

RESOURCES
—Go RVing Canada, RV park directory, ✆ www.gorving.ca
—RV Park, RV park directory, ✆ www.rvpark.com
—📖 *2005 National Repair and Remodeling Estimator*, Albert S. Paxton (Craftsman Book Company, 2004)

Cruise Ship Travel Agent

Here is your opportunity to cash in on the fastest growing segment of the travel industry by planning and booking cruise vacations of a lifetime for your clients, all while working from the comforts of a homebased office. Alaska, Mexico, and the Caribbean are just a few of the hot port-of-call destinations attracting millions of cruise ship travelers every year. There is a lot to know about the cruise travel industry. Consequently, travel consulting experience or training is recommended. You can contact the National Association of Commissioned Travel Agents to inquire about available travel consultant training classes in your area, or you might consider purchasing a "turn-key" cruise agent franchise business. The advantage of the franchise business is the franchisee provides new business owners with cruise travel marketing, administration, and reservation booking training, as well as ongoing support and new product sales programs. Like all travel-related businesses, marketing is the key to success. You have to develop strategies enabling you to tap into the groups of people most likely to purchase cruise vacation holidays, namely the 50-plus crowd and newlyweds. But at the same time, you might also want to consider specializing in a niche area of the cruise holiday industry, such as single-only cruises, family cruises, or alternative lifestyle cruises.

AT A GLANCE

INVESTMENT: Under $10K

$ INCOME: $15+

SKILL LEVEL: 2–3

RESOURCES
—★ Cruise One, ☎ (800) 892-3928, ✇ www.cruiseonefranchise.com
—★ Cruise Planners, ☎ (888) 582-2150, ✇ www.cruiseagents.com
—The National Association of Commissioned Travel Agents,
✇ www.nacta.com

Tour Guide

Galleries, amusement parks, ski resorts, and hotels commonly hire or contract with independent tour guides to explain attractions and acquaint customers with on-site amenities as well as local attractions. If you live in an area frequented by tourists and are a real people person, why not consider starting a personal tour guide service? Whether you contract with a local business or start an independent tour guide service, the business can be started for peanuts and has the potential to generate an income that can easily top $50,000 per year if you work at it full time. Promote the service aggressively by building alliances with businesses and people such as coach and taxi drivers, event planners, hotels, restaurants, and travel agents so they can refer your personally guided tours to their clients. In addition to the usual tour stops at the oldest and most architecturally interesting buildings, the best beaches, the pedicab ride through the park, and area museums, also show off a few of the more unusual sights of your community— crime scenes, movie or television set locations, and past or present celebrity houses. Personal tour guides charge $150 to $200 for half-day tours and up to $350 for full-day tours, plus the cost of transportation and tickets to events and attractions. Providing clients with an unforgettably fun experience combined with incredible service gives you the two main ingredients needed to secure referral and repeat business. Also be sure to market your services to corporations that want to treat their visiting out-of-town customers, employees, and executives to a special event.

 AT A GLANCE

 INVESTMENT: Under $10K

 INCOME: $15+

 SKILL LEVEL: 1–2

 RESOURCES
—Canadian Tour Guide Association, ☎ (416) 410-8621, ♂ www.ct gaoftoronto.org
—National Federation of Tourist Guide Associations U.S.A, ☎ (210) 684-3523, ♂ www.nftga.com
—☆ Rezcity.com, ☎ (201) 567-8500, ♂ www.rezcity.com
—📖 *Start and Run a Profitable Tour Guide Business*, Barbara Braidwood, Susan Boyce, and Richard Cropp (Self-Counsel Press, 2000)

Kayak Tour Operator

Stay active, have fun, and turn your passion for ocean, lake, or river kayaking into a profitable full- or part-time enterprise by starting a kayak tour business. Offer outdoor enthusiasts various kayak tour packages—half-day beginners course, full day paddling with basic training and lunch, and weeklong paddling excursions with meals, activities, and overnight campouts on islands and beaches. Ideal locations for this type of venture are coastal areas of the United States and Canada, as well as states and provinces surrounding the Great Lakes. You will need to invest in five or six fiberglass or plastic touring kayaks and related equipment such as life jackets, dry bags, spray skirts, and paddles, as well as suitable transportation, a van capable of carrying six people and towing a trailer outfitted for carrying the kayaks and other gear. Current kayak tour rates are in the range of $65 per person for half-day tours, $120 for full-day tours, and $1,200 for weeklong tours inclusive of transportation, overnight gear, and meals. Multiply this by six, and you have the ability to generate up to $5,000 per week or more having fun, enjoying your sport, and living it up in the great outdoors.

AT A GLANCE

 INVESTMENT: Under $25K

 INCOME: $50+

 SKILL LEVEL: 2

 RESOURCES
—Kayak Online, industry information portal, ✍ www.kayakonline.com
—Ocean Kayak, sea kayak manufacturer, ☎ (360) 366-4003, ✍ www.ocean kayak.com
—See Kayak, industry information portal, ✍ www.seekayak.com
—Trade Association of Paddlesports, ☎ (800) 755-5228, ✍ www.go paddle.org

Bed and Breakfast Host

If you have a big enough house, convert your home into a moneymaking machine by starting a bed and breakfast that caters to both pleasure and business travelers. Just think, the money you earn renting rooms out by the day, week, or month can be used to pay down your mortgage faster, send the kids to college, or to supplement your postretirement income. B&B rates are in the range of $40 in low season to more than $100 per night per person in the high season and include a light (or sometimes a full and hearty) breakfast, hence the name. Discounted rates are typically provided to travelers who stay for a week or longer. Promote your bed and breakfast through local tourist associations, via online bed and breakfast and travel accommodation directories, and by establishing alliances with independent and chain travel agents and brokers. The biggest obstacle you might need to overcome in turning your home into a B&B is zoning regulations. Some municipalities encourage B&Bs, whereas others prefer to keep guest accommodations within the confines of an established hotel/motel zone and out of residential neighborhoods. A trip to the city hall planning and zoning department will be your first stop to find out about local bylaws. Also consider creating a theme for the entire B&B or for individual rooms—Western, rock n' roll, castle, and space—because themed B&Bs have recently become very popular and captured lots of valuable publicity in travel and leisure magazine articles.

AT A GLANCE

 INVESTMENT: Over $25K

 INCOME: $35–$120 per night

 SKILL LEVEL: 1

 RESOURCES
   —American Bed and Breakfast Association, ♂ www.abba.com
   —Bed and Breakfast Center, worldwide B&B directory, ♂ www.bedand
     breakfastcenter.com
   —Bed and Breakfast Inns Online, worldwide B&B directory, ♂ www.bb
     online.com
   —📖 *Start Your Own Bed & Breakfast*, Rob Adams (Entrepreneur
     Press, 2004)

Party Planner

Event and party planners share common personality traits; they are detail-oriented, well-organized, good communicators, and very creative. If this sounds like you and if you love to plan and host parties and special events, then starting an event and party planning service will be right up your alley. In a nutshell, event and party planners are responsible for organizing and hosting special events such as wedding anniversaries, birthdays, graduations, corporate events, and award ceremonies for their clients, which can include consumers, organizations, clubs, and corporations. Typical duties of the party planner include creating and sending out invitations, selecting event locations, purchasing and hanging decorations, arranging entertainers and speakers, selecting caterers and menus, and just about every thing else that is required to pull a special event or party together, put it on without a hitch, and get everything cleaned up at the end. Networking, networking, and more networking will be your main marketing tool for attracting new business, peppered liberally with advertising in newspapers, the Yellow Pages, and direct mail fliers. You will also need to build a reliable team of contractors, businesses and individuals whom you can call on and rely on to supply products and services required for hosting events on-time and on-budget. The more reliable your team is, the more successful and profitable your event and party planning service will be.

AT A GLANCE

 INVESTMENT: Under $10K

 $ INCOME: $25+

 SKILL LEVEL: 2

 RESOURCES
—The Great Event, event planning information portal, ♂ www.the greatevent.com
—US Event Guide, event planning information portal, ♂ www.usevent guide.com
— 📖 *Start Your Own Event Planning Business*, Krista Turner (Entrepreneur Press, 2004)

Vacation Property Rental Agent

If you live in a busy tourist area, there is a good chance that you can start and flourish operating a vacation property rental agency. It is not uncommon for people to purchase vacation homes and condominiums in hopes of renting them for part or all of the year to help offset their costs. Unfortunately, rental income often fails to materialize because the property owners do not understand how much time and work is involved in renting the properties—marketing, booking, cleaning, repairs, and lots more. And most owners are usually hundreds—if not thousands—of miles away. As a result, many vacation properties sit vacant when not being used by the owners. This creates a terrific opportunity to handle rentals for the owners on a revenue-splitting basis. In addition to marketing and renting the properties, you will also be responsible for cleaning and light maintenance to ensure the properties stay in tiptop condition and get top dollar for rentals. Start small, representing one or two vacation property owners, and run the service from home. As the business grows, so too can your time commitment, until you find yourself operating a profitable, full-time, business concern. The same business concept can be applied toward other properties, houseboat rentals or recreation vehicle rentals.

AT A GLANCE

 INVESTMENT: Under $10K

INCOME: $15+

 SKILL LEVEL: 1

 RESOURCES
—Vacation Rental Owners Association, ✆ www.vroa.org
—Vacation Rentals by Owner, industry information portal, ✆ www
.vrbo.com

Film Extra

The motion picture and television film production industry is booming, and you can cash in and secure your 15 minutes of fame by becoming a film extra, otherwise known as a background performer. What makes working as a film extra a great way to supplement your retirement income is that people of every age, size, ethnicity, and look are needed as background performers. The work schedule is very flexible, and you do not need any previous acting experience. Motion pictures, television shows, commercials, and music videos are filmed just about anywhere but the big film production centers in North America are Los Angeles, Vancouver, New York, Toronto, Miami, and Montreal. In fact, if you live in one these cities, it is possible to work full-time as a film extra. Becoming a film extra is simple. You can get started by visiting the SAG or ACTRA web sites (contact information below) to get a list of "extras casting services and agents." The next step is to contact one of these services and sign up as a client. That's about it. When they have work for you, they will call and give you the details, such as casting call time and location, as well as special requests such as wardrobe needs. You will start out as a nonunion extra until you qualify to be a member of the Screen Actors Guild (SAG) in the United States, or Alliance of Canadian Cinema Television and Radio Artist (ACTRA) in Canada. Nonunion performers earn substantially less than union performers. Rates for extra work start about $10 an hour, with a minimum of eight hours' pay guaranteed, but can be as high as $20 an hour for stand-in extra work.

AT A GLANCE

 INVESTMENT: Under $2K

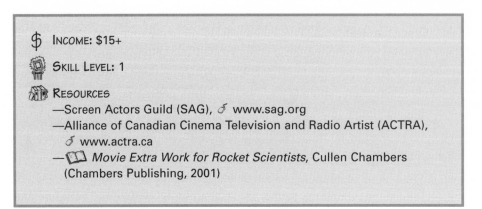

$ INCOME: $15+

SKILL LEVEL: 1

RESOURCES
—Screen Actors Guild (SAG), ♂ www.sag.org
—Alliance of Canadian Cinema Television and Radio Artist (ACTRA),
  ♂ www.actra.ca
— *Movie Extra Work for Rocket Scientists*, Cullen Chambers
(Chambers Publishing, 2001)

Disc Jockey Service

Disc jockey services are in high demand in a growing industry, which makes starting and operating a disc jockey service a wise decision for people looking for a fun way to supplement their retirement income. Even better, age has no bearing on the business. It doesn't really matter if you are 25, 50, or 75, just as long as you love music and like to entertain. DJ rates are in the range of $250 to $500 per event, plus gratuities, which is an excellent return on the initial investment, especially when you consider that the business can be started for less than $10,000, including equipment, music, business setup, and advertising. You will need an excellent and varied music selection, DJ equipment, and reliable transportation, as well as an outgoing personality and talent for public speaking. Potential clients include event and wedding planners, tour operators, restaurant and nightclub owners, corporations, and individual consumers who want a disc jockey for a special event. Picking a music specialty, such as big band or country and western, is also a good idea because it helps to brand your business.

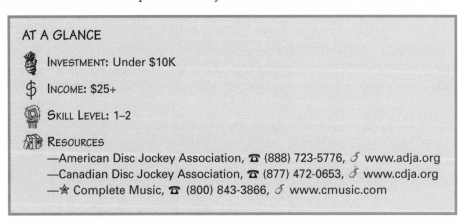

AT A GLANCE

INVESTMENT: Under $10K

$ INCOME: $25+

SKILL LEVEL: 1–2

RESOURCES
—American Disc Jockey Association, ☎ (888) 723-5776, ♂ www.adja.org
—Canadian Disc Jockey Association, ☎ (877) 472-0653, ♂ www.cdja.org
—★ Complete Music, ☎ (800) 843-3866, ♂ www.cmusic.com

Freelance Writer

If you enjoy writing, but are not quite ready to pen the next great American novel, you might want to give freelance writing a try to sharpen your word-smithing skills and earn some extra money. As a writer, I can tell you firsthand that freelance writing is very competitive; some writing sources peg the number of freelancers in the United States alone at more than 100,000 and growing fast. There is lots of competition, but for those who make it, freelance writing can offer a fulfilling postretirement career. The majority of successful freelance writers will tell you that if you want to make it, you must specialize. Pick a topic that you know, write about it, write about it lots more, and keep on writing about it and submitting your work until you find your voice and a market for your information. You could specialize in business, sports, entertainment, real estate, finance, health, retirement and seniors, or travel or venture into more specialized niche markets based on your specific experiences, such as engineering. Writers are typically paid in two ways: per word or a fixed amount per story. Sometimes further royalties are paid, depending on negotiated republishing rights. To get the ballpoint pen rolling and some publishing credits, expect to write a few freebies in order to get your name out. The best paying markets tend to be major monthly magazines. The least attractive pay is usually content for web publishing. Other options include trade and consumer journals, books, e-books, national and local newspapers, e-zines, and newsletters.

AT A GLANCE

 INVESTMENT: Under $2K

 INCOME: $15+

 SKILL LEVEL: 2–3

 RESOURCES
—Absolute Write, freelance writers' information portal, ♂ www.abso
lutewrite.com
—Freelance Online, information and resources, ♂ www.freelanceon
line.com
— *2005 Writer's Market*, Kathryn S. Brogan and Robert Lee Brewer
(Writer's Digest Books, 2004)

Freelance Photographer

If you are a hobby photographer and would love to make a living snapping and selling photographs, you'll be happy to know that there are two very good reasons why the internet has breathed new life into the freelance photography industry: First, using e-mail, it is now very easy to send pictures to publishers, editors, copywriters, marketers, and designers all around the globe in a matter of moments. Second, billions of photographic images are needed to fill the now more than four billion (and climbing) web pages. In addition to the internet, there are also millions of print publications, media companies, retailers, marketers, organizations, and government agencies which need new photographs every day to add meaning to newspapers, newsletters, magazines, brochures, catalogs, and presentations. Needless to say, people with fantastic photographic skills and a bit of marketing savvy have the opportunity to earn a great living taking and selling photographs. You can contract with publishers and others needing photographic images directly or post your photos on any one of the many stock photography services online. On these sites, people browse the selection and purchase photographic images that they need. You are paid a one-time fee or a royalty each time the image is downloaded, depending on your agreement with the image broker.

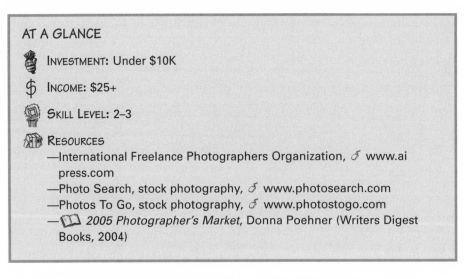

AT A GLANCE

INVESTMENT: Under $10K

INCOME: $25+

SKILL LEVEL: 2–3

RESOURCES
—International Freelance Photographers Organization, ♂ www.ai press.com
—Photo Search, stock photography, ♂ www.photosearch.com
—Photos To Go, stock photography, ♂ www.photostogo.com
—📖 *2005 Photographer's Market*, Donna Poehner (Writers Digest Books, 2004)

Children's Party Organizer

The two most important prerequisites for starting and operating a children's party service are love of children and love of party planning. Becoming a children's party organizer is a red-hot business opportunity with an excellent profit potential and growth outlook! Just think of all of the reasons a party is thrown for kids—birthdays, milestones, school-is-out, back-to-school, holidays like Halloween, special achievements in sports, arts, and academics, and recovery from illness. There are basically two options for starting and operating this business. First, operate the service on a mobile basis, throwing the party at your clients' locations. Second, organize and host parties at a fixed location requiring partygoers to come to you. This location could be your home, a rented commercial space, or at a restaurant or children's retailer with whom you have an arrangement. Regardless of whether you operate from a mobile or fixed location, your duties remain the same—plan the party; decorate with balloons, streamers, and party favors; provide entertainment like clowns, music, and magicians; serve lots of food, beverages, and desserts; stage fun games and contests giving away lots of neat prizes; and make the event one heck of a lot of fun for kids and their parents. Rates will vary depending on the menu, entertainments, games, and frills, but start at about $20 per guest and can go as high as $100 per guest for highly specialized and themed parties.

AT A GLANCE

INVESTMENT: Under $2K

INCOME: $15+

SKILL LEVEL: 1

RESOURCES
— *The Ultimate Birthday Party Book: 50 Complete and Creative Themes to Make Your Kid's Special Day Fantastic*, Susan Batters (Chariot Victor Publishing, 2002)

Boardinghouse Operator

If you are like many people, you probably spent the better part of 25 years becoming mortgage free, or close to mortgage free. Now it's time for your home to start paying you to help supplement your retirement income, and one of the best ways to make your home pay you is to start renting rooms by the week, month, or year. Just think what you could do with an extra $400, $500, or even $1,000 every month—travel, invest, help the kids or grandkids, take up a new hobby, or just have fun doing anything that makes you happy. In urban centers, you can expect to receive in the range of $300 to $750 per month per room, which generally includes a furnished room, access to other areas of your home such as a television room and kitchen, as well as utilities, cable, and use of laundry facilities, but excludes meals and telephone. In a perfect situation, your home will be large enough that both you and your boarders will have privacy. Private washroom facilities are especially useful. Boarders can be people from all walks of life—students, pleasure travelers, business people on assignment, and just about anyone else looking for short-term, economical accommodations. As a rule of thumb, renting rooms generally requires nothing more than running "room for rent" classified advertisements, but be sure to check references and credit for all would-be boarders before handing them keys to your home.

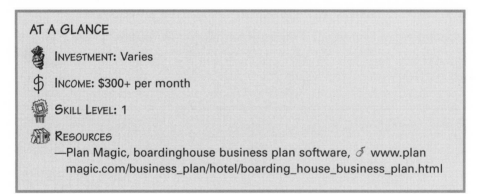

AT A GLANCE

INVESTMENT: Varies

INCOME: $300+ per month

SKILL LEVEL: 1

RESOURCES
—Plan Magic, boardinghouse business plan software, ♂ www.plan magic.com/business_plan/hotel/boarding_house_business_plan.html

House Sitter

There are lots of people who regularly or just occasionally need house-sitting services, including people going on vacations lasting longer than a week, traveling business owners and executives, people having major renovations who do not want to be there but still want the home to be occupied for security reasons, to name just a few. House sitting is an excellent way to earn postretirement income because the service is easy to market, demand is proven, the business is cheap to start, and no one is excluded because of physical limitations. House sitters not only provide peace of mind security, but also provide clients with other valuable services while on the job, such as watering plants and the lawn, feeding the cat, collecting mail, light cleaning duties, and taking care of emergency situations that may arise, such as a burst pipe.

If you want to expand the business beyond yourself, the next logical question is, Who would house sit? There are quite a few people interested in house-sitting positions, including students, singles, other retirees, and the occasional odd duck looking for a change of pace. You have a couple of options in terms of how you establish a house-sitting service. First, you can operate as a referral service, bringing together people who want house-sitting services and those who want to house sit. Second, you can employ yourself and contract house sitters on an on-call basis, posting them to jobs as they come available. Increasing revenues can be as easy as adding additional, but complementary, services like pet sitting, dog walking, babysitting referrals, and a nanny service.

AT A GLANCE

INVESTMENT: Under $2K

INCOME: $15+

SKILL LEVEL: 1

RESOURCES
— ☆ Hawkeye's Home Sitters, ☎ (888) 247-2787, ♂ www.homesitter.com
—House Carers, industry information portal, ♂ www.housecarers.com
—House Sit World, industry information portal, ♂ www.housesit world.com

Pet Sitter

Lots of people have pets that are not suited to being boarded at kennels or left with friends or family. For example, it is difficult to find boarding facilities for pets with chronic health conditions or exotic pets. And, many people prefer to have their dogs, cats, and other pets in the safe and familiar surroundings of home. When these pet owners need to be away from home, there is only one available solution—hire a pet-sitting service to come to their homes to care for their beloved pets. If you want to work on a small scale, you can be the pet sitter, but if your intentions are to operate full time with an eye for growth, you will need to hire or contract additional pet sitters. Good candidates for the job include pet-loving retirees and students. Market your pet-sitting services through pet-related businesses in your community: veterinarians, pet food retailers, dog trainers, dog walkers, and pet-grooming services. Remember, many people also hire pet sitters for short periods of time—a weekend away, a night out, or time off for family events. Therefore, you will need to develop a fee schedule for both long- and short-term pet sitting jobs.

AT A GLANCE

💰 INVESTMENT: Under $2K

$ INCOME: $15+

🎛 SKILL LEVEL: 1

🏚 RESOURCES
 —American Dog Owners Association, ✆ www.adoa.org
 —☆ Pets Are Inn, ☎ (800) 248-7387, ✆ www.petsareinn.com
 —📖 *Start Your Own Pet-Sitting Business*, Cheryl Kimball (Entrepreneur Press, 2004)

Singles-Only Event Promoter

Two things make starting a singles-only event promotion business a safe bet in terms of the potential for success and profitability—a 50 percent (and climbing) divorce rate in North America, and people choosing to stay single much longer than in decades past. Lots of 25-, 30-, 35-, and even 40-year-olds are still looking for Mr. or Mrs. Right before they take the plunge into a union. The result is a whole bunch of single people looking to meet other singles for fun, friendship, and maybe even love. The business concept is very straightforward. Plan, promote, and host singles events such as pub nights, group outings to concerts and sporting events, local and international travel destinations, bingo nights, Saturday morning wilderness hikes, Thursday night potluck dinners, and dog-walking outings. Providing the events are unique, fun, and exciting, word will spread fast, negating a need for a lot of costly advertising and promotion once the business is established. And, to separate your singles-only events from others, you might even want to specialize, planning events for single seniors, singles with dogs, alternative lifestyle singles, or singles with disabilities. There are lots of options, because there are lots of single people looking for companionship.

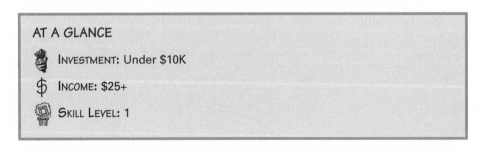

AT A GLANCE

💰 INVESTMENT: Under $10K

$ INCOME: $25+

🎛 SKILL LEVEL: 1

RESOURCES
—Entrepreneur, small business information portal, ♂ www.entrepre
neurpress.com
—Singles On The Go, singles event directory, ♂ www.singleson
thego.com
—Singles Stop, singles event directory, ♂ www.singlesstop.com

Personal Shopper

Calling all shopping fanatics! Earn great money and have fun by starting a personal shopping service assisting people who are too busy to shop, who don't like to shop, or who can't get out to do their own shopping. Lots of busy and well-heeled people hire personal shoppers to select gifts for any number of special occasions, including birthdays, births, weddings, Christmas, and anniversaries. And it's not just new products they're after: personal shoppers are also hired by interior designers and collectors to rummage through flea markets, consignment shops, antique dealers, and garage sales for collectibles, art, books, antiques, and funky home and office décor items. Corporations hire personal shoppers to purchase the perfect gifts for customers, prospects, business partners, investors, employees, and executives, as well as to purchase products for gift bag giveaways at events, ceremonies, and seminars. Seniors and people with disabilities who may find it difficult to get around or who can't get out of their homes hire personal shoppers to purchase groceries, clothing, and other home and personal products. Best of all, no experience is required to get started. If you love to shop, are creative, and don't mind networking with business owners, corporate executives, and people from all walks of life, you're qualified to become a personal shopper and get paid to shop till you drop.

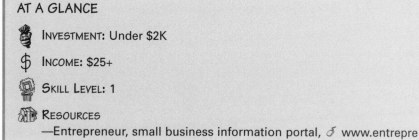

AT A GLANCE

INVESTMENT: Under $2K

$ INCOME: $25+

SKILL LEVEL: 1

RESOURCES
—Entrepreneur, small business information portal, ♂ www.entrepre
neurpress.com

—Elance Online, outsourcing and services marketplace, ♂ www
.elance.com
—📖 *Get Paid to Shop: Be a Personal Shopper for Corporate America*,
Emily Lumpkin (Forte Publishing, 1999)

Backcountry Hiking Tour Guide

North America is blessed with an abundance of incredible national, state, and provincial parks, stretching coast-to-coast. They provide an excellent opportunity for fitness fanatics with a love of hiking and knowledge of the great outdoors to start and operate a backcountry hiking tour guide business. Offer half-day, full-day, or overnight hiking expeditions catering to all outdoor enthusiasts, or offer specialized hiking trips catering to seniors, kids, or people with disabilities. Tours can be general fitness and fun sightseeing outings or focused on educating clients about the environment, wildlife, or significant geographical features. If you have the training and skills, you could even specialize in training recreational hikers outdoor survival skills, as well as marketing this end of the business to corporations that want to enroll employees and managers in team-building exercises. You will need to invest in equipment, including safety equipment, but overall this is a very inexpensive business to start with excellent seasonal income potential that can even be operated four seasons with the addition of snowshoe hiking.

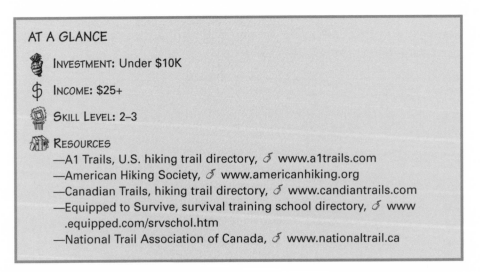

AT A GLANCE

INVESTMENT: Under $10K

INCOME: $25+

SKILL LEVEL: 2–3

RESOURCES
—A1 Trails, U.S. hiking trail directory, ♂ www.a1trails.com
—American Hiking Society, ♂ www.americanhiking.org
—Canadian Trails, hiking trail directory, ♂ www.candiantrails.com
—Equipped to Survive, survival training school directory, ♂ www
.equipped.com/srvschol.htm
—National Trail Association of Canada, ♂ www.nationaltrail.ca

Adventure Travel Agent

How about skiing glaciers in India, paddling a class five river in Argentina, deep-sea fishing off Australia, base-jumping in Africa, or a Mayan ruins tour in a hot-air balloon? Don't let age stand in the way of your having fun and earning incredible profits arranging adventure getaways of a lifetime for clients by starting a specialty adventure travel agency. Forget about run-of-the-mill bus tours of London and mundane amenity-packed hotels in Mexico; concentrate instead on matching your clients' need for adventure by offering the most unique vacation adventures available on the planet. Get the word out about your adventure travel services by marketing in company newsletters, online chat rooms and forums, advertising in specialty sports and recreation publications, exhibiting at sports and recreation shows, and using e-mail broadcasting to reach adventure enthusiats around the globe. Once established, repeat business and referrals should go a long way toward attracting a steady flow of bookings and profits. Income is earned either by charging clients a fee for organizing the adventure trip or by charging adventure companies, outfitters, and accommodation providers a fee for marketing their accommodations and activities to your clients. You can charge both, but you will need to establish a standard fee formula. With a little imagination, motivated entrepreneurs can make big bucks arranging adventure vacations for people seeking something out of the ordinary for their next vacation. This business can be really fulfilling, especially if you also share the same enthusiasm for adventure travel and recreation.

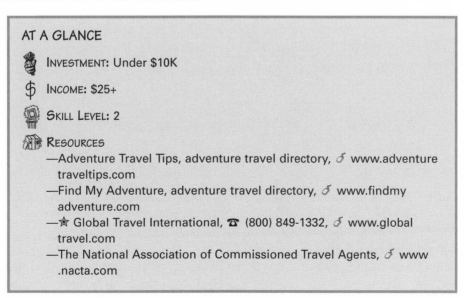

AT A GLANCE

INVESTMENT: Under $10K

INCOME: $25+

SKILL LEVEL: 2

RESOURCES
—Adventure Travel Tips, adventure travel directory, ✎ www.adventure traveltips.com
—Find My Adventure, adventure travel directory, ✎ www.findmy adventure.com
—✪ Global Travel International, ☎ (800) 849-1332, ✎ www.global travel.com
—The National Association of Commissioned Travel Agents, ✎ www .nacta.com

Arcade Games Business

There are three ways to profit from an arcade games business. But before you can earn a profit, you have to make an investment to purchase arcade games, which can be substantial if you elect to buy brand-new machines. If you decide to purchase secondhand games, expect to pay about 50 percent of the cost of new. Secondhand machines can be purchased from arcade games dealers, arcade closeouts, and auction sales. A few resources for new and used games are listed below. The first way to profit is to open a traditional arcade, stocked with the latest games and a few of the older, more popular ones. This route requires a substantial investment, over $100,000, but also has the potential to generate fabulous profits, especially in the right location. The second way to profit is to purchase arcade games, jukeboxes, and pool tables to place in locations with existing businesses, such as taverns. Revenues are earned by charging a monthly rental fee for the equipment or by splitting machine earnings with the business owners. The third way to profit is to rent the arcade games on a long- or short-term basis, depending on your customer's needs. Potential customers include people hosting house parties and corporations hosting events, as well as clubs, schools, and charities hosting events. All three options can be profitable, but ultimately your investment budget will determine the right option for you.

AT A GLANCE

💰 INVESTMENT: Varies

$ INCOME: Varies

🖳 SKILL LEVEL: 1

🗄 RESOURCES
—Arcade Games Online, ♂ www.arcadegames.com
—Arcade Games U.S.A., ♂ www.arcadegamesusa.com
—BMI Gaming Wholesale, ♂ www.bmigaming.com
—Cuestix International Wholesale, ♂ www.cuestixint.com
—Game Room Antiques, ♂ www.gameroomantiques.com

Mobile Makeup Artist

There are numerous occasions when professional makeup artistry is needed—for the bride on her wedding day, for people working in the fashion industry, for people going for important job or organizational interviews, and for many others when looks are especially important. And some people just want a makeover to feel more confidant within. What makes makeup artistry such as great opportunity is the flexibility it offers. You can work on a mobile basis, full or part time, and travel to your client's location. You can establish an independent shop or join forces with one or more established hair salons, day spas, or nail studios booking appointments at each location on specific days of the week. You can even freelance for cosmetic companies and work from retail cosmetic counters in department and drug stores. To get the word out about your service, you will want to build working relationships with wedding planners, event planers, and people in the fashion industry because they can all be a fantastic source of referrals. Cosmetology training is recommended, if you do not already have it. Contact the associations listed below to inquire about class availability in your area.

AT A GLANCE

INVESTMENT: Under $2K

INCOME: $25+

SKILL LEVEL: 2–3

RESOURCES
—Beauty Schools Directory, www.beautyschoolsdirectory.com
—Canadian Cosmetics Career Association, www.cccacosmetics.com
—National Cosmetology Association, www.salonprofessionals.com

Public Relations Specialist

An outstanding PR person representing an individual, business, politician, celebrity, product, or service can be the equivalent of having someone in your corner that can pick the winning lottery numbers long before the draw. Public relations specialists help clients establish a high profile and positive image in the public eye. Some deal with many industries and professions, whereas others focus on a specific niche, such as politicians, corporations, celebrities, or online communications. Public relations specialists offer clients various services depending on the client's needs and objectives. Services can include preparing and distributing press releases to the media, organizing and hosting press and media conferences, attending networking and business events for clients, organizing grand openings and product launches, public speaking and image consulting, and performing damage control services when things go awry. Because the public relations industry is fiercely competitive, consider starting small and representing one or two clients on a local basis until you have mastered the art. It could be your current employer, a businessperson, someone running for election, or a local celebrity. Remuneration is generally by way of a flat fee plus additional fees depending on the services rendered, frequency, and length of contract. Experience in the newspaper or television industries is especially helpful.

AT A GLANCE

INVESTMENT: Under $10K

INCOME: $50+

SKILL LEVEL: 2–3

RESOURCES
—Canadian Public Relations Society, ☎ (416) 239-7034, ♂ www.cprs.ca
—PR Web, information and resources, ♂ www.prweb.com
—Public Relations Society of America, ☎ (212) 460-1490, ♂ www.pr
sa.org

Image Consultant

Help people look and feel great by becoming an image consultant. Working as an image consultant, you can help people land a new job, spruce up for an important occasion, make a great impression on others, or feel great about the way they look and the image they project. Image consultants assist people on many fronts. They provide wardrobe consulting and updating services. They analyze their clients' current image and develop a new image program for each based on particular needs and objectives. They supply etiquette training that can be utilized in business and social circles. They assist clients in developing better communication skills through vocabulary enhancement and voice projection. They also provide assistance in developing nonverbal skills, such as the perfect handshake and perfect posture. If you think only women enlist the services of a professional image consultant, you would be wrong. In fact, the numbers are evenly split, 50 percent women and 50 percent men. Potential clients include corporate executives, people looking to land new jobs, politicians, people recovering from major illnesses and injuries, television and radio personalities, public speakers, sales professionals, and singles in or reentering the dating scene. Market your services by building a strong network of alliances, including corporations, hair and makeup profession-als, doctors, fitness trainers, and public relations consultants, able to refer their clients and contacts to your business.

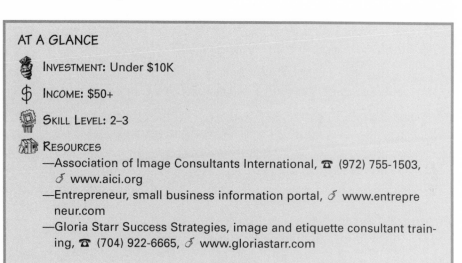

AT A GLANCE

INVESTMENT: Under $10K

INCOME: $50+

SKILL LEVEL: 2–3

RESOURCES
—Association of Image Consultants International, ☎ (972) 755-1503, ♂ www.aici.org
—Entrepreneur, small business information portal, ♂ www.entrepreneur.com
—Gloria Starr Success Strategies, image and etiquette consultant training, ☎ (704) 922-6665, ♂ www.gloriastarr.com

Laundry Service

Starting and operating a laundry wash and fold service might not be glamorous, but it is a great way to supplement your retirement income. Even better, if you already have laundry equipment, the investment needed to start the business from home adds up to nothing more than a few hundred dollars to cover business cards, fliers, and an initial advertising budget. Eventually, you might want to invest in commercial grade washers and dryers if your volume warrants, but to get started, you can use your own laundry equipment to keep costs to a minimum. To really kick-start marketing efforts, offer customers free, fast, and convenient laundry pickup and delivery. Post fliers describing your service on community bulletin boards commonly found at fitness centers, grocery markets, and gas stations. Also run cheap classified ads, and most importantly, call on businesses such as police and fire services, restaurants, grocers, fitness clubs, spas, and hair salons that use laundry services to land large volume accounts. Most commercial laundries charge by the pound, so check around your area to see what the competition is charging, and remember, you can charge extra for services such as ironing, stain removal, zipper repair, alterations, and button replacements.

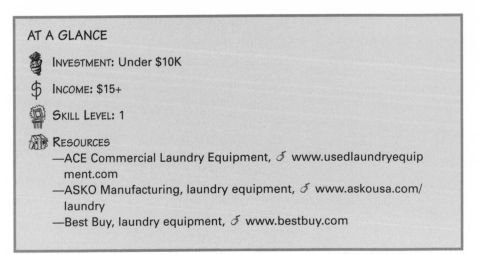

AT A GLANCE

INVESTMENT: Under $10K

$ **INCOME:** $15+

SKILL LEVEL: 1

RESOURCES
—ACE Commercial Laundry Equipment, ♂ www.usedlaundryequip
ment.com
—ASKO Manufacturing, laundry equipment, ♂ www.askousa.com/
laundry
—Best Buy, laundry equipment, ♂ www.bestbuy.com

Professional Organizer

Today's busy lifestyles often leave little time for working people to get themselves organized, let alone organize family members, their homes, or businesses. Capitalizing on your own organizational and time management skills are the two main prerequisites needed to start a professional organizer consulting service. Focus on helping clients get and stay organized, both in terms of their physical surroundings and how they manage their time for work and day-to-day tasks. Aim your organizational efforts at two separate, but equally important topics—physical organization of space, better known as decluttering, and time management. On the physical side, focus on issues such as clearing clutter (things) from the home, office, or business develop storage solutions, reorganize office furniture and equipment for maximum visual appearance and productivity, and rearrange closet space. Basically, reorganize your client's surroundings by priority to achieve maximum productivity. On the time management side, assist clients in developing routines and schedules to eliminate duplication of tasks, streamline operations, and squeeze the most productivity out of each hour so they no longer have to work nights and weekends just to stay on top of everything. Without question, networking at business and social functions is the best way to get the word out about your service and to start building a valuable contact and referral base.

AT A GLANCE

INVESTMENT: Under $2K

INCOME: $25+

 SKILL LEVEL: 1–2

RESOURCES
—Guru, outsourcing and services marketplace, ♂ www.guru.com
—National Association of Professional Organizers, ☎ (770) 325-3440,
   ♂ www.napo.net
—Professional Organizers in Canada Association, ♂ www.organizersin
   canada.com

Calligrapher

Turn your talent for exquisite handwriting into a profitable business by providing customers with calligraphy services and selling calligraphy products. Even people with minimal artistic ability can learn to master the art of calligraphy. There are numerous books and kits available to help you as well as many classes offered by schools around the country. Calligraphy can be used to create one-of-a kind handwritten wedding and event invitations, restaurant menus, gift basket cards, high-end product labels, business cards, award certificates, greeting cards, thank you cards, and stationery and to design business and club logos. Likewise, print shops and stationery retailers are often asked for special designs requiring calligraphy, and because the majority only offer machine-printed calligraphy, there is a great opportunity to subcontract your services to fill to this void in the marketplace. Also be sure to create a portfolio of work that can be distributed to wedding consultants, restaurants, banquet facilities, associations, and clubs throughout your community, as well as print and stationery shops. This is a low-cost business that can be started right from your kitchen table. Rates are in the range of $25 to $50 per hour, which also makes this opportunity a profitable pasttime.

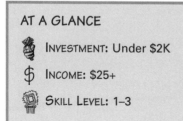

AT A GLANCE

INVESTMENT: Under $2K

INCOME: $25+

SKILL LEVEL: 1–3

RESOURCES
—Calligraphy Centre, industry information portal, ♂ www.calligraphy
centre.com
—Society for Calligraphy, ♂ www.societyforcalligraphy.com
—📖 *The Calligrapher's Bible: 100 Complete Alphabets and How to Draw Them*, David Harris (Barron's, 2003)

Dog Groomer

Calling all dog lovers! Here is your chance to tap into a highly lucrative industry by becoming a dog groomer or as groomers prefer to be called, a *canine cosmetologist*. This is a service that can easily be operated from a homebased grooming studio, a commercial storefront location, or even on a mobile basis working from a well-equipped van, which would enable you to service customers without transportation or with dogs facing health issues that keep them from traveling. There are an estimated 30,000,000 pet dogs in North America, and most owners think nothing of spending a bundle on a regular basis to keep their pampered pooches well-groomed. In fact, professional grooming rates start at about $35 for a small dog and can go as high as $125 for large breeds. Not all dog groomers are professionally trained and certified. I do recommend, however, that you invest in the training to become a professional dog groomer if this is a business that truly interests you. Dog owners are a fickle and conscientious bunch and most do not like to leave their best friends in the care of the inexperienced. The National Dog Groomers Association of America and the Western Professional Dog Groomers Association in Canada both offer training to become a Certified Master Groomer. The profit potential is excellent, as many groomers report earnings in the range of $50,000 after expenses.

AT A GLANCE

INVESTMENT: Varies

$ INCOME: $25+

SKILL LEVEL: 1–3

RESOURCES
—National Dog Groomers Association of America, ☎ (724) 962-2711, ♂ www.nationaldoggroomers.com

—★ Wag 'n' Tails, ☎ (631) 513-0304, ♂ www.wagntails.com
—Western Professional Dog Groomers Association, ☎ (604) 476-6637, ♂ www.wags.ca
—📖 *From Problems to Profits: The Madson Management System for Pet Grooming Businesses,* Madeline Bright Ogle (Madson Group, 1997)

Dog-Walking Service

A dog-walking service is perfectly suited for people with the time, patience, and a love for dogs. Best of all, with an investment of just a few hundred dollars you can be up and running your own full- or part-time business in no time. There are numerous styles of multilead dog walking collars and leashes available that will allow three or more dogs to be walked at the same time without becoming tangled in the leash, and most cost less than $100. Acquiring this equipment is important because it will reduce frustration and enable you to walk multiple dogs at the same time, which in turn will increase revenues and profits. And it's the law. In most areas of the United States and Canada, dogs must be on a lead while walking in public spaces. Design a promotional flier detailing your dog-walking service and qualifications, and distribute the fliers to businesses that are frequented by dog owners: dog grooming locations, kennels, pet food stores, community animal shelters, and community centers. Once word is out about your service, it should not take long to establish a base of 20 or 30 regular clients. Dog-walking rates are in the range of $6 to $12 per hour, per dog. Obviously, walking several dogs at a time gives you the best income and profit potential.

AT A GLANCE

💰 INVESTMENT: Under $2K

$ INCOME: $15+

▦ SKILL LEVEL: 1

▥ RESOURCES
—American Dog Owners Association, ♂ www.adoa.org
—★ Fetch! Pet Care, ☎ (510) 527-6420, ♂ www.fetchpetcare.com
—National Association of Professional Dog Walkers, ♂ www.napdw.com

Pooper-Scooper Service

It may not be sexy, but believe it or not, you can actually make a very comfortable living operating a doggie pooper-scooper service in your community. Pooper-scooper services have taken off in a big way over the last few years, and new pooper-scooper services are popping up daily across the country. This is an easy business to get into, requiring little investment, no special skills, and minimal equipment to operate. You need reliable transportation, a cell phone, garbage buckets, shovels, gloves, and a good pair of rubber boots, but that's about it. Basically, if you can handle a shovel and plastic bags and can put up with less than aromatic smells, you are qualified to start and run a pooper-scooper service. If not, you can still cash in on this booming business by marketing and managing the service, while hiring others to do the proverbial dirty work. Get the word out about your pooper-scooper service by running low-cost classified advertisements in local newspapers, pinning promotional fliers to bulletin boards, and by informing dog-related businesses in the community, such as pet food retailers, groomers, dog walkers, and veterinarians, about your service. Most pooper-scooper services charge a flat monthly rate of between $30 and $60, which includes a once-per-week visit to clean up the yard, typically taking no more than ten minutes.

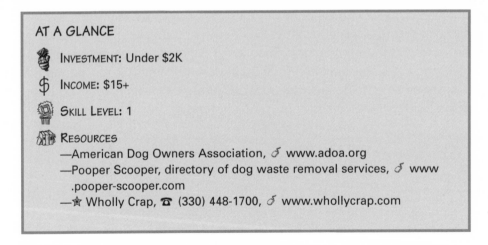

AT A GLANCE

INVESTMENT: Under $2K

$ INCOME: $15+

SKILL LEVEL: 1

RESOURCES
—American Dog Owners Association, ♂ www.adoa.org
—Pooper Scooper, directory of dog waste removal services, ♂ www
.pooper-scooper.com
—☆ Wholly Crap, ☎ (330) 448-1700, ♂ www.whollycrap.com

Appliance Repair

Appliance repair is a great moneymaking opportunity for mechanically inclined entrepreneurs of any age. Stoves, fridges, dishwashers, washers, dryers, central vacuum systems, and freezers are just a few of the home appliances that you can repair at rates as high as $75 per hour. You will need home-appliance repair training, but certification courses can be completed in less than a year. Contact the associations listed below to find classes in your area. Further training in commercial kitchen equipment will enable you to repair restaurant and food services equipment such as gas grills and ranges, deep fryers, and commercial coolers. Advertise in the Yellow Pages and in your community newspaper classifieds to get the ball rolling. Offering customers a 24-hour emergency repair service, as well as an ironclad warranty on all work, is sure to get the telephone ringing. Also market your services to apartment landlords and property managers. This is a venture that is perfectly suited to a homebased business with major repairs done in your workshop and minor repairs completed onsite. Extra income can be earned by purchasing appliances in need of repair at auctions and garage sales and from classified ads. In fact, in more cases than not, appliances that are not working can be picked up for free. Once repaired, they can be resold for a handsome profit.

AT A GLANCE

INVESTMENT: Under $25K

INCOME: $50+

SKILL LEVEL: 2–4

RESOURCES
—Canadian Electronic & Appliance Service Association, ☎ (905) 629-7907, ♂ www.ceasa.org
—☆ Mr. Appliance, ♂ www.mrappliance.com
—National Appliance Repair Association, ☎ (765) 453-1820, ♂ www.nasa1.org

Painting Service

Interior and exterior residential and commercial painting is a surefire winner in terms of generating lots of extra income. In fact, house painters who are not afraid to roll up their sleeves and get to work can earn as much as $60,000 per year, and more if they employ others. Even better, starting and operating a painting service is perfectly suited for baby boomers, both women and men, because compared to other home improvement businesses, house painting is not physically demanding and just about everyone has painted some. Of course, key to success in this business is giving clients uncompromising quality and service, which in turn helps to secure more repeat and referral business than most painters can handle. Ideally, you should have some prior painting experience to get started, but much about the trade can be learned as you go. Paint your own home and those of friends and family for practice before you start charging. Tool and equipment requirements add up to nothing more than good-quality ladders, brushes, roller trays, sanding blocks, and reliable transportation.

AT A GLANCE

INVESTMENT: Under $10K

INCOME: $25+

SKILL LEVEL: 1–2

RESOURCES
—★ Certa Pro Painters, ☎ (800) 462-3782, ♂ www.gocerta.com
—★ Fresh Coat Painters, ♂ www.freshcoatpainters.com
—Painting and Decorators Contractors Association, ♂ www.pdca.org

Community Handyperson Service

Cash in on the multibillion-dollar home repair industry by starting your own handyperson service. Handyperson services require little explanation. The main requirements for starting such a service, of course, are being handy with tools, having the required tools and equipment, and having a good understanding and working knowledge of many trades—painting, carpentry, flooring, plumbing. Basically, you should be a jack-of-all-trades, although not necessarily master of any. Currently, handyperson billing rates are in the range of $25 to $40 per hour, plus materials and a markup to cover costs associated with handling and delivery. The service can be promoted and marketed to both residential and commercial clients through traditional advertising and marketing such as the Yellow Pages, newspaper classified advertisements, fliers and door hangers, site and vehicle signage, door knocking, and attending home and garden shows to generate inquiries. Also, be sure to work with general contractors and renovation firms, as more often than not, they will send small jobs your way rather than bother with them. Repeat business and word-of-mouth referrals will become your main source of new business once you are established, providing you offer clients good value and excellent service.

AT A GLANCE

 INVESTMENT: Under $10K

 INCOME: $25+

 SKILL LEVEL: 2

 RESOURCES
— ★ House Doctors, ☎ (800) 319-3359, 🖊 www.housedoctors.com
— 📖 *2005 National Repair and Remodeling Estimator*, Albert S. Paxton (Craftsman Book Company, 2004)

Yard Maintenance Service

If you are looking for a great way to stay fit and active, love the outdoors, and want to earn a little money to help supplement your retirement income, you can offer a host of yard and property clean up and maintenance services by starting a general yard maintenance service. Cut grass, provide rubbish removal, trim trees and hedges, and offer lawn aeration and garden tilling. Concentrate your marketing efforts on securing customers who are prepared to sign up for a regular weekly or monthly maintenance service, and offer financial incentives to persuade them to do so, such as a 10 percent discount. Most of the equipment needed to operate a yard maintenance service is relatively inexpensive. To keep start-up costs to a minimum, equipment such as mowers, tillers, leaf blowers, and weed eaters can be purchased secondhand or rented on an as-needed basis until you have earned enough to buy them. On average, you should have no problem charging in the range of $20 to $30 per hour, providing you offer quality and reliable services. If you will be operating in northern climates, offer leaf raking in the fall and snow clearing and de-icing services in the winter for a year-round operation, or work only in the summer months and spend the money you earn traveling the rest of the year.

AT A GLANCE

 INVESTMENT: Under $10K

 INCOME: $15+

 SKILL LEVEL: 1

RESOURCES
—How to Start a Lawn Care Business, ♂ www.mowing4money.com
—★ Jim's Mowing, ☎ (604) 878-0787, ♂ www.jimsmowing.com
—★ Weed Man, ☎ (416) 269-5754, ♂ www.weed-man.com

Gardening Consultant

If you enjoy working in the great outdoors, playing in the dirt, and know a whole lot about flowers, trees, shrubs, and veggie gardens, then chances are you are the perfect candidate to start a gardening consulting business. The focus of the service is to help teach other would be green-thumbers everything they need to know so they can design, plant, and maintain a decorative or productive vegetable and herb garden. During the first consultation with clients, you ask questions to determine the type of garden and landscape features they want, their budgets, their time frames, and whether they want to do the work to install the garden or hire others. From this point, based on your knowledge about plants, plant placement, soil, rocks, and fertilizers, you create a garden plan in step-by-step detail suited to each client's needs and garden criteria. This is a terrific opportunity for green-thumb entrepreneurs to stay active and fit because gardening work can be somewhat physically demanding, but at the same time earn an income in the range of $25 to $50 an hour doing something you love. This is very much a business that will thrive on repeat business and referrals once established. To get the ball rolling, advertise your services locally using newspaper advertisements. Then build a network of alliances at garden product retailers so they refer your services to their clients.

AT A GLANCE

 INVESTMENT: Under $2K

 INCOME: $25+

 SKILL LEVEL: 2–3

 RESOURCES
—Garden Seeker, industry information portal, ♂ www.garden seeker.com
—Gardener's Supply Company, ♂ www.gardeners.com
—Plant Ideas, industry information portal, ♂ www.plantideas.com

Garden Tilling Service

If you are looking for a simple seasonal enterprise that has great income potential, then starting a garden tilling service might be right up your alley. You will need to invest in a rototiller, as well as a truck or trailer for transportation. In total, you can easily get started for less than $1,000 if you already have suitable transportation. Tilling the garden performs a number of necessary functions, such as mixing organic matter and fertilizer into garden soil and controlling weeds that compete with vegetables for moisture and nutrients. Most gardening gurus agree that you do not want to overtill a garden, but at the same time tilling is best done once in the spring and again in the fall after all vegetables have been harvested. Advertise by posting notices at garden centers, joining gardening clubs, posting fliers on community bulletin boards, and by running low-cost classified ads in your local newspaper in the spring and fall. This is very much a business that will be supported by referrals and repeat business once established. Expect to earn in the range of $15 to $25 per hour.

AT A GLANCE

 INVESTMENT: Under $2K

 INCOME: $15+

 SKILL LEVEL: 1

 RESOURCES
—ABE Supply, new and used garden tillers, www.abesupply.com
—Canadian Business Service Center, www.cbsc.org
—Cub Cadet, garden tillers, www.cubcadet.com

Wedding Planner

With the cost of a typical wedding now easily $10,000, $20,000, and even $30,000, it's easy to understand why many couples are more than happy to spend $1,000 to hire a professional wedding consultant. Not only is this money wisely spent, but it is also a very cheap insurance policy on a substantial wedding investment. What are the duties of a professional wedding planner? Lots. But more specifically, wedding planners hire caterers, screen musicians or disc jockey services, book the reception hall, find a florist and help create table centerpieces and bouquets, make a lot of suggestions, and fix a myriad of last-minute crises. In other words, wedding planners do everything that is required to plan and carry out an unforgettable, perfect wedding. If you like to plan a party, are well organized, and thrive in a chaotic atmosphere, it's likely that this business is right up your alley. There are more than 8,000 professional wedding planners in the United States, and needless to say, the industry is competitive. At the same time, however, more than 2.5 million people get hitched each year, so there is more than ample opportunity to carve off a piece of the very lucrative wedding cake for yourself, especially if you are prepared to work hard and smart to get the job done.

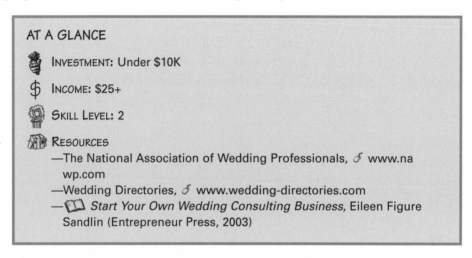

AT A GLANCE

INVESTMENT: Under $10K

INCOME: $25+

SKILL LEVEL: 2

RESOURCES
—The National Association of Wedding Professionals, ♂ www.nawp.com
—Wedding Directories, ♂ www.wedding-directories.com
—📖 *Start Your Own Wedding Consulting Business*, Eileen Figure Sandlin (Entrepreneur Press, 2003)

Errand Service

It comes as no surprise that today's busy lifestyles mean many working folk just don't have time for even the simplest of errands, such as taking the family pet to the veterinarian for a routine checkup, buying Aunt Sue a birthday present, buying groceries, picking up dry cleaning, or fetching the kids after school, all of which can be difficult sometimes. That's great news if you're a reliable multitasker looking to start your own simple, inexpensive, yet potentially very profitable business. An errand service can be operated with nothing more than a cellular telephone and reliable transportation. Land clients by networking and by creating a simple marketing brochure explaining the services you provide, along with your contact information. The brochures can be pinned to community bulletin boards, hand delivered to homes and businesses, and distributed with the local newspaper. A few promotional items such as pens and memo pads emblazoned with your company logo, name, and telephone number given out to potential customers will go a long way as a gentle reminder of your fast, reliable, and affordable errand services. This is the kind of business where growth is fuelled by referrals, so customer service and satisfaction are the most important goals.

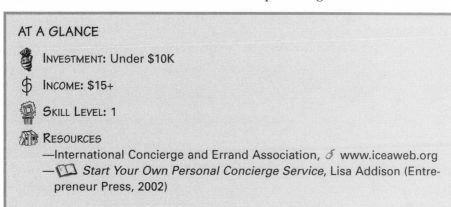

AT A GLANCE

INVESTMENT: Under $10K

$ INCOME: $15+

SKILL LEVEL: 1

RESOURCES
—International Concierge and Errand Association, ✆ www.iceaweb.org
—📖 *Start Your Own Personal Concierge Service*, Lisa Addison (Entrepreneur Press, 2002)

Glass Etching Business

Glass etching is a great moneymaking opportunity for may reasons, but mainly because glass etching is easy to learn, equipment and supplies are inexpensive, you can work from a garage workshop, and demand for decorative etched glass is high. There are several techniques that can be used to decoratively etch glass—acid wash, engraving, laser etching, and sandblasting. At present, sandblasting remains the most popular choice. The glass is covered with a stencil pattern and sand is then blown against the surface; glass surfaces not protected by the pattern are etched. Products that can be etched with elegant designs, patterns, and images for resale include window glass, cabinet glass, glass awards, and most other glass products. Many people also want glass etched with codes and identification marks for security purposes. There are many ready-made etching stencil designs and letter stencils available through craft retailers, or you can make your own by purchasing stenciling vinyl and cutting your own patterns. In addition to selling etched glass products online and at home décor shows, you can also do custom one-of-a-kind glass etching work for interior designers, kitchen cabinet installers, and automotive dealers.

AT A GLANCE

INVESTMENT: Under $2K

$ INCOME: $15+

SKILL LEVEL: 1–2

RESOURCES
—The Crafters Mall, craft products marketplace, ♂ www.procrafter.com
—Martronics Corporation, glass etching tools and supplies, ☎ (800) 775-0797, ♂ www.glass-etching-kits.com
—📖 *Easy Glass Etching*, Marlis Cornett (Sterling, 2004)

Holiday and Event Decorating Service

One of the hottest new services to sell is holiday and event decoration services. Not only is there the potential to earn big bucks and have a lot of fun, but the business also has minimal start-up investment and skill requirements. Holiday and event decorators offer clients a wide variety of services—everything from installing Christmas lights, to decorating banquet halls for wedding receptions, to "creeping-out" a house, business, or office for Halloween celebrations. Establishing working relationships with wedding planners, event planners, and retailers can go a long way in gaining valuable work and referrals. In addition to Christmas and special occasions, you can also help decorate customers' homes, stores, and offices for milestone celebrations such as anniversaries, Halloween, Easter, New Years, and Fourth of July celebrations. To provide clients with holiday and special event decorating services, you will need basic tools like ladders, a cordless drill, and hand tools, along with a creative design flair and suitable transportation. Decorations may be purchased wholesale and marked up providing an additional revenue source. Ultimately, your work decorating will be your greatest advertisement, so be sure to use site signs promoting your service, hand out lots of business cards, and send out press releases to the media when you have really done a bang-up decorating job on a business, house, or office.

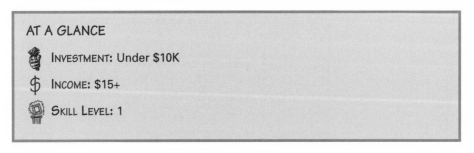

AT A GLANCE

INVESTMENT: Under $10K

$ INCOME: $15+

SKILL LEVEL: 1

Balloon Service

With an investment of less than $1,000, you can start a part-time party balloon service and earn big profits on weekends and during holidays, or you can even turn the business into a full-time, lucrative money generator depending on your goals and ambitions. Corporate events, grand openings, children's birthday parties, special occasions, graduations, retailer sales, weddings, community events, concerts, and parades, the demand for party balloons is gigantic and continually growing. Marketing a party balloon service is best achieved by creating a basic yet detailed promotional flier describing your service and rates and distributing the flier to party and event planners, wedding planners, children's stores, restaurants, banquet facilities, day-care centers, and catering companies. There are also many balloon manufacturers and printers who offer custom balloon printing services, enabling you to sell balloons direct to businesses that want to advertise sales and special events with their names and logos emblazoned on the balloons. Great add-on services that can be used to increase revenues include a party cleanup service, streamer and decoration supplies, and event planning services, especially for children's birthday parties. You will need reliable transportation and basic equipment such as helium tanks for gas-filled balloons and air compressors for blowing up cold-air balloons. But don't worry. This equipment is cheap to buy or rent.

AT A GLANCE

 INVESTMENT: Under $10K

$ INCOME: $15+

 SKILL LEVEL: 1

RESOURCES
—Balloons Online, wholesaler, ☎ (800) 239-2000, ♂ www.balloons.com
—Wholesale Balloons, wholesaler, ☎ (919) 676-5998, ♂ www.whole
saleballoons.com

Honeymoon Consulting Service

Without question, the honeymoon trip is the most important trip that people take in their lifetimes. Lots of research and planning is required to make sure it is as perfect as the wedding. Unfortunately, that's not always the case. Why? Simply because newlyweds spend so much time fussing over wedding plans, they do not have the time or energy left to plan for the perfect honeymoon. Operating as a honeymoon consultant, you can make sure your client's honeymoon vacation is the experience of a lifetime. Help couples select a destination that is suited to their personalities, make travel arrangements, book accommodations, and arrange activities and events, as well as planning for even the smallest details like a camera, film, currency conversions, travel and health insurance, and passports, in short, every detail that goes into planning and executing the honeymoon trip of a lifetime. Remember, there is no cookie cutter honeymoon stuff here. The honeymoon package you create for your clients must be unique and developed specifically for each client. You may even want to specialize in 50-plus newlyweds.

AT A GLANCE

 INVESTMENT: Under $10K

$ INCOME: $25+

 SKILL LEVEL: 1–2

 RESOURCES
—☆ Enchanted Honeymoons, ☎ (800) 253-2863, ♂ www.enchanted
honeymoons.com
—The National Association of Wedding Professionals, ♂ www.na
wp.com
—Wedding Directories, ♂ www.wedding-directories.com
—📖 *Fodor's FYI: Plan Your Honeymoon: Experts Share Their Secrets*, Karen Cure and Melissa Klurman (Fodor's, 2001)

Product Assembly Service

Furniture, lawn and garden products, fitness equipment, and computers. Far too many products sold today require assembly, which is never as easy as advertised. Everyone has been in the annoying situation of fighting and struggling to get three or four boxes home, only to fight and struggle for another few hours to assemble a product. But opportunity can be born out of circumstance. In this case, opportunity is the chance to offer product assembly services and earn a very good income in the process. The business can be started for less than $500 and marketed through retailers who do not currently offer product assembly services to their customers; additional revenues can be earned if you also provide delivery services at the same time. You need to buy basic tools such as a cordless drill, hand tools, and a socket set, along with moving equipment like blankets, a dolly, and suitable transportation if you will also be offering delivery services. Retailers of products that must be assembled after purchase will be your big market. At the same time, do not overlook the possibility of building alliances with home and office movers; moving often requires furniture and equipment to be disassembled for the move and then reassembled.

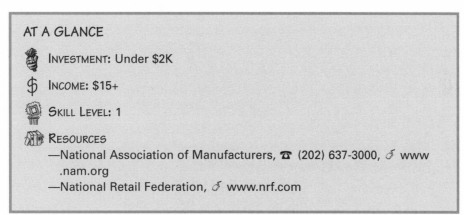

AT A GLANCE

INVESTMENT: Under $2K

INCOME: $15+

SKILL LEVEL: 1

RESOURCES
—National Association of Manufacturers, ☎ (202) 637-3000, ♂ www
.nam.org
—National Retail Federation, ♂ www.nrf.com

Floral Designer

The floral industry generates a whopping $20 billion a year in sales, and according to the U.S. Bureau of Labor Statistics, demand for floral designers is at an all-time high, and will increase 12 percent in the next five years alone! If you love flowers and need to earn money to supplement your retirement income, then this just might be the right opportunity for you. If you have an eye for design, you are qualified to start your own floral design business. However, formal training is an asset, and there are a number of schools and community continuing education programs that offer floral design classes. Floral designers select flowers, greenery, and decorations to be used to create appealing floral arrangements, such as bouquets, wreaths, and table centerpieces for any number of occasions—weddings, funerals, social events, restaurants, and business functions. Designers also use a variety of tools and materials, such as various knives and shears to produce the desired cut and shape, as well as foam, wire, tape, and all kinds of containers to hold and showcase their designs. Market your services by establishing alliances with event planners, wedding planners, catering companies, and funeral homes.

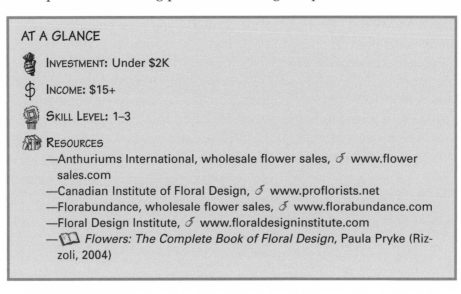

AT A GLANCE

INVESTMENT: Under $2K

INCOME: $15+

SKILL LEVEL: 1–3

RESOURCES
—Anthuriums International, wholesale flower sales, ♂ www.flower sales.com
—Canadian Institute of Floral Design, ♂ www.proflorists.net
—Florabundance, wholesale flower sales, ♂ www.florabundance.com
—Floral Design Institute, ♂ www.floraldesigninstitute.com
—📖 *Flowers: The Complete Book of Floral Design*, Paula Pryke (Rizzoli, 2004)

Entertainment Booking Service

Starting and operating an entertainment booking service is an opportunity that is sure to prove fun and profitable. Just think about all the talented performers that your service could represent and book—from singers to public speakers to animal acts. You can help celebrate many special occasions—from children's birthdays, to bachelor and bachlorlette parties, to charity events. The business concept is very straightforward. You find performers and sign them to a nonexclusive representation agreement (which means they can work for anyone else or have anyone else they choose represent them). The next step is to advertise the service by utilizing newspaper classifieds and Yellow Pages advertisements, and by building alliances with wedding planners, event planners, restaurants, nightclubs, and banquet halls. Clients call, book the type of performer they need, and you pass on the information to the performer who completes the contract with the client. As a rule of thumb, the booking service retains 15 to 20 percent of the performer's fee for providing the booking service. This is very much a business that thrives on referral and repeat business, so A-1 customer service is a must.

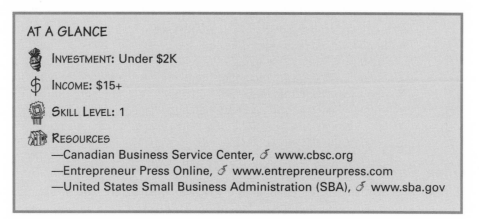

Fabric Restoration

Fabric restoration is big business for both residential and commercial applications, mainly because, if you stop to think about it, fabric covers just about everything in the home and office. Working from a well-equipped van on a mobile basis, you can repair and restore torn, cracked, faded, stained, and burned fabrics like leather, suede, vinyl, cloth, plastic, carpet, and velour. Market your fabric restoration services through traditional advertising media, like the Yellow Pages and classified ads, and build working relationships with other businesses that have the potential to utilize your services on a regular basis. These businesses include hotels, motels, movie theaters, hospitals, carpet cleaners, and similar businesses where many customers, not all careful, use the facilities. There is quite a bit of learning needed in terms of mastering the fabric restoration trade because there is lots to know about chemicals, fabrics, dyes, and patching, which makes starting a franchise fabric restoration operation a good choice because initial training and ongoing support is provided. At the same time, entrepreneurs with handyperson skills can master the trade on their own through trial and error, and practice, practice, and more practice.

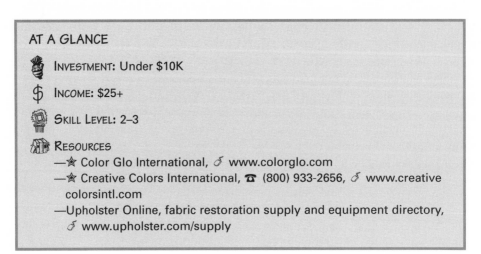

Cleaning Service

Residential and commercial cleaning is a multibillion-dollar industry, and getting your piece of this very lucrative pie is very easy because cleaning requires no special skills or start-up investment, equipment costs are minimal, and there is no shortage of work. Residential cleaners perform standard household duties and some also offer interior window washing. For the most part, residential cleaners provide all supplies and equipment needed to perform these services. So you will need to invest in a vacuum cleaner, buckets, dusters, mops, rags, cleaning solvents, a stepladder, and reliable transportation. Ideally, you want customers who will use the service on a regular basis—daily, weekly, monthly—not occasionally. Market your services with flier and coupon drops, as well as with classified advertisements in your local newspaper. Referrals will also make up a large percentage of new business, so quality and excellent customer service are a must. On average, residential cleaners charge in the vicinity of $15 to $25 per hour. Like residential cleaning, commercial cleaning is also a booming industry generating billions in sales. Commercial cleaners perform the same services as residential cleaners—dusting, vacuuming, and polishing—but on a larger scale and with additional services like replenishing paper product supplies and soaps, washing windows, stripping floors, and emptying trash and recycling receptacles. The only real downside to commercial cleaning is most of the cleaning is done nights and/or weekends after the business or office closes. Commercial cleaning rates tend to be higher than residential cleaning rates, in the range of $20 to $30 per hour, plus paper and other specialized supplies. Securing commercial cleaning contracts requires nothing more than getting out and knocking on doors to pitch your services to business owners and managers.

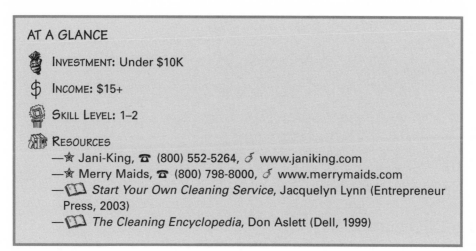

AT A GLANCE

INVESTMENT: Under $10K

$ INCOME: $15+

SKILL LEVEL: 1–2

RESOURCES
—★ Jani-King, ☎ (800) 552-5264, ♂ www.janiking.com
—★ Merry Maids, ☎ (800) 798-8000, ♂ www.merrymaids.com
—📖 *Start Your Own Cleaning Service*, Jacquelyn Lynn (Entrepreneur Press, 2003)
—📖 *The Cleaning Encyclopedia*, Don Aslett (Dell, 1999)

Power-Washing Service

There are hundreds of items that can be cleaned using power-washing equipment. Driveways, patios, vehicles, mobile homes, signs, metal roofs, construction and farm equipment, and lots of other things can benefit from a good cleaning. Not only is there a nearly unlimited number of items to pressure wash, rates are also excellent. It is not uncommon to earn as much as $400 per day pressure washing. The only fixed costs to operating the service are a telephone, liability insurance, transportation, occasional equipment repair, and a bit of initial advertising until repeat business and referrals kick in and make up the lion's share of your work. A helpful hint to keep in mind when you start marketing is to aim your efforts at clients who will become repeat clients. These include companies with fleet vehicles and retailers who want to keep their storefronts and parking lots spic-n-span. The reason you want to target repeat business is obvious: It costs 100 times as much to find 100 clients as it does to find one client and provide service 100 times. You can also visit marinas, trailer parks, and RV campgrounds on weekends and offer your pressure-washing services to boat, trailer, and recreational vehicle owners at reduced rates because you can make up the difference (and more) through volume pressure washing.

AT A GLANCE

 INVESTMENT: Under $10K

 INCOME: $25+

 SKILL LEVEL: 1

 RESOURCES
—E-Power Wash, industry information portal, ♂ www.epower wash.com
—Higher Power Supplies, power washing equipment, ☎ (877) 389-3131, ♂ www.higherpowersupplies.com
—★Sparkle Wash International, ☎ (800) 321-0770, ♂ www.sparkle wash.com

Patio Landscaping Service

Condominiums, townhouses, and lofts are being constructed in record-breaking numbers across the United States and Canada. This building boom has spawned an entirely new and super red-hot industry—small-spaces landscaping. Where are these small spaces? They include sundecks, patios, decks, balconies, rooftops, and courtyards for both residential and commercial locations. Home and property owners want to have beautiful outdoor spaces to enjoy, but when the outdoor space is limited to a ten-by-ten foot balcony, most do not know how they can combine both function and flowers in such a small space. That's when they call in a professional small-spaces landscaper. Capitalizing on your knowledge of plants, flowers, and design, you can offer customers a specialized landscaping service transforming their small outdoor spaces into a lush, yet highly functional living spaces. Planters, gazebos, seats, water features, flowers, ivy, sunshades, heaters, and barbeques are just a few of the elements you will have to work with and plan for. Income is earned in three ways: (1) planning and installing the small-space garden; (2) purchasing products wholesale that will be used in the garden and selling them to clients at retail prices; and (3) ongoing monthly fees to maintain and upgrade the garden area as required.

AT A GLANCE

 INVESTMENT: Under $2K

INCOME: $25+

 SKILL LEVEL: 2

RESOURCES
—Associated Landscape Contractors of America, ♂ www.alca.org
—Garden Seeker, industry information portal, ♂ www.garden seeker.com
—Gardener's Supply Company, ♂ www.gardeners.com
—📖 *Gardening in Small Spaces: Creative Ideas from America's Best Gardeners* (Taunton Press, 2002)

Bicycle Repair

Mechanically inclined entrepreneurs with a love of cycling can earn a great supplemental income repairing bicycles right from the comfort of a homebased workshop. In addition to big profit potential, there are many other advantages to operating a bicycle repair service, including low overhead, huge demand for service in an ever-growing sport (and commuter option as fuel prices continue to skyrocket), and flexible full- or part-time hours. Even if you are not experienced in bicycle repairs, there are a number of schools offering bicycle mechanic courses that take only a few weeks to complete, such as those offered by United Bicycle Institute in Oregon. Key to marketing your services is to join bicycling clubs and organizations in the community, largely because their members can become customers and refer other bicycling enthusiasts to your business. When you are not busy repairing your own customers' bikes, you can also work on a contract basis for bicycle retailers, handling their overflow repair and warranty work. Advertising your services in your community newspaper and distributing fliers detailing the services you provide—perhaps an introductory offer for a spring time bicycle tune-up at a very low-cost—is sure to attract new business, which can be converted into long-term repeat customers.

AT A GLANCE

 INVESTMENT: Under $10K

 INCOME: $25+

CHAPTER 7: *202 Ways to Supplement Your Retirement Income* ■ **175**

Skill Level: 2–3

 Resources
—Barnett Bicycle Institute, bicycle repair training school, ♂ www.bb institute.com
—Park Tool, professional bicycle repair tools and equipment, ♂ www .parktool.com
—United Bicycle Institute, Oregon-based training school offering students certification courses in bicycle mechanics, ♂ www.bike school.com
—📖 *Barnett's Manual: Analysis and Procedures for Bicycle Mechanics*, John Barnett (Velo Press, 2003)

Dry-Cleaning Delivery

Dry-cleaning delivery services have recently exploded in popularity. In addition to starting your own dry-cleaning delivery service from scratch, there are also a number of franchise opportunities available across the country for those who prefer a strength-in-numbers approach to business. Armed with nothing more than a cell phone to handle customer calls, and reliable transportation, you can earn substantial profits picking up and delivering dry-cleaning. Revenues are earned by charging customers a small fee for pick-up and delivery, as well as by charging dry cleaners a fee for supplying business, generally 10 to 15 percent of the dry cleaning bill. The benefit to customers is they do not have to worry about dropping off or picking up their dry cleaning, which is delivered right to their homes, businesses, or offices. The benefit to dry cleaners is they don't have to spend money on marketing to find new customers, because that's your job. In addition to advertising the service in the newspaper, through flier and coupon drops, and in your local Yellow Pages telephone directory, also be sure to call on large-volume clients such as police departments, fire stations, hospitals, restaurants, corporations, and basically any other business or organization that requires employees to wear uniforms that must be regularly dry-cleaned.

AT A GLANCE

 Investment: Under $10K

 Income: $15+

SKILL LEVEL: 1

 RESOURCES
—✩ 1-800-Dry Clean, ☎ (866) 822-6115, ✂ www.1-800-dryclean.com
—Dry Cleaners Directory, ✂ www.drycleanersdirectory.biz
—✩ Pressed 4 Time, ☎ (800) 423-8711, ✂ www.pressed4time.com

Seniors' Employment Agency

Outsourcing, downsizing, and consolidating are the norm in today's corporate business world, and the result is a lot of people are losing their jobs. If it happens when you're younger, it is not too difficult to bounce back and find a new job or start a new career. Unfortunately, the same does not hold true for older displaced workers. For them it can be very difficult to find new work, and even harder to find work at their previous career level. Of course, there is a solution for every problem, and in this case the solution is to start an employment agency for people aged 50 and over. Even though finding a job after the age of 50 is difficult, there are still lots of employers that want to hire older employees so they can utilize on their wealth of talent, experience, and skills. Your job is to locate these employers and find the right senior employees to fill the job openings. You should probably not charge job seekers fees; instead, charge companies seeking employees a fee to list their job openings. If you also provide job seekers with additional services such as creating resumes and interview coaching, you should charge for these services.

AT A GLANCE

 INVESTMENT: Under $25K

$ INCOME: $25+

 SKILL LEVEL: 2

 RESOURCES
—American Association of Retired Persons (AARP), ✂ www.aarp.org
—Canadian Association of Retired Persons (CARP), ✂ www.50plus.com
—Canadian Business Service Center, ✂ www.cbsc.org
—Entrepreneur Online, small business portal, ✂ www.entrepreneur.com
—United States Small Business Administration (SBA), ✂ www.sba.gov

Association Management Services

Many clubs, associations, and organizations simply do not have the time, money, or people-power to manage the day-to-day operations of their enterprises, and when an association grows beyond the size that its volunteer officers can effectively handle, they often turn to an association management service to provide organizational and financial continuity. Needless to say, a fantastic opportunity exists to provide these small organizations with management services that run the gamut: from database management to membership recruitment, to bookkeeping, to writing and publishing association newsletters and all the activities in between. Associations may be nonprofit groups, seniors' groups, or sports clubs. The easiest way to market association management services is to compile a list of all of the clubs and associations in your community regardless of size, create a complete package detailing all services you provide, set appointments, and present your services to each. There are a few requirements to be effective. You need great organizational, strong marketing, administration, and management skills, and a fully equipped office. Depending on the size of the association and how efficient you are, you should have no problem managing several associations at one time.

AT A GLANCE

INVESTMENT: Under $10K

INCOME: $25+

SKILL LEVEL: 2

RESOURCES
—Guru, online marketplace for freelance talent, ☞ www.guru.com
—Marketing Source, directory listing over 5,000 associations, ☞ www
.marketingsource.com

Executive Recruiter

A star executive is vital to a corporation's or organization's success, just as a star pitcher is to a baseball team's chances of winning the World Series. If you want to win in today's super-competitive global marketplace, you need the right executives to lead the team to victory. This is why executive recruiting services are in big demand as corporations worldwide scramble to build the best executive team to guide their ships in the new global economy. An executive recruiter is nothing more than a fancy term for a headhunter. The objective of the executive recruiter is to locate the best candidate to meet each client's needs and executive criteria. Many executive recruiters wisely choose to specialize in a specific field such as investment and finance, manufacturing, technology, or food services. You would also be well advised to do the same. So where do you find the right executives for your clients? The answer is simple—everywhere. You run advertisements on behalf of clients, you source out great talent at other corporations and lure them away with superior contracts and benefits, and you never stop networking and building your database of potential candidates.

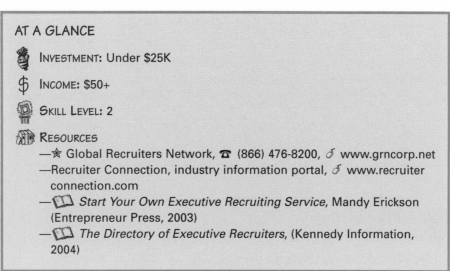

AT A GLANCE

INVESTMENT: Under $25K

INCOME: $50+

SKILL LEVEL: 2

RESOURCES
—☆ Global Recruiters Network, ☎ (866) 476-8200, ♂ www.grncorp.net
—Recruiter Connection, industry information portal, ♂ www.recruiter connection.com
—📖 *Start Your Own Executive Recruiting Service*, Mandy Erickson (Entrepreneur Press, 2003)
—📖 *The Directory of Executive Recruiters*, (Kennedy Information, 2004)

Copywriting Service

If you have a talent for writing in a clear and concise manner that can build excitement and interest and motivate readers, listeners, and viewers to take the desired action, then starting a copywriting service might be just the right moneymaking opportunity for you. Copywriters prepare copy or text for advertising, marketing materials, press releases, TV and radio commercials, catalogs, web sites, and packaging labels, just to mention a few. The demand for copywriting services is excellent, as most business owners, managers, and marketers do not have the time, skills, or inclination to prepare highly effective copy. Most also realize paying a professional copywriter is not an expense, but the best way to ensure a good return on investments in advertising and marketing materials. Establishing alliances with graphic designers, publishers, editors, advertising agencies, and public relations firms is a good way to get your foot in the door and the telephone ringing. Copywriting fees vary greatly depending on what is being prepared and the size of the assignment, but nonetheless average out in the range of $50 per hour. If you have the required skills, additional income can also be earned by providing a full-complement of editing services, including proofreading, indexing, and production.

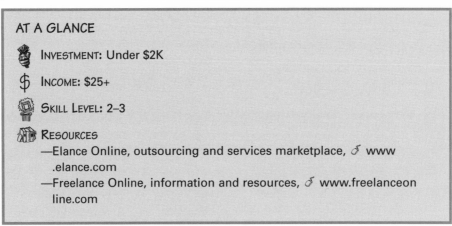

AT A GLANCE

INVESTMENT: Under $2K

$ INCOME: $25+

SKILL LEVEL: 2–3

RESOURCES
—Elance Online, outsourcing and services marketplace, ♂ www
.elance.com
—Freelance Online, information and resources, ♂ www.freelanceon
line.com

Business Plan Writer

Did you know that a recent survey of new business owners revealed that fewer than 25 percent of the 250 owners surveyed had created a business plan for their new venture? Asked why they hadn't, the number-one reason was that they simply did not know how. Couple this with an SBA statistic that approximately 750,000 new businesses are started each year in the United States, and you have an outstanding opportunity for entrepreneurs with business planning experience to capitalize by providing new businesses with research and business plan development services. Marketing business plan writing services is not terribly difficult. Start by attending business networking meetings. Obtain a list of all new and renewal business registration licenses through your local business service center or registration office. In addition to new businesses, you can also aim marketing efforts at existing businesses and professionals that are expanding or that need to update or create a new business plan. This service costs little to start and can be operated part- or full-time depending on your needs. Billing rates vary depending on the size and scope of the business plan being developed and range anywhere from a few hundred dollars for a basic business plan to as much as $10,000 for a highly sophisticated plan. On average, expect to earn in the vicinity of $75 to $100 per hour.

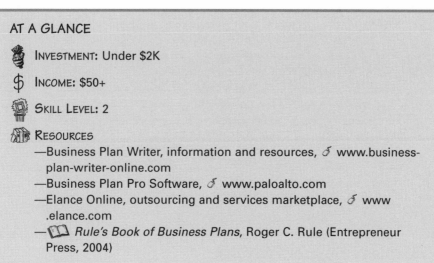

AT A GLANCE

💰 INVESTMENT: Under $2K

💲 INCOME: $50+

🗳 SKILL LEVEL: 2

🏛 RESOURCES
—Business Plan Writer, information and resources, ♂ www.business-plan-writer-online.com
—Business Plan Pro Software, ♂ www.paloalto.com
—Elance Online, outsourcing and services marketplace, ♂ www.elance.com
—📖 *Rule's Book of Business Plans*, Roger C. Rule (Entrepreneur Press, 2004)

Venture Capitalist

Most people's perception of a venture capitalist is a wealthy person that takes financial risks funding start-up companies in hopes of making big profits overnight. In truth, a venture capitalist is typically one investor in a group that invests in companies with an opportunity for a good return on investment within ten years. Venture capitalists are not static players; most take an active hands-on role in helping to guide the business to profitability. That second role is often the more important role for new business start-ups. If you have previous business experience and substantial capital that can be invested without negatively effecting your retirement funds and income, then becoming a venture capitalist might be the right opportunity for you. Of course, there is also a second option, which is to become an angel investor. Angel investors play a similar role, but on a smaller scale. Venture capitalist generally only deal in business investments of $100,000 and more, whereas angel investors invest in business deals of $1,000 to $100,000. Still, no less research and planning is required to ensure that you are investing in a business with good growth and profit potential. When considering any business investment, carefully screen the technical and business merits of the proposed company and the management team, whether you are investing $5,000 or $5,000,000.

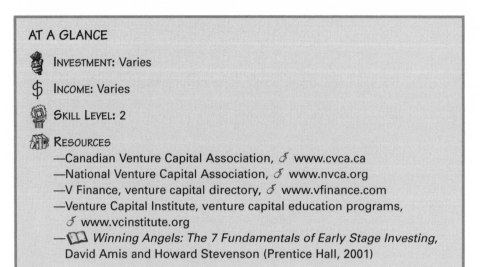

> **AT A GLANCE**
>
> 💰 INVESTMENT: Varies
>
> $ INCOME: Varies
>
> 🗄 SKILL LEVEL: 2
>
> 🗄 RESOURCES
> —Canadian Venture Capital Association, ♂ www.cvca.ca
> —National Venture Capital Association, ♂ www.nvca.org
> —V Finance, venture capital directory, ♂ www.vfinance.com
> —Venture Capital Institute, venture capital education programs,
>   ♂ www.vcinstitute.org
> —📖 *Winning Angels: The 7 Fundamentals of Early Stage Investing*,
>   David Amis and Howard Stevenson (Prentice Hall, 2001)

Small Business Support Service

In the United States and Canada, homebased and small businesses are opening at a record pace, some 800,000 new businesses each year, which means the time has never been better to start a business support service. Most new businesses are small operations with few, if any, employees and more often than not lack a support team to properly handle all of the work involved with running a business on a day-to-day basis. Business support services offer clients a wide range of services, such as bookkeeping, inventory management, on-call support staff, and many more. It is not necessary to be proficient in all areas because you can employ specialists as needed to service clients on a contract basis. One of the best ways to find clients is to join small and homebased business associations, such as the chamber of commerce, ♂ www.uschamber.com, and SOHO (Small Office Home Office), ♂ www.soho.org, to network with other small and homebased business owners and inform them about the business support services you offer.

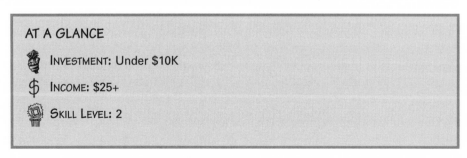

> **AT A GLANCE**
>
> 💰 INVESTMENT: Under $10K
>
> $ INCOME: $25+
>
> 🗄 SKILL LEVEL: 2

RESOURCES
—American Home Business Association, ☎ (800) 664-2422, ♂ www
.homebusiness.com
—International Association of Virtual Office Assistants, ♂ www
.iavoa.org
—International Virtual Assistants Association, ♂ www.ivaa.org
—📖 *Start Your Own Business Support Service* (Entrepreneur Press,
2003)

Homebased Promotional Products Printing

The promotional products industry generates billions in annual sales, and demand continues to grow for advertising novelties as more and more businesses look for unique ways to promote and brand their products and services in a cost efficient way. Getting in on this profitable action is easier than most people think, because pad printing equipment and supplies are widely available, easy to use, and relatively inexpensive, especially if you purchase secondhand equipment. And for entrepreneurs who want flexibility, this opportunity can provide it. The business can be operated from home part-time or even seasonally to allow for pursuit of other interests such as travel. Utilizing pad printers, silk-screening equipment, and hot stamping, you can print a wide variety of novelty advertising products for businesses—coffee mugs, mouse pads, compact discs, pens, and hundreds of other items. Promotional advertising products can be sold online, at business-to-business trade shows, and from a homebased showroom. You can even hire commissioned sales reps to call on businesses and sell products.

 AT A GLANCE

 INVESTMENT: Under $10K

 INCOME: $25+

 SKILL LEVEL: 1–3

 RESOURCES
—ITW Imtran, printing equipment and supplies, ♂ www.itwimtran.com
—Pad Printing Machinery of Vermont, printing equipment and supplies,
♂ www.padprintingmachinery.com
—Press Xchange, used printing equipment marketplace, ♂ www.press
xchange.com

—Printex USA, printing equipment and supplies, ♂ www.printex usa.com

—Promotional Products Association International, ☎ (972) 258-3206, ♂ www.ppa.org

Mystery Shopper

Do you have an eye for good and bad customer service? If so, you can turn that skill into a moneymaking opportunity by starting a mystery shopper service. More and more chain and independent retailers, and even some service providers, are using mystery shoppers to uncover shortcomings in the service that they offer clients and customers in stores and on the phone. Go undercover, and mystery-shop at clients' retail businesses, eat at clients' restaurants, and have clients' employees provide you with services, all in an effort to assess quality of employees and management, operational procedures, and customer-service policies. Many companies have introduced mystery-shopper programs to their businesses, and for good reason. Mystery shopper programs work extremely well at uncovering customer service, employee, or product and service problems. Mystery shoppers prepare a document detailing their findings, relaying their experiences, and making recommendations to clients. Recently, some have even begun to use small and concealed digital cameras to document their work and present their clients with an audiovisual record of their findings. Expanding the business is as easy as hiring additional mystery shoppers to work on a subcontract-as-needed basis. The industry is competitive, so the more relevant experiences and training you can bring to the table, the better. Particularly valuable are managerial training, prior customer service postings, retail selling, human-resources experience, and operations specialties. There are even mystery-shopper training courses available that can put you on the path to starting and operating your own mystery-shopper service.

AT A GLANCE

INVESTMENT: Under $2K

$ INCOME: $15+

SKILL LEVEL: 1–2

ATM Business

At one time, not too long ago, banks and credit unions monopolized the ATM
(Automated Teller Machine) industry, but no more. Since deregulation of the ATM
industry, any ambitious entrepreneur with the drive to succeed can own and operate an ATM business and earn excellent profits in the process. The business opportunity is very straightforward. Purchase new or used ATMs, place in high-traffic
locations throughout the community, stock them with cash, and return on a
weekly or daily basis (depending on volume) to replenish the cash supply. If you
are worried about walking around town with lots of cash, don't. Most armored car
services also provide cash restocking services for ATMs. Money is earned every
time a customer uses the machine to withdraw cash from his or her bank account.
The fee can range from a low of 50 cents to as much as $2 per transaction. This fee
is generally split with the owner of the property or business where the ATM is
installed. It can range from a 50–50 split to a 90–10 split in your favor. Some business and property owners, however, prefer a flat monthly rent, so you will need
to negotiate with each on an individual basis. Good locations for ATMs are places
like taverns, convenience stores, and locations with high foot traffic counts.

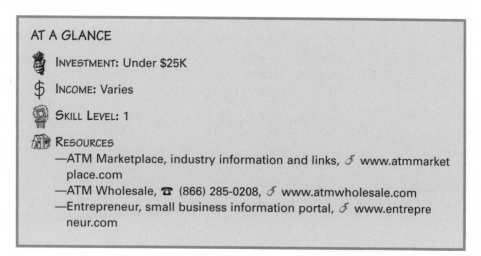

AT A GLANCE

💰 INVESTMENT: Under $25K

$ INCOME: Varies

🏧 SKILL LEVEL: 1

🏦 RESOURCES
—ATM Marketplace, industry information and links, ♂ www.atmmarket
place.com
—ATM Wholesale, ☎ (866) 285-0208, ♂ www.atmwholesale.com
—Entrepreneur, small business information portal, ♂ www.entrepre
neur.com

Liquidated Inventory Sales

Savvy entrepreneurs can earn a bundle simply by buying liquidated inventory and government surplus equipment at dirt-cheap prices and reselling it at staggering markups. In terms of liquidated inventory, retailers, distributors, and manufacturers liquidate inventory for any number of reasons—slow moving, out-of-season, damaged, relocating, merging, or going out of business. In fact, billions of dollars worth of inventory becomes available every year at fire sale prices. The best types of liquidated inventory to purchase are power and hand tools, music and movie discs, toys, kitchen and bath accessories, fashion accessories, and electronics. Stay clear of products that have limited shelf life or special warehousing and transportation requirements. Products can be resold for a profit through eBay and other online marketplaces, at weekend flea markets, as well as to dollar store retailers, flea market vendors, and eBay sellers. Purchasing government surplus and seized merchandise for pennies on the dollar of the original value and reselling to consumers at marked-up prices can also make you very rich. Government agencies such as the Internal Revenue Service (IRS), U.S. Postal Service, U.S. Small Business Administration (SBA), U.S. Marshals Service, and the U.S. Treasury Department often sell off used and surplus equipment, as well as items seized for nonpayment or for criminal activity, through auction sales and sealed bid tenders. And many more government agencies at various levels also routinely hold auction sales to dispose of property. Items that are routinely auctioned by government agencies include computers, real estate, automobiles, machinery and tools, jewelry, furniture, electronics, and boats. Sell the larger items you buy from home using classified ads and through eBay and the smaller items at weekend flea markets.

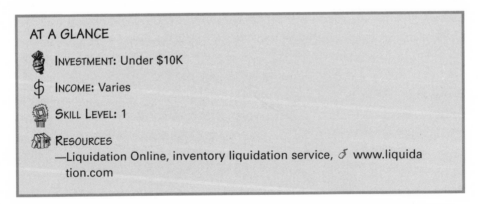

AT A GLANCE

INVESTMENT: Under $10K

$ INCOME: Varies

SKILL LEVEL: 1

RESOURCES
—Liquidation Online, inventory liquidation service, ✆ www.liquidation.com

—Merchandise USA, inventory liquidation service, ♂ www.merchandiseusa.com

—Public Works and Government Services Canada. Crown Assets Distribution, sales of government surplus and seized property by auctions, tenders, and public sales, including real estate, equipment, automobiles, furniture, boats, jewelry, clothing, furniture, and electronics, ☎ (905) 615-2025, ♂ http://crownassets.pwgsc.gc.ca/text/index-e.cfm

—Quitting Business, inventory liquidation portal, ♂ www.quittingbusiness.com

—U.S. Department of the Treasury, seized property auctions including automobiles, boats, jewelry, electronics, and furniture, ☎ (202) 622-2000, ♂ www.ustreas.gov/auctions/customs

—U.S. General Services Administration, government owned asset sales, ☎ (800) 473-7836, ♂ www.propertydisposal.gsa.gov.Property/About/

—U.S. Postal Service, damaged and unclaimed items auctions, ♂ www.usps.com/auctions

Career Guide Writer

There are lots of good reasons to start writing and selling career guides to help boost your retirement income. Career guides have always been hot sellers, they are very cheap to produce in print or electronic formats, and best of all, they sell for as much as $100 each! The best careers to write about are specialized jobs that are either very high paying, very exciting, or ideally, very exciting and high paying. Some of the better careers to write are jobs in the travel industry such as cruise ship jobs, airline jobs, and "sunny destination" tour, hotel, food, and beverage jobs. Specialized construction jobs and trade careers are also popular, as are high-tech, medical services, and television and feature film production careers. What type of information should be included with each career guide? Lots. Excellent research skills are needed. Start by creating a full description of the career, including typical job duties, education or certification requirements, expected salary range, available training courses, industry association and union information if applicable, and lots of contact resource information relevant to the career. The guides can be produced in print format, which are best sold by posting classified newspaper and magazine ads describing the guides for mail order sales as well as by exhibiting at career expositions. Or, the guides can be produced in a downloadable e-book format and promoted and sold via online marketplaces.

AT A GLANCE

INVESTMENT: Under $2K

INCOME: $25+

SKILL LEVEL: 2

RESOURCES
—Fab Job, ♂ www.fabjob.com
—Hot Job, ♂ www.hotjob.com
—Monster, ♂ www.monster.com

Seniors' Business Opportunity Finder

The fact that you are reading this book should be a good indication to you that there is a real need and demand for helping people aged 50-plus locate the right business opportunity to meet their specific needs and objectives. Capitalizing on your small business experience, you can provide seniors with business opportunity finder services and build a profitable business for yourself in the process. The first step is to analyze each client's situation—what they want to do, how much income they need to earn, how much money they have to invest, what their current experiences and skills are, and other issues such as health. Using this information, you can research on your client's behalf to find a suitable business, a business opportunity to pursue, a business to buy, or a suitable franchise to purchase. You can also provide additional services such as assisting in business and marketing planning, developing and managing product and consumer research projects, creating marketing strategies, and preparing financial budgets and forecasts.

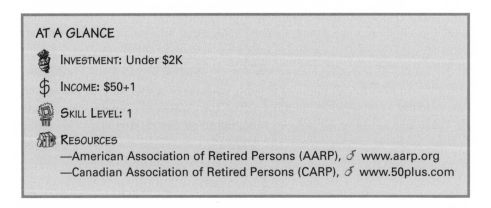

AT A GLANCE

INVESTMENT: Under $2K

INCOME: $50+1

SKILL LEVEL: 1

RESOURCES
—American Association of Retired Persons (AARP), ♂ www.aarp.org
—Canadian Association of Retired Persons (CARP), ♂ www.50plus.com

Seniors' Support Services

Information is a very valuable asset. The more information you have, the more valuable it becomes to you. Excellent profits can be earned operating a seniors' support services business. The key to success is information. You have to be able to coach both seniors and children of elderly parents about issues, programs, and information pertaining to seniors. This includes information on local activities and clubs, medical and pharmacy insurance options, travel and tours, recreational activities, available living accommodations, medical and nomedical home care, and lots more. Basically, you need to become a walking talking encyclopedia about all of the issues, challenges, assistance programs, and activities that seniors need to be informed about. You can work from home as well as meet with clients at their homes. Market your service by running advertisements in publications and web sites catering to seniors, as well as by joining seniors' groups and associations. Once established, word-of-mouth referrals will easily support the service and generate most new client business.

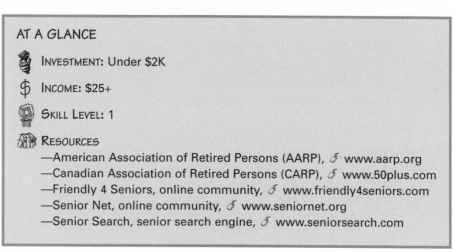

AT A GLANCE

INVESTMENT: Under $2K

INCOME: $25+

SKILL LEVEL: 1

RESOURCES
—American Association of Retired Persons (AARP), ♂ www.aarp.org
—Canadian Association of Retired Persons (CARP), ♂ www.50plus.com
—Friendly 4 Seniors, online community, ♂ www.friendly4seniors.com
—Senior Net, online community, ♂ www.seniornet.org
—Senior Search, senior search engine, ♂ www.seniorsearch.com

Community Advertising Newsletter

Writing, publishing, and distributing a community information and advertising newsletter is a great way to earn extra money. The information you supply in the advertising newsletter can be whatever you think will benefit readers—entertainment, sports, real estate, anything. To keep start-up, equipment, and printing costs to a minimum, use 11- by 17-inch paper folded in half as your newspaper. This format will give you four pages, with content in the center and 24 business-card size advertisements around the perimeter. The paper is supported financially by local advertisers, and charging $150 per month for each ad space will generate revenues of $3,600, of which approximately 20 percent will be needed to cover paper, printing, and distribution costs. Deliver the newspaper weekly free of charge to community gathering places such as restaurants, community centers, coffee shops, fitness centers, and pubs for clients to read on location and/or take home with them. A computer, software such as Adobe PageMaker, and a printer capable of printing 11- by 17-inch pages will be needed. Once you have typeset in all content and ads, you can print one copy of the paper and use a local copy shop to complete the run for pennies apiece.

AT A GLANCE

INVESTMENT: Under $10K

$ INCOME: $15+

SKILL LEVEL: 1–2

RESOURCES
—Adobe, desktop publishing software, ♂ www.adobe.com
—★ Coffee News, ☎ (207) 941-0860, ♂ www.coffeenews.com
—▭ *Design It Yourself Newsletters: A Step-by-Step Guide*, Chuck Green (Rockport Publishers, 2002)

Small Business Bookkeeper

Bookkeeping is the process of recording every time money comes into or goes out of a business. Providing you have money management and bookkeeping experience, or are willing to take bookkeeping training, a very comfortable postretirement living can be earned by providing clients with bookkeeping services. Clients will mostly be small business owners and professionals without the time, skills, or inclination to keep their own books and file and remit tax forms and the like. A secondary market for bookkeeping services is helping families balance their household expenses and keep track of where all of the money is currently going and where it should be going. Accounting software such as QuickBooks, ♂ www.quickbooks.com, is, of course, a mandatory tool of the trade for every bookkeeper. Attracting clients requires a combination of traditional advertising in newspapers, and getting out in the community and talking to business owners to inform them about the services you provide. Work can be completed at your clients' locations, or you can work from home offering free pickup and delivery of documents and forms. Rates are in the range of $25 to $40 per hour depending on services provided and your qualifications.

AT A GLANCE

INVESTMENT: Under $2K

INCOME: $25+

SKILL LEVEL: 2–3

RESOURCES
—American Institute of Professional Bookkeepers, ☎ (800) 622-0121, ♂ www.aipb.com
—Canadian Bookkeepers Association, ☎ (250) 334-2427, ♂ www.c-b -a.ca
—★ Ledger Plus, ☎ (888) 643-1348, ♂ www.ledgerplus.com

Marketing Consultant

It is no secret that without marketing, businesses cannot survive. So it is no surprise that topnotch marketing consultants are in high demand across North America. Consequently, if you are an experienced marketer, the time has never been better to put that experience to work leading other businesspeople down the path to marketing success. Marketing consultants offer clients a wide range of services, including developing marketing plans, establishing marketing budgets, hiring and training salespeople, and developing advertising, telemarketing, and direct marketing programs to suit each individual client's needs and budgets. Marketing consultants also help businesses expand into new markets, and even new countries, as well as build new distribution channels and profit centers. In short, marketing consultants are the jack-of-all-trades for helping clients build their businesses, revenues, and profits. Market your services through networking activities and by setting appointments with business owners and managers to explain how your services will ultimately profit their businesses. Expanding the business is as easy as hiring additional marketing consultants, especially people like you that have put in the years to gain a vast knowledge in sales and marketing, the kind of knowledge and experience that cannot be taught in schools.

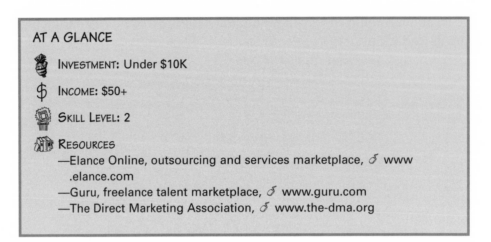

AT A GLANCE

INVESTMENT: Under $10K

$ INCOME: $50+

SKILL LEVEL: 2

RESOURCES
—Elance Online, outsourcing and services marketplace, ♂ www
.elance.com
—Guru, freelance talent marketplace, ♂ www.guru.com
—The Direct Marketing Association, ♂ www.the-dma.org

Flier Delivery Service

Small business owners, salespeople, and marketers of all sorts have utilized promotional fliers for decades as a fast and frugal, yet highly effective, method of advertising their products and services. After all, you can fit an enormous amount of promotional information, pictures, and contact details on one flier, especially if both sides are used. A flier delivery service is easy to start and operate. It requires no more than a telephone and a good pair of walking shoes to get started, while at the same time has the potential to generate a great full- or part-time income. Flier delivery services charge in the range of 5 to 10 cents for each flier individually hand delivered. Of course, revenues increase exponentially if you delivery more than one flier to each home. Imagine delivering five fliers for separate clients all in the same area. You could be raking in up to 50 cents per delivery and spending less than 30 seconds to get the job done. As a method of increasing revenues, hire students, other retirees, and homemakers to deliver fliers during busy times, while concentrating your efforts on marketing and managing the business. Create your own flier detailing the services you offer as well as rate information, and deliver it to businesses and professionals in your community. That will get the telephone ringing and clients lining up to get their promotional fliers hand delivered by your service.

AT A GLANCE

INVESTMENT: Under $2K

$ INCOME: $15+

SKILL LEVEL: 1

RESOURCES
—Entrepreneur Online, small business portal, ✆ www.entrepre
neur.com
—Guru, freelance services marketplace, ✆ www.guru.com

Bulletin Board Service

Take flier delivery to the next level by starting a community bulletin board service. The bulletin board business concept is very straightforward. In exchange for a flat monthly fee, you post promotional fliers for local retailers, professionals, and service providers on bulletin boards throughout the local trading area. Community bulletin boards are typically found at supermarkets, schools, laundries, libraries, gas stations, community centers, and fitness centers. Most, however, have a policy of removing fliers after one week so that boards do not get overcrowded with outdated information and products for sale and to allow space for new fliers to be posted. Even though most small business owners realize that posting fliers on community bulletin boards is a fast, frugal, and effective way to advertise their products and services, most do not do it simply because they do not have the time necessary to drive around town posting fliers; they are too busy operating their businesses. Like hand delivering fliers to homes and businesses, this service can also be very profitable because you have the potential to post fliers for more than one client at a time. Charging clients $20 (not including the cost of the fliers) per week to post fliers on 50 bulletin boards may not seem like a lot of money, but if you have 50 clients, that equals $52,000 a year! And, at 40 cents per flier posted with the potential for thousands of people to read it, you will find little resistance in selling the service to small business owners.

AT A GLANCE

INVESTMENT: Under $2K

$ INCOME: $15+

SKILL LEVEL: 1

RESOURCES
—Guru, freelance services marketplace, ✆ www.guru.com

Greeting Card Service

The majority of business owners, salespeople, and service professionals know that one of the keys to successful customer retention is regular contact. But at the same time, many are so busy working 60 hours a week running their businesses that it leaves little time to even send a simple thank you, thinking of you, or congratulations-on-this-special-day greeting card. By starting a greeting card service, you will be able to help your clients stay in regular contact with all of their clients, and in all probability, they will retain a higher percentage of customers for the effort. You will need to build a database and create files for all clients. Each client file should include full contact information for their customers including telephone, e-mail, and mailing address, as well as more specific information such as birthdays and anniversaries. Having this information will enable you to automatically send your clients' customers greeting cards regularly—Christmas, birthdays, Fourth of July—and to announce special sales or other information that your clients want to include periodically. Additionally, you should work with a graphic designer and print shop so that each greeting card can be specific to each of your clients' businesses. Ideal candidates for a greeting card service include car dealers, real estate brokers, corporations, associations, and clubs to send to members, lawyers, accountants, and doctors. Rates will vary depending on the quantity of cards sent for each client, frequency, as well as each client's greeting card design and selection.

AT A GLANCE

INVESTMENT: Under $2K

$ INCOME: $25+

SKILL LEVEL: 1

RESOURCES
—SNAFU Design, custom greeting card design, ♂ www.snafu designs.com
—The Greeting Card Association, ♂ www.greetingcard.org
—📖 *Designing Handcrafted Cards: Step-by-Step Technique for Crafting 60 Beautiful Cards*, Claire Sun-Ok Choi (Quarry Books, 2004)

Litter Pickup Service

If you are looking for an easy business to start, one that requires no special skills or experience, needs a start-up investment of only a few hundred dollars yet still has excellent income potential, a litter pickup service might be just what you have been searching for. Armed with nothing more than the basic tools of the trade—rake, shovel, garbage can, and gloves—you can be cleaning up litter for paying customers in your community and staying physically active in the process. For the most part, target customers will be retailers, professionals, and other business owners who need to project a good business image. Litter in and around businesses, their parking lots, lawns, flowerbeds, and sidewalks, is not the positive image businessowners want to project. Design and produce a flier outlining your service and fee schedule, and distribute the fliers to retailers, service providers, and professionals with storefronts and parking lots. In exchange for a flat monthly fee, visit your customers' business locations daily to pick up any litter lying in close proximity to their shops. It won't take long for word to spread, and in no time you will probably be inundated with more work than you can handle.

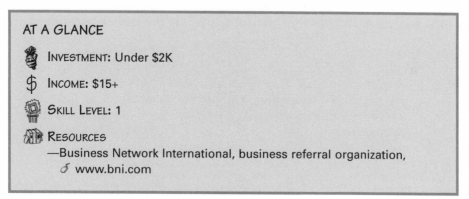

AT A GLANCE

INVESTMENT: Under $2K

$ INCOME: $15+

SKILL LEVEL: 1

RESOURCES
—Business Network International, business referral organization,
  www.bni.com

Aerial Photography

Aerial photography is the perfect business to combine with pleasure travel because you can tow a trailer filled with aerial photography equipment behind an RV or travel van. Just think, you can travel through Mexico, Canada, and the United States, and pay for it by taking and selling aerial photographs. Aerial photography equipment is available in various styles, including telescopic aluminum masts that can be outfitted with a camera and extended to heights reaching over 100 feet. There are also helium-filled blimps available in sizes from 5 to 25 feet that can be outfitted with cameras and still reach heights up to 1,000 feet. The blimps are safely operated from the ground by a tether line or remote control. Surprisingly, the blimp option is not very expensive. Good quality blimps, complete with photographic gear and a transportation trailer, can be purchased new for less than $10,000 or as much $25,000, depending on features. Regardless of whether you choose to use a telescopic mast or a helium blimp, both can be outfitted with film or digital still cameras or video cameras. Potential clients range from government agencies to homeowners to outdoor event organizers, basically any person or business that wants or needs aerial photographs of their homes, buildings, events, or property. There is a bit of a learning curve to operating the equipment, but the manufacturers listed below do provide basic training. Rates are excellent because this is a highly specialized niche service.

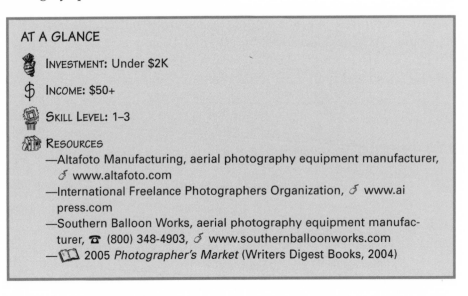

AT A GLANCE

INVESTMENT: Under $2K

$ INCOME: $50+

SKILL LEVEL: 1–3

RESOURCES
—Altafoto Manufacturing, aerial photography equipment manufacturer, ♂ www.altafoto.com
—International Freelance Photographers Organization, ♂ www.aipress.com
—Southern Balloon Works, aerial photography equipment manufacturer, ☎ (800) 348-4903, ♂ www.southernballoonworks.com
— 2005 *Photographer's Market* (Writers Digest Books, 2004)

Small Sign Installation

If you find yourself searching for a simple, part-time, low-cost business that requires no previous experience or special skills, a small sign installation service might just fit the bill. Small, or site, signs are temporary signs typically used by realtors to advertise a home for sale, politicians to promote their runs for office, and firms like painters, roofers, and landscapers to promote the products and services they sell and/or install These signs are typically stuck in the ground in front of homes so that passing motorists and pedestrians will take notice of what is being advertised or promoted. Installing small site signs is very easy and only requires basic tools such as a sledge hammers and shovels, sometimes not even those tools if the signs have preformed metal wire feet that push easily into the ground. You will also need suitable transportation such as a pickup truck, van, station wagon, or hatchback car. Current rates for small sign installations are in the vicinity of $20 to $30 each, including delivery, installation, and removal at a later specified date. Install just 10 per week and you'll earn an extra $10,000 per year. The easiest way to get started is to call on real estate broker and businesses in your area that typically use small site signs and pitch the benefits of your services—fast, convenient, reliable, and fair prices. To boost income and profit, you can also offer clients flier delivery and promotional door hanger services.

AT A GLANCE

INVESTMENT: Under $2K

INCOME: $15+

SKILL LEVEL: 1

RESOURCES
—Canadian Real Estate Association, ♂ www.crea.ca
—Entrepreneur, small business information portal, ♂ www.entrepre neur.com
—National Association of Realtors, ♂ www.realtor.com

Coin and Stamp Dealer

Excellent part-time profits can be earned dealing in collectible coins and stamps. In fact, stamp collecting is the number-one collectible hobby in the United States, and coin collecting is number-three, after doll collecting. Needless to say, with millions of people collecting coins, paper money, and stamps, the potential to strike it rich as a dealer is available for motivated entrepreneurs. There is a real possibility you can find valuable coins, paper money, and stamps at garage sales, estate sales, auctions, private seller classified ads, private collectors liquidating their collections, and at flea markets. But to be able to do so, you need to educate yourself not only about the value of coins, paper money, and stamps, but also about how they are graded by condition for valuation. This can be accomplished by purchasing and studying up-to-date price guides and by reading coin and stamp collectors' publications. Timing often comes into play as well, and deals can be had when no other parties are interested in the sale. You might have to hang on to your purchases for a while, but in time they can appreciate substantially. Coins, paper money, and stamps can be sold through online coin and stamp marketplaces and eBay, as well as at coin and stamp shows in the bricks and mortar world. By joining collecting clubs, you will have the ability to sell your finds directly to other collectors.

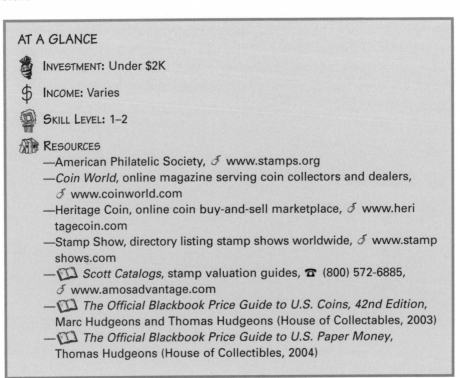

AT A GLANCE

INVESTMENT: Under $2K

$ INCOME: Varies

SKILL LEVEL: 1–2

RESOURCES
—American Philatelic Society, ♂ www.stamps.org
—*Coin World*, online magazine serving coin collectors and dealers, ♂ www.coinworld.com
—Heritage Coin, online coin buy-and-sell marketplace, ♂ www.heritagecoin.com
—Stamp Show, directory listing stamp shows worldwide, ♂ www.stampshows.com
—📖 *Scott Catalogs*, stamp valuation guides, ☎ (800) 572-6885, ♂ www.amosadvantage.com
—📖 *The Official Blackbook Price Guide to U.S. Coins, 42nd Edition*, Marc Hudgeons and Thomas Hudgeons (House of Collectables, 2003)
—📖 *The Official Blackbook Price Guide to U.S. Paper Money*, Thomas Hudgeons (House of Collectibles, 2004)

Expert Witness

With more than 160 million lawsuits filed each year in the United States, expert witnesses are always in high demand. By definition, an expert witnesses is a person who gives opinions based on his or her special knowledge or skill. Who uses expert witnesses? Insurance companies, defense lawyers, activities, politicians, public prosecutors, health-care providers, unions, law enforcement agencies, government agencies, hospitals, and corporations often use expert witnesses to substantiate or refute claims and testimonies via their expertise on the topic or subject matter. The most common expert witnesses are defense, prosecution, compelled, meta-experts, and expert-advisors in the fields of forensic science, weapons, military, engineering, medicine, aviation, maritime, construction, investment, computer sciences, security, environmental, psychiatrist, transportation, and business.

At the same time, experts from just about any profession and trade are often needed. Who can become an expert witness? Anybody can become an expert witness, providing she can establish that she possesses some particular experience, training, or education beyond the experience of the layman. How can you become an expert witness and earn up to $250 per hour, depending on your qualifications? The easiest way is to list with one or more online expert witness directories, such as the ones listed below. People looking for expert witnesses search these directories to find a suitable match.

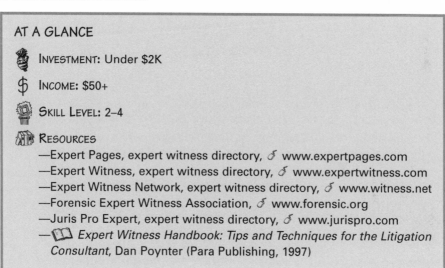

AT A GLANCE

INVESTMENT: Under $2K

INCOME: $50+

SKILL LEVEL: 2–4

RESOURCES
—Expert Pages, expert witness directory, ♂ www.expertpages.com
—Expert Witness, expert witness directory, ♂ www.expertwitness.com
—Expert Witness Network, expert witness directory, ♂ www.witness.net
—Forensic Expert Witness Association, ♂ www.forensic.org
—Juris Pro Expert, expert witness directory, ♂ www.jurispro.com
— *Expert Witness Handbook: Tips and Techniques for the Litigation Consultant*, Dan Poynter (Para Publishing, 1997)

Professional Greeter

Thanks to Wal-Mart, an entirely new profession has been created—the professional greeter. Wal-Mart pioneered and perfected using greeters at its stores to make shoppers feel welcome and part of the community. Obviously, this approach has worked with great success. Now many other retailers, corporations, and organizations have themselves jumped on the bandwagon, employing professional greeters to make customers and guests feel welcome and part of the family. Starting a freelance professional greeter service is perhaps one of the best money-making opportunities discussed in this book because there are few requirements to get started; if you are personable, like to smile, and like to help people even more, then you are qualified to be a professional greeter. In addition to department stores, other retailers such as car dealers, building supply retailers, or restaurants are enlisting the services of professional greeters. Corporations and charitable organizations like to have greeters present during events. This is very much a business that is built one step at a time because it will take time to build a reputation and a solid customer base. But the investment to get started is virtually zero, as are the operating overheads; yet you can charge anywhere up to $25 per hour for your services and have the flexibility of working full-time, part-time, or even seasonally.

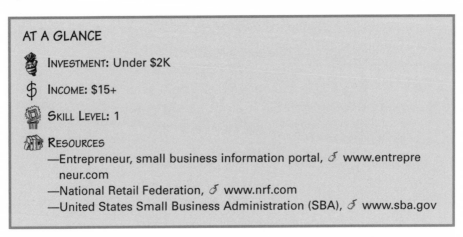

AT A GLANCE

INVESTMENT: Under $2K

INCOME: $15+

SKILL LEVEL: 1

RESOURCES
—Entrepreneur, small business information portal, ♂ www.entrepreneur.com
—National Retail Federation, ♂ www.nrf.com
—United States Small Business Administration (SBA), ♂ www.sba.gov

Resume Service

Finding the perfect words to describe why people's experiences, special skills, and interests make them the right candidate for the job is difficult work. That's why resume services continue to flourish in spite of the fact that just about everyone has or has access to a computer and a word processing program. If you are a wordsmith with a human resources, management, or administration background, then this may be the perfect postretirement moneymaking opportunity for you. One of the best aspects about starting a resume service is you can start small, part-time, and keep costs to a minimum by working at home and utilizing existing resources. That makes this the perfect opportunity for people looking to earn an extra few hundred dollars a month. In addition to resumes, you can also write cover, sales, and follow-up letters for clients, and offer duplication and binding services, which will help boost revenues. As a way to separate your resume service from others, consider creating a tips booklet to help clients land their dream jobs. This might include how to dress for interviews, handle a stressful interview situation, make follow-up telephone calls, prepare for interviews, and network for that dream job. Advertise locally, online, and through career expos. Once established, word-of-mouth advertising will go a long way in keeping you busy.

AT A GLANCE

INVESTMENT: Under $2K

INCOME: $15+

SKILL LEVEL: 1–2

RESOURCES
—WinWay, resume software, ♂ www.winway.com
— *The Resume Handbook: How to Write Outstanding Resumes & Cover Letters for Every Situation*, Arthur D. Rosenberg and David Heizer (Adams Media Corporation, 2003)

Freelance Sales Consultant

It does not really matter if you have experience selling shoes, houses, cars, clothing, or vacuum cleaners in your preretirement career. If you are an experienced salesperson, you are qualified to start a freelance sales consulting business in your postretirement years. Freelance sales consultants who produce results, meaning lots of profitable sales, are in high demand and earn annual incomes that go well into the six-figure range. Freelancers represent companies selling products and services ranging from manufactured goods and equipment, to services that include home improvements and internet technology, as well as associations seeking to expand their membership base. Freelance sales consultants find securing clients very easy because they generally supply all the tools of the trade needed to find new customers and close the sale—transportation, communications, and computer hardware. And almost all also generate and qualify their own sales leads. So clients have little to lose by having freelance sales consultants representing them because the consultants supply the needed sales tools, leads, and are paid only if they sell, i.e., by commission. Commissions range between 10 and 25 percent of the total sales value, depending on what is being sold.

AT A GLANCE

INVESTMENT: Under $10K

$ INCOME: $50+

▨ SKILL LEVEL: 2

▨ RESOURCES
—Guru, freelance talent marketplace, ✆ www.guru.com
—The Training Registry, consultants and trainers marketplace, ✆ www
.tregistry.com

Engraving Service and Product Sales

Engraving and selling products such as trophies, awards, wedding gifts, and identification tags is a great way to supplement your retirement income working from home, a mall kiosk or storefront, or a flea market vending booth. In fact, engraving services and engraved products can even be sold online via your web site, internet malls, and eBay. Products that can be engraved can be purchased cheaply from wholesalers, yet once engraved can be retailed for as much as ten times the wholesale cost. You need to invest in engraving equipment, but these machines are not very expensive and readily available. Engraving is also a very easy skill to learn. Most equipment manufacturers also supply engraving manuals and videos, and some also offer in-classroom training. In addition to engraving and selling products, extra income can be earned by engraving security identification names and codes onto home and business equipment and products such as bicycles, computer cases, silver, tools, and construction equipment.

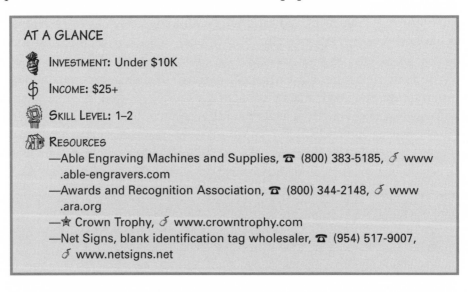

AT A GLANCE

▨ INVESTMENT: Under $10K

$ INCOME: $25+

▨ SKILL LEVEL: 1–2

▨ RESOURCES
—Able Engraving Machines and Supplies, ☎ (800) 383-5185, ✆ www
.able-engravers.com
—Awards and Recognition Association, ☎ (800) 344-2148, ✆ www
.ara.org
—☆ Crown Trophy, ✆ www.crowntrophy.com
—Net Signs, blank identification tag wholesaler, ☎ (954) 517-9007,
✆ www.netsigns.net

Cartridge Refill Business

One of the fastest growing businesses today is ink cartridge recycling. Ink and toner cartridges used in most photocopiers, fax machines, and laser and inkjet printers can be recycled by simply replenishing the ink or toner supply, thus keeping them out of the landfill and putting profits in your pockets. So start a toner cartridge recycling service operating from home, on a mobile basis, or from a small retail location such as a mall kiosk or storefront. The requirements to operate the business are basic. You will only need simple tools, which are very inexpensive, and the ability to refill cartridges with new ink, which is easily learned. To start off with a bang, offer clients fast and free delivery of recycled cartridges to their offices, stores, or homes. That can save them as much as 50 percent of the cost of new cartridges and the time in line to purchase them. These two benefits alone can become your most convincing marketing tools for landing new business. Be bold. Don't be afraid to go after large accounts with hundreds of machines that regularly must have ink and toner cartridges renewed.

AT A GLANCE

💰 INVESTMENT: Under $10K

$ INCOME: $25+

SKILL LEVEL: 1

RESOURCES
—American Cartridge Recycling Association, ☎ (305) 539-0701
—★ Full Circle Image, ☎ (800) 584-7244, ♂ www.fullcircleimage.com
—📖 *Recharger Magazine Online*, ♂ www.rechargermag.com

Homebased Carpentry Shop

Carpentry shop services are in big demand. A terrific opportunity exists for carpenters of every skill level to earn a substantial full- or part-time income by setting up and operating a fully equipped carpentry shop at home. Offer customers a wide range of woodworking and carpentry services, from lumber milling, to shaping, to wooden window sash and door construction. Commercial grade carpentry equipment will be required. Most, if not all, tools can be purchased in good condition secondhand for about half the cost of new by attending auction sales, scanning newspaper classified ads, and watching for shop closeouts. Potential customers include both homeowners in need of custom milling and woodworking to commercial clients such as contractors and renovators who need similar services. Stocking and selling exotic hard and softwoods, tools, design plans, and supplies for hobbyists and craftspeople can boost bottom-line revenues and profits substantially. Advertise services locally utilizing cheap classified ads, Yellow Pages directories, and by a direct mail campaign aimed at renovation companies and general contractors.

AT A GLANCE

INVESTMENT: Under $25K

INCOME: $50+

SKILL LEVEL: 2

RESOURCES
—Mammoth Tool, ☎ (516) 942-0905, ✒ www.mammothtools.com
—My Crazy Tools, ☎ (416) 944-8605, ✒ www.mycrazytools.com

Picture Framing and Matting

What must you have and know in order to sell framing and matting services? Framing and matting experience is helpful, but with a little bit of practice, framing and matting can be mastered by just about everyone with a desire to do so. Some tools and equipment are necessities. If you are purchasing standard-size picture frames from wholesalers, only basic tools will be needed. If you plan on building custom frames, you will need a power miter saw, glass cutters, clamps, and other hand tools, along with suitable workshop and storage space. You can set up your workshop at home or rent appropriate space. Set up at home and work part-time to keep overheads low until the business is self-supporting; then move to a larger space if required. In addition to customers looking to have only one or two photographs or paintings framed, you can also market your services to higher volume customers, including photographers, artists, retailers of prints and posters, schools (for framing diplomas and awards), and interior designers.

AT A GLANCE

INVESTMENT: Varies

INCOME: $25+

SKILL LEVEL: 2–3

RESOURCES
—★ Big Picture Framing, ☎ (800) 315-0024, ♂ www.bigpicturefram ing.com
—★ The Great Frame Up, ♂ www.thegreatframeup.com
—📖 *Home Book of Picture Framing: Professional Secrets of Mounting, Matting, Framing and Displaying Artworks, Photographs, Posters, Fabrics, Collectibles, Carvings and More*, Kenn Oberrecht (Stackpole Books, 1998)

Furniture Maker

Artistic freedom can also be practiced when designing and building furniture because beauty is in the eye of the beholder. Trading on your carpentry skills and working from a well-equipped homebased workshop, you can design and build all sorts of furniture for a profit. What kind of handcrafted furniture sells the best? Almost anything wooden sells in almost any style. Stretch your creative wings a bit to come up with a few truly amazing designs incorporating both visual and functional design elements, and use a wide variety of construction materials, including exotic hardwoods, softwood, plastic, iron, pre-cast cement, marble, stone, fiberglass, and fabric. Handcrafted furniture can be sold online, by advertising in home furnishings magazines, by displaying at home décor and furniture shows, by establishing a homebased furniture showroom, and by making contact with residential and commercial interior designers to secure referral business. Consignment placement or wholesale sales to home furnishing retailers and even art galleries are also possibilities. Additionally, don't overlook the commercial market; unique and finely crafted furniture is often needed to furnish offices and waiting rooms.

AT A GLANCE

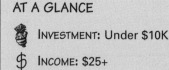 INVESTMENT: Under $10K

INCOME: $25+

SKILL LEVEL: 2–3

RESOURCES
—American Home Furnishings Alliance, ☎ (336) 884-5000, ♂ www.af
ma4u.org
—Futon Furniture Plans, ♂ www.futonfurnitureplans.com
—Furniture Plans, ♂ www.furnitureplans.com
—The Furniture Wizard, industry information portal, ♂ www.furniture
wizard.com
—U-Bild, furniture plans, ♂ www.u-bild.com

Furniture Repairs and Refinishing

Providing you have the skills, equipment, time, and a love for working with your hands, big bucks can be earned repairing office, residential, and antique furniture. The furniture repair side of the business can be operated on a mobile basis working from a fully equipped van at a customer's location. Customers commonly requiring furniture repair services include home and office movers, business owners, property managers, restaurants, hotels, institutions, government offices, and retailers of new and used furniture. The furniture refinishing side of the business, namely antiques refinishing, is perfectly suited to a well-equipped home workshop. Develop this side of the business by advertising locally as well as by establishing alliances with antique dealers and interior designers who can utilize your services or refer their clients to your service. Truly ambitious entrepreneurs can earn extra income by attending auction and garage sales to buy furniture and antiques in need of repair and refinishing. Once repaired and refinished, these pieces can be sold for a profit by posting classified ads in your local newspaper, selling on eBay, and renting kiosk space at antique malls and consumer shows.

AT A GLANCE

INVESTMENT: Under $10K

$ INCOME: $25+

SKILL LEVEL: 2–3

RESOURCES
—★ Furniture Medic, ☎ (901) 820-8600, ♂ www.furnituremedicfran
chise.com

—The Furniture Wizard, industry information and resources portal,
♂ www.furniturewizard.com

—📖 *Furniture Repair and Refinishing*, Brian Hingley (Creative Homeowner Press, 1998)

Patio Furniture Manufacturing

An easy business to start and operate, lawn and garden patio furniture manufacturing also has the potential to be one of the most profitable. Consumer demand
is proven, so there is no need to reinvent the wheel. Just design and build a good
quality product, and sales will follow. Patio furniture can be constructed from various materials—wood, plastic, iron, pre-cast cement, marble, and fiberglass—or
combinations. Wood is the easiest to work with and requires the least amount of
specialized equipment and construction materials to get started. Especially popular is wooden Adirondack patio furniture constructed of cedar. Whatever the type
of patio furniture you decide to manufacture and sell, great selling methods
include a homebased showroom (your patio), direct to businesses such as restaurants, home-and-garden shows, and sales via online marketplaces such as eBay
and internet malls. You might want to consider concentrating on the high-end
market, supplying only the best custom patio furniture and catering to those with
substantial enough budgets to make the purchase. If you choose this route, be sure
to establish working relationships with designers, architects, and deck builders as
all can refer business to you.

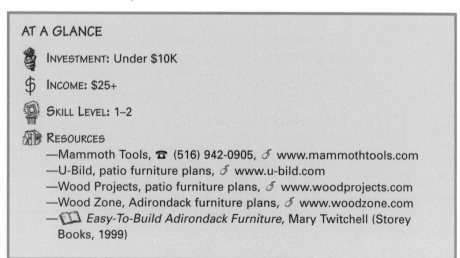

AT A GLANCE

INVESTMENT: Under $10K

INCOME: $25+

SKILL LEVEL: 1–2

RESOURCES
—Mammoth Tools, ☎ (516) 942-0905, ♂ www.mammothtools.com
—U-Bild, patio furniture plans, ♂ www.u-bild.com
—Wood Projects, patio furniture plans, ♂ www.woodprojects.com
—Wood Zone, Adirondack furniture plans, ♂ www.woodzone.com
—📖 *Easy-To-Build Adirondack Furniture*, Mary Twitchell (Storey
Books, 1999)

Pet Products Manufacturing

American's spend more than $30 billion every year on products for their cherished pets. Needless to say, you don't have to be a rocket scientist to figure out that big bucks can be earned by designing, manufacturing, and selling all sorts of products for pets. What types of pet products can you make? Anything from furniture, to clothing, to memorials. The granddaddy of them all is treats for pets from your own homebased bakery. In fact, you can turn your passion for pets into a profitable pastime by manufacturing and selling just about any kind of pet product imaginable. For the most part, no special skills are needed because with a little practice all of these products are very easy to make working from a small homebased workspace with basic tools and equipment. Sell your pet products online via internet pet product malls and eBay, and in the bricks and mortar world through pet fairs, craft shows, and a homebased boutique. There is also great potential to build a wholesale arm of the business by contacting pet product boutiques, pet shop retailers, veterinarians, and groomers to carry your products or at least accept consignments to test the waters. Word travels fast among dog owners. When they find a great product for their pets they are quick to spread the word to other pet owners.

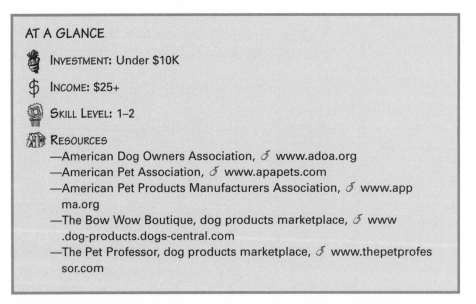

AT A GLANCE

INVESTMENT: Under $10K

$ INCOME: $25+

SKILL LEVEL: 1–2

RESOURCES
—American Dog Owners Association, ✆ www.adoa.org
—American Pet Association, ✆ www.apapets.com
—American Pet Products Manufacturers Association, ✆ www.app
 ma.org
—The Bow Wow Boutique, dog products marketplace, ✆ www
 .dog-products.dogs-central.com
—The Pet Professor, dog products marketplace, ✆ www.thepetprofes
 sor.com

Fashion Designer

The vast majority of internationally known fashion designers were once just like you are now, dreaming of starting their own fashion houses and sharing their designs with fashion enthusiasts from around the world. If they can make it big, so can you, regardless of your age! What does it take to break into the world of high fashion clothing? Great designs, determination to succeed, and persistence to ensure you do succeed. To get started, there are basically three routes you can choose. One, design and manufacture fashion clothing to sell to department stores or chain fashion retailers. Two, design and manufacture fashion clothing to sell to small independent fashion boutiques. Three, design and manufacture fashion clothing for private clients. Each route has advantages and disadvantages, but all three share a common thread: great fashions start with great designs. Initially, concentrate on creating sketches of the clothing you want to make. Pick a few of your best designs and make sample garments, which can be shown to fashion buyers. If you do not sew at the level needed for fashion clothing, contract with a local seamstress to sew the garments. Once you have secured orders, you can interview and contract with a suitable clothing manufacturer able to sew garments in larger quantities. Likewise, you will probably want to specialize in specific fashion styles, such as high, casual, sports, or work fashions, and aim at a specific target audience, such as children, teens, young adults, professionals, or seniors.

 AT A GLANCE

 INVESTMENT: Under $10K

 INCOME: $25+

 SKILL LEVEL: 2–3

 RESOURCES
—Bright Notions, sewing equipment and supplies, ♂ www.bright notions.com
—Fashion Schools Online, fashion schools and programs directory, ♂ www.fashionschools.com
—National Association of Fashion and Accessory Designers, ♂ www.na fad.com
—📖 *High Fashion Sewing Secrets from the World's Best Designers: A Step-By-Step Guide to Sewing Stylish Seams, Buttonholes, Pockets, Collars, Hems, and More*, Claire B. Shaeffer (Rodale Books, 2004)

Fashion Accessories Designer

If you have a flair for design, then why not break into the fashion accessories designers industry? It is not as difficult as you might think. Get started by picking a fashion accessory to design, produce, and sell. It could be just about anything, including bridal veils, handbags, shoes, belts, belt buckles, costume jewelry, wraps, or wallets, and everything from high fashion to vintage reproductions of top designers like Fendi, Gucci, and Prada. Don't worry if your sewing or tooling skills are not up to par, because there are numerous fashion accessory manufacturers that will manufacture your designs under your name. The options for selling fashion accessories are also numerous. You can organize and host in-home fashion accessory sales parties, sell from a homebased showroom, sell online utilizing eBay and internet malls, sell at craft fairs and consumer shows, or if you're a big thinker, sell your products wholesale to fashion accessory retailers.

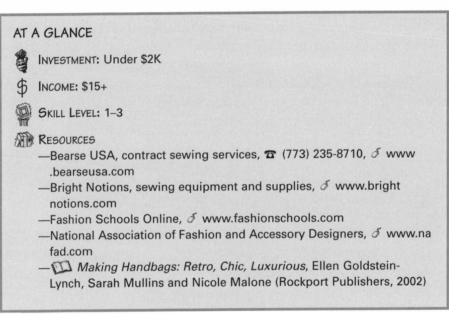

AT A GLANCE

INVESTMENT: Under $2K

INCOME: $15+

SKILL LEVEL: 1–3

RESOURCES
—Bearse USA, contract sewing services, ☎ (773) 235-8710, ✂ www.bearseusa.com
—Bright Notions, sewing equipment and supplies, ✂ www.brightnotions.com
—Fashion Schools Online, ✂ www.fashionschools.com
—National Association of Fashion and Accessory Designers, ✂ www.nafad.com
— 📖 *Making Handbags: Retro, Chic, Luxurious,* Ellen Goldstein-Lynch, Sarah Mullins and Nicole Malone (Rockport Publishers, 2002)

Homebased Alteration Service

Calling all people with sewing skills and a sewing machine! It's time to capitalize on your sewing skills by providing garment and fabric alteration services right from the convenience of a home workspace, and earn a bundle of money in the process. Dry cleaners, fashion retailers, uniform retailers, bridal boutiques, costume shops, drapery studios, and consignment clothing shops—all are potential customers for your service. In fact, any businesses that retail or rent clothing of any sort are potential customers, and for that matter so is any person who is in need of alteration services. As a quick-start marketing method, put on a comfortable pair of shoes and start calling on businesses most likely to require alteration services. Offer free pick-up and delivery, fast turnaround times, great service, and quality workmanship, all at fair prices. Your business clients benefit because they can offer alteration services to customers for free, ensuring repeat business. Or, they can make it in to a profit center by marking up what you charge. Along your sewing skills, you will need the tools of the sewing trade along with reliable transportation.

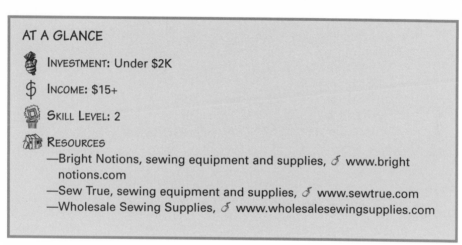

AT A GLANCE

INVESTMENT: Under $2K

INCOME: $15+

SKILL LEVEL: 2

RESOURCES
—Bright Notions, sewing equipment and supplies, ♂ www.brightnotions.com
—Sew True, sewing equipment and supplies, ♂ www.sewtrue.com
—Wholesale Sewing Supplies, ♂ www.wholesalesewingsupplies.com

Building Custom-Fitted Golf Clubs

Golf is the fastest growing sport and recreational pastime in North America. You can earn a small fortune building and selling custom-fitted golf clubs. Making custom golf clubs is easier than most think. Not only are there numerous classes available nationwide, but also because equipment needed to build golf clubs is widely available and relatively inexpensive. You can purchase club components such as heads, shafts, and grips wholesale and assemble the clubs at home to meet each of your customers' specific needs. The sport is so popular that finding customers is not difficult, especially if you are an avid golfer. This is a business that can largely be built and supported by referral and repeat business. Run advertisements locally as well as in specialty golf publications and web sites. Forge working relationships with golf courses and pro shops that do not currently offer custom golf club building and sales. They sell, you build, and each profits. Equipment is small enough that a garage or basement space is suitable. If you really want to blow your clients away by providing a complete package, install a practice putting green and a driving net in your backyard so that clients can test their new clubs before they leave to ensure proper fit and total satisfaction.

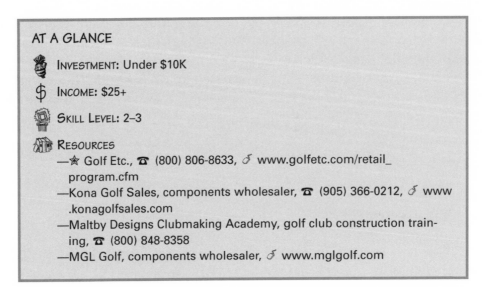

AT A GLANCE

INVESTMENT: Under $10K

INCOME: $25+

SKILL LEVEL: 2–3

RESOURCES
—★ Golf Etc., ☎ (800) 806-8633, ♂ www.golfetc.com/retail_
  program.cfm
—Kona Golf Sales, components wholesaler, ☎ (905) 366-0212, ♂ www
  .konagolfsales.com
—Maltby Designs Clubmaking Academy, golf club construction train-
  ing, ☎ (800) 848-8358
—MGL Golf, components wholesaler, ♂ www.mglgolf.com

Toy Maker

Building and selling children's toys is a great way to create cherished memories for children and to supplement your retirement income at the same time. Just think of all of the toys that you can make—wooden toys, dollhouses, die cast toys, antique toy replicas and puzzles, to name just a few. In fact, handcrafted toys often become treasured family heirlooms passed down to each new generation to enjoy. Fortunately, you do not need much in the way of special skills or equipment to start making and selling handmade toys, just a workshop space outfitted with basic hand and power tools, and toy design plans, which are widely available from a number of sources. Due to the fact that handcrafted toys are always in demand, they can be sold many ways, including online using eBay, internet malls, and toy marketplaces, and in the bricks and mortar world by selling at craft shows, toys shows, flea markets, kiosk space in malls, and even factory direct by setting up a small toy boutique at your home. You can also consign toys with retailers, or sell toys at wholesale pricing to toy retailers.

AT A GLANCE

INVESTMENT: Under $2K

INCOME: $15+

SKILL LEVEL: 1–2

Specialty Tree and Shrub Grower

People with green thumbs, a backyard, and some time, take notice: Growing and selling trees and shrubs right from home is a fantastic way to earn an extra few thousand dollars every year, or even every month if you are ambitious. Surprisingly, not much yard space is required to generate excellent profits. Consider that you can purchase Japanese maple seedlings for about 75 cents each wholesale, plant them in pots or in burlap in the ground, wait a season or two while they grow, and resell them for $25 to $50 each. A 20-foot square garden area is large enough to support 300 seedlings, which in turn can produce approximately 150 saleable trees annually when planting is alternated. That is as much as $7,500 every year from just a small patch of ground in your backyard. Imagine what you can earn by planting a 50-, 60-, or 100-square foot seedling tree garden. In addition to selling directly to consumers from home and through garden shows, you can also sell the trees and shrubs to garden centers and landscape contractors in volume at wholesale pricing.

AT A GLANCE

 INVESTMENT: Under $2K

 INCOME: Varies

 SKILL LEVEL: 1

 RESOURCES
—Brooks Tree Farms, wholesale seedlings, ☎ (503) 393-6300, ♂ www
  .brookstreefarm.com
—May Trees, wholesale seedlings, ☎ (888) 383-3708, ♂ www.maytree
  enterprises.com

—Meadow Lake Nursery, wholesale seedlings, ☎ (503) 435-2000, ♂ www
.meadow-lake.com
—Mike's Backyard Growing System, ♂ www.freeplants.com/starting-a
-plant-nursery.htm

Lawn and Garden Products Manufacturing

Manufacturing lawn and garden products is a fantastic retirement business venture that will let you capitalize on your creative abilities and stay active. There are a plethora of highly saleable lawn and garden products that you can easily manufacture from a homebased workshop, from garden arbors to concrete lawn ornaments to garden ponds. Most of these products only require basic tools to construct and can be easily tackled by the novice handyperson with the aid of design plans and material lists. Utilize your own lawn and garden as an outdoor showroom displaying the products you make. And to get the telephone ringing, run classified advertisements and post fliers on bulletin boards promoting your products. Additionally, display your products at home and garden shows, and sell to a worldwide audience by listing products for sale on eBay, in internet malls, and through e-commerce sites specializing in home and garden products. If you are truly ambitious, you can even mass produce lawn and garden products and sell them to garden centers and retailers on a wholesale basis.

AT A GLANCE

INVESTMENT: Under $10K

$ INCOME: $15+

SKILL LEVEL: 1–2

RESOURCES
—Garden plans, ♂ www.gardenplans.com
—Handyman Plans, ♂ www.handymanplans.com
—Mammoth Tools, ☎ (516) 942-0905, ♂ www.mammothtools.com
—North American Wholesale Lumber Association, ♂ www.lumber.org
—U-Bild, garden product plans, ♂ www.u-bild.com
—Woodworkers Workshop, garden products plans, ♂ www.freewood
workingplans.com

Birdhouse Builder

Birdhouses are very easy to build, even for the novice handyperson with limited carpentry skills. In fact, all you really need to get started building birdhouses are design plans, a small workshop, and an assortment of basic power and hand tools. But because there are numerous types of birdhouses for various bird species, a bit of research will be needed to pinpoint the types of birdhouses you build. To separate your birdhouses from those of competitors, you might also want to consider using only recycled materials in the birdhouse construction. Doing so will give you a very powerful marketing tool (environmentally friendly) as well as keep costs to a minimum because used wood can often be acquired for free or very inexpensively. Displaying samples of all of the birdhouses you make and sell at your home with bold attention-grabbing signage ensures people and motorists passing by will stop in and browse through the selection. In addition to selling from home, birdhouse can also be sold on eBay and internet malls, as well as at weekend flea markets, home and garden shows, and crafts shows. Building and selling birdhouses is not likely to make you rich, but it does have the potential to generate a few extra hundred dollars a month to help supplement your retirement income.

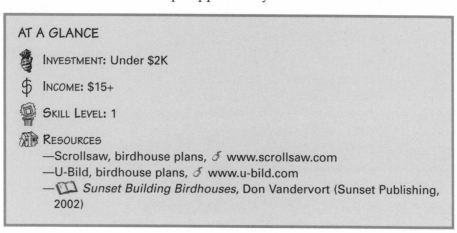

AT A GLANCE

INVESTMENT: Under $2K

INCOME: $15+

SKILL LEVEL: 1

RESOURCES
—Scrollsaw, birdhouse plans, ♂ www.scrollsaw.com
—U-Bild, birdhouse plans, ♂ www.u-bild.com
—📖 *Sunset Building Birdhouses*, Don Vandervort (Sunset Publishing, 2002)

Garden Curbing Business

Stay physically active and fit by starting a garden curbing manufacturing business and also cash in on the highly lucrative garden-curbing craze. Raw materials to produce garden curbing are very cheap, and business overheads are very low because this is a mobile business that can easily be operated by one person. This combination makes for a potentially very profitable moneymaking opportunity for entrepreneurs prepared to get out and hustle up new business. The best way to make concrete garden curbing is to use specially designed extrusion machines that produce a continuous concrete curb right on location, so there are no shipping costs. Simply load the equipment onto a truck or trailer and make the product at your customer's home. It's that easy. The same curbing can be used to edge flowerbeds, driveways, and walkways, and it is available in a number of concrete curb profiles and color choices. Sell concrete garden curbing by exhibiting the product and collecting sales inquiries at home and garden shows, by advertising in your local newspaper and Yellow Pages directory, and by building alliances with landscape and building contractors who can refer their clients to your business or subcontract with you to supply and install garden curbing. This is a fantastic opportunity for people who want to earn enough money in a few months of the year to supplement their income and travel plans for the balance of the year.

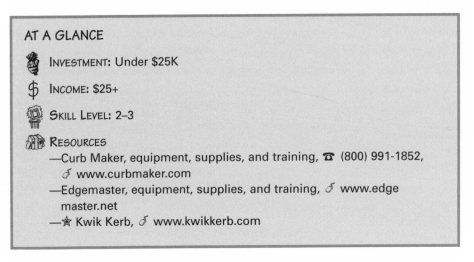

AT A GLANCE

INVESTMENT: Under $25K

INCOME: $25+

SKILL LEVEL: 2–3

RESOURCES
—Curb Maker, equipment, supplies, and training, ☎ (800) 991-1852, ♂ www.curbmaker.com
—Edgemaster, equipment, supplies, and training, ♂ www.edge master.net
—★ Kwik Kerb, ♂ www.kwikkerb.com

Window Screen Repairs and Replacements

Starting a screen repair and replacement business could put you on the road to riches, especially in light of the recent mosquito-borne West Nile virus and the possible threat of killer bees. This is the perfect postretirement business because window screens are very easy to repair or replace. You will need basic tools and materials to get started—a miter saw, screen rollers, various screen replacement parts, and a selection of fiberglass and aluminum screen rolls in various widths. Screen repair and screen making can be self-taught by repairing or replacing the screens in your own home and your friends and family members' homes for practice. The business can be operated from an enclosed trailer or van to provide protection from inclement weather for on-site screen repairs and installations. Or, you can operate from a homebased workshop: Pick up the screens, repair them at the workshop, and return to install them. To market your service, contact companies and individuals that require screen repairs and replacements on a regular basis. These include residential and commercial property management firms, condominium/strata corporations, apartment complexes, government institutions, and renovation contractors. The profit potential is excellent as there is limited competition, and consumer demand for screen repairs and replacements is high.

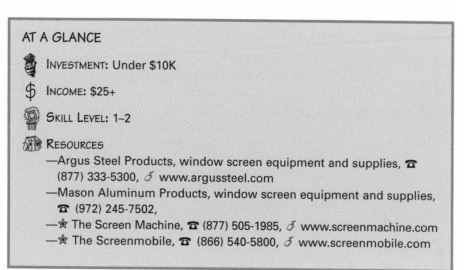

AT A GLANCE

INVESTMENT: Under $10K

$ INCOME: $25+

SKILL LEVEL: 1–2

RESOURCES
—Argus Steel Products, window screen equipment and supplies, ☎ (877) 333-5300, ✆ www.argussteel.com
—Mason Aluminum Products, window screen equipment and supplies, ☎ (972) 245-7502,
—✩ The Screen Machine, ☎ (877) 505-1985, ✆ www.screenmachine.com
—✩ The Screenmobile, ☎ (866) 540-5800, ✆ www.screenmobile.com

Garden Stepping-Stone Business

Making and selling garden stepping-stones is a little known, yet simple manufacturing opportunity that can generate excellent supplementary income, and the business can also be a whole lot of fun. The main supplies you need to make garden stepping-stones are molds, cement, reinforcement mesh, and items such as tiles, glass, colored stones, or embossed designs to decorate the surface. Molds, as well as the rest of the supplies needed, are widely available, including through the sources listed below. You can also make your own molds out of wood, plastic, or metal. There is not much involved in making stepping-stones—fill the mold half full with concrete, lay in the reinforcing mesh, pour in the balance of the concrete, wait about 30 minutes to add decorations on top, and let dry for a couple days. Presto, a completed stepping-stone ready to sell. In total, each costs approximately $2 to $3 each to make and retails in the range of $15 to $25 each, depending on size and complexity of design. Expect to sell wholesale to garden centers for about half of the retail sale price. In addition to wholesale sales, stepping-stones can also be sold directly to consumers at gift shows, home and garden shows, craft fairs, online via internet malls and eBay, and at flea markets. Selling from home supported by signage and local advertising is a good idea because you can create elaborate stepping-stone walkways to show customers and really showcase the beauty and functionality of the product.

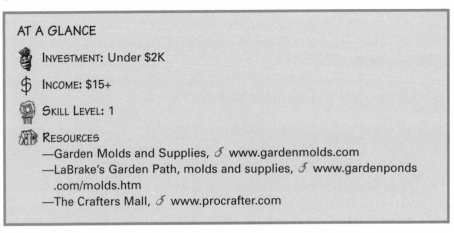

AT A GLANCE

INVESTMENT: Under $2K

INCOME: $15+

SKILL LEVEL: 1

RESOURCES
—Garden Molds and Supplies, ☎ www.gardenmolds.com
—LaBrake's Garden Path, molds and supplies, ☎ www.gardenponds.com/molds.htm
—The Crafters Mall, ☎ www.procrafter.com

Mosaic Tile Art

Mosaic tile art products are always in high demand because they are unique and colorful, are great gifts, and make fantastic home, garden, or office decorations. More importantly, making and selling mosaic tile art products can become the basis for a very profitable postretirement business venture. Mosaic art products are made out of broken ceramic tiles and/or glass arranged to form an abstract design or scene, and placed over a substrate such as wood or plastic mesh, and held together with grout in the cracks between the pieces of tile. Mosaic art products can include tabletops, floor and wall tiles, wind chimes, and many other unique interior or exterior decorative items. The learning curve to make mosaic tile art products is quick and mostly obtained through practice, practice, and more practice. However, artistic abilities and creative design flair are definite assets. Selling mosaic tile art products is also very easy. Sell them where people go to shop for gifts and home decorations—craft shows, home shows, flea markets, eBay, internet malls, and mall kiosks. Consigning or wholesaling your products to gift retailers, garden centers, and building stores are also viable options.

AT A GLANCE

INVESTMENT: Under $2K

$ INCOME: $15+

SKILL LEVEL: 1

RESOURCES
—Mosaic Art Supply, ✆ www.mosaicartsupply.com
—Mosaic Basics, tools and supplies, ✆ www.mosaicbasics.com
—Mosaic Tile Supplies, ✆ www.mosaictilesupplies.com

Sign Business

Now is your chance to cash in on the ever-growing demand for advertising and marker signs by starting your own sign-making business. There are lots of options available to would-be sign makers, including making and selling hand carved or machine sandblasted wooden signs, computer generated and cut vinyl stick-on semi-permanent signs, removable magnetic signs, handpainted signs and banners, sandblasted stone signs, custom designed and built illuminated box signs, square, round, and angled awning signs, futuristic or vintage replica neon signs, silk-screened banner signs, or mix-media signs constructed from various materials such as plastic, foam, wood, and metal. Wow, as I said, lots of options! Even with little sign making experience or basic training, you can get started from home and grow your business as you hone your skills. In addition to retail store and office signs, you can also target others that commonly need signs, such as boat owners and trade show exhibitors. Extra income can also be earned installing the signs you make and sell, and by offering monthly, quarterly, or annual sign maintenance services such as changing light bulbs, cleaning sign surfaces, and painting sign posts and hangers.

AT A GLANCE

INVESTMENT: Under $25K

$ INCOME: $25+

SKILL LEVEL: 2–3

 RESOURCES
—✫ Sign-A-Rama, ☎ (800) 286-8671, ♂ www.signarama.com
—Sign College, sign making training classes, ♂ www.signware house.com/sign_college
—Sign Warehouse, sign making equipment, tools, information, and supplies, ☎ (800) 699-5514, ♂ www.signwarehouse.com
—📖 *Sign Industry Magazine Online*, ♂ www.signindustry.com

Manufacturing Essential Oils

Manufacturing and selling essential oils from home is a unique business opportunity that will appeal to eco-friendly entrepreneurs. By definition, essential oils are the volatile essences extracted from aromatic plants. Essential oils can be applied topically or inhaled, and act on physical, emotional, and psychological processes. Essential oils are up to one hundred times more concentrated than the oils found in dried herbs and can be used as fragrant ingredients in a wide variety of health and beauty products, including cosmetics, body lotions, soaps, candles, aromatherapy burners, perfume, and aromatic potpourri products. There are basically two ways to extract essential oils from herbs and flowers: distillation and expression. Distillation is the most common, using steam to break down plant tissue, causing it to release essential oil in a vaporized form. The vapors travel from the distillation chamber into cooling tanks and become liquid. The essential oil is then separated from the water, resulting in pure essential oil. You can make your own distiller, although it's best to spend about $1,000 to purchase a commercially manufactured distiller. The expression, or cold pressing extraction, method involves mixing the plants with citrus oils and pressing the mixture, the resulting liquid is then filtered to separate the pure essential oils. This method yields much less essential oil than distillation per plant volume. The retail price of essential oils is directly related to how much plant material is needed for distillation. Essential oils can be sold in bulk to companies manufacturing and selling health and beauty products, or sold to consumers online utilizing eBay, internet eco and health malls, or offline at craft fairs, health and beauty fairs, from your home, and through mail order sales.

AT A GLANCE

 INVESTMENT: Under $2K

 $ INCOME: $15+

 SKILL LEVEL: 1

RESOURCES
—National Association for Holistic Aromatherapy, ♂ www.nhha.org
—The Essential Oil Company, professional distillation equipment, ☎ (800) 729-5912, ♂ www.essentialoil.com
—The Journal of Essential Oil Research, ♂ www.perfumerflavorist.com
—📖 *The Complete Book of Essential Oils and Aromatherapy*, Valerie Ann Worwood (New World Library, 1991)

Soap Making

An investment of less than $500 can set you up in a specialty soap manufacturing and sales business, giving you the opportunity to make and sell everything from aromatherapy soaps to novelty soaps to soap gift baskets sets. There are just as many ways to sell soap as there are soaps to make. For instance, you can sell part time from a homebased soap boutique, hire salespeople to organize and host in-home soap sales parties, sell through eBay and internet malls, and display and sell your soaps at craft shows, farmers' markets, and health shows. You can also sell direct to the public at kiosk space in malls and by starting a suds club in which you collect customer information and send out a new bar of specialty soap every month as a free gift with a catalog of your products and three order forms: one for the customer and two for friends. On a larger scale, you can make and package specialty soaps and sell to gift shops, bed and bath retailers, and natural health products retailers on a wholesale basis.

 AT A GLANCE

 INVESTMENT: Under $2K

 $ INCOME: $15+

SKILL LEVEL: 1

RESOURCES
—The Handcrafted Soap Makers Guild, ☎ (866) 900-7627, ✄ www.soap guild.org
—John C. Campbell Folk School, soap making classes, ☎ (800) 365-5724, ✄ www.folkschool.com
—National Craft Association, ✄ www.craftassoc.com
—📖 *Soapmaking for Fun & Profit*, Maria Nerius (Prima Lifestyle, 1999)

Candle Business

Just think of all the different candles that you can easily make at home and sell for big profits—aromatherapy, scented jar, floating, wedding, novelty, 100 percent beeswax, citronella, and decorative bowl and crock candles. Of course, you can specialize in one kind. But why, when all of these candles are so easy to make and sell? The learning curve is short, which makes this an excellent opportunity for everyone. Get started by getting candle-educated. Purchase books and videos, attend classes, mystery shop candle-making studios, and network with others to learn the secrets of their craft. Sell your candle creations online utilizing eBay, internet malls, and your own web site. Display and sell candles at home and gift shows, and advertise in magazines for mail-order sales. You can even sell at flea markets, in-home parties, and mall kiosks during holidays. To increase sales and profits, buy candle accessories such as holders, stands, snuffers, coil incense, and lamp oils wholesale, and sell along with your wide selection of candles. Don't overlook the possibility of mass-producing candles so that you can establish wholesale accounts with gift and home décor retailers right across the county.

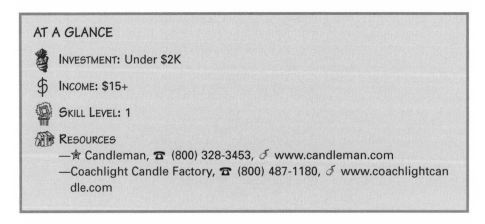

AT A GLANCE

INVESTMENT: Under $2K

INCOME: $15+

SKILL LEVEL: 1

RESOURCES
—☆ Candleman, ☎ (800) 328-3453, ✄ www.candleman.com
—Coachlight Candle Factory, ☎ (800) 487-1180, ✄ www.coachlightcandle.com

—Country Star Candles Manufacturing, ☎ (661) 269-5828, ♂ www
.countrystarcandles.com
—National Candle Association, ♂ www.candles.org
— 📖 *Candlemaking for Fun & Profit*, Michelle Espino (Prima
Lifestyles, 2000)

Stained Glass

Making and selling original stained glass products such as lamps, window, door
and cabinet inserts, and sun catchers is an excellent way to supplement your
retirement income. Don't worry if you have no experience working with stained
glass because there are very affordable stained glass classes available in every
community, and the leaning curve is quick. Equipment and startup raw materials are inexpensive. For less than a total investment of $2,000, you can be set up
making great stained glass products and earning excellent profits. Not much
workspace is needed, which means you can convert just about any spare room in
your home into a stained glass studio. Completed products can be sold in a number of ways: via internet malls and eBay, wholesale to retailers, direct to interior
designers and builders, and direct to consumers from a homebased showroom,
at crafts shows, and at home shows. Also, keep in mind that you can target businesses such as restaurants, retailers, and professionals seeking to jazz up their
shops and offices with artistic stained glass items. If there are no stained glass
supply shops in your area, the online sources below let you purchase stained
glass, equipment, product patterns, and training videos and books at wholesale
prices.

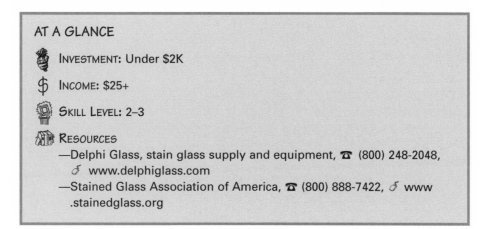

AT A GLANCE

💰 INVESTMENT: Under $2K

💲 INCOME: $25+

🏛 SKILL LEVEL: 2–3

🎁 RESOURCES
—Delphi Glass, stain glass supply and equipment, ☎ (800) 248-2048,
♂ www.delphiglass.com
—Stained Glass Association of America, ☎ (800) 888-7422, ♂ www
.stainedglass.org

—📖 *390 Traditional Stained Glass Designs*, Hywel G. Harris (Dover Publications, 1996)

Pottery Business

Designing and producing fabulous decorative art and functional pottery products is certainly not a craft that is mastered overnight; it takes lots of practice to hone your skills. There are also pottery classes available in every community as well as a plethora books and videos to get you up and running. Those who do invest the time and money necessary to learn and master the craft are often rewarded with very profitable and personally fulfilling businesses. What types of pottery and ceramics products can you make and sell? Lots, from planting pots to picture frames to sculptures. The list goes on and on because just about any product can be made from pottery. You will need to invest in the tools of the potter's trade: pottery wheel, slab roller, clay extruder, kiln, mixers, glazing tools, and ware racks, all of which are widely available through pottery supply companies. Or they can be purchased secondhand at half the cost of new if you are prepared to scour classified ads and web sites selling used equipment. Pottery can be sold in many ways—consigned with home furnishing, garden, and gift retailers, or sold wholesale to these same retailers at discounted prices. Alternately, pottery products can be sold to consumers by establishing a homebased pottery showroom, selling at craft fairs and home and garden shows, and utilizing online marketplaces such as eBay and internet craft products malls.

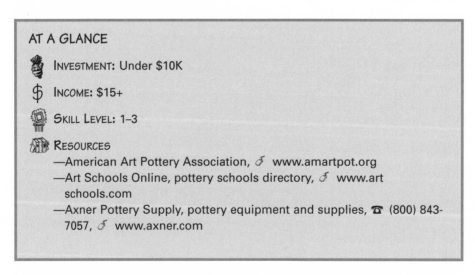

AT A GLANCE

INVESTMENT: Under $10K

$ INCOME: $15+

SKILL LEVEL: 1–3

RESOURCES
—American Art Pottery Association, ♂ www.amartpot.org
—Art Schools Online, pottery schools directory, ♂ www.art schools.com
—Axner Pottery Supply, pottery equipment and supplies, ☎ (800) 843-7057, ♂ www.axner.com

—Bailey Pottery, pottery equipment and supplies, ☎ (800) 431-6067, ✆ www.baileypottery.com
—Pottery Auction, ✆ www.potteryauction.com

Woodcrafts Manufacturing

Woodcrafts are big business. If you have basic woodworking skills and equipment, you have the potential to earn an excellent supplementary income making and selling woodcraft products. Almost anything can be made of wood, from small items like clock cases and picture frames to larger ones like storage boxes and canoe paddles. Design and construction plans for woodcraft products are readily available through the resources listed below, or if you are creative, you can design your own products. In addition to making products from rare and exotic woods, try also to incorporate recycled wood. Doing so will give you a powerful marketing tool (environmentally friendly) as well as keep costs to a minimum. Woodcrafts can be sold online via eBay, at internet malls, and through online craft malls, as well as from a homebased showroom, at flea markets, craft shows, and wholesale to gift and décor retailers.

AT A GLANCE

 INVESTMENT: Under $2K

 INCOME: $15+

 SKILL LEVEL: 1–2

 RESOURCES
—Craft Mall, craft products marketplace, ✆ www.craftmall.com
—Mammoth Tools, ☎ (516) 942-0905, ✆ www.mammothtools.com
—Scrollsaw, woodcraft plans, ✆ www.scrollsaw.com
—The American Association of Woodturners, ✆ www.woodturners.org
—U-Bild, woodcraft plans, ✆ www.u-bild.com

Quilting

What is a symphony of thread, fabric, shape, color, and creativity? Quilted products. Hot-selling quilted products such as blankets, handbags, throws, and the like can be produced by hand or by quilting machines. The latter is much more economically viable from a business standpoint. According to the National Quilting Association, quilters can expect to earn on average about $150 profit on the sale of every machine sewn; queen size quilt after expenses have been paid. This provides an excellent return on invested time when you consider that a quilt can be machine made in a day. Therefore, the potential is there to earn $40,000 to $50,000 per year by producing just one quilt at day, Monday through Friday. Quilting is a skill that can be self-taught with lots of practice and reading books on the topic, or you can take the fast track and enroll in quilting classes. Quilted products can be consigned with retailers, sold at craft, gift, and home décor shows, or sold online. If your production is good, you can also hire sales reps, working on a profit sharing arrangement, to host quilting products sales parties in their own homes.

AT A GLANCE

INVESTMENT: Under $2K

INCOME: $25+

SKILL LEVEL: 1–3

RESOURCES
—Hands On Sewing Schools, ☎ (888) 739-6395, ♂ www.handson sewingschools.com
—Quilters Coupon, quilting equipment and supplies, ♂ www.quilters coupon.com
—Start Your Own Machine Quilting Business, ♂ www.machine-quilt ing-business.com
—The National Quilting Association, ☎ (614) 488-8520, ♂ www.nqa quilts.org

Basket Making

Basket making is a centuries old craft that continues to flourish. Little has changed in the way handmade baskets are made. What has changed is the way baskets are used. At one time baskets were used everyday to carry goods and often as a system for measuring quantities of goods such as eggs, meat, vegetables, and bread. Today, baskets are more artistic than utilitarian, which is reflected in the prices. It is not uncommon for highly artistic handcrafted baskets to fetch $500 or more. Learning to make baskets can be accomplished by teaching yourself the craft through trial and error and with the aid of instructional books and videos, or you can enroll in classes, which are offered in just about every community through colleges, clubs, and private instruction. Regardless of your approach to learning the craft, you will need to invest in basic tools such as a measuring tape, scissors, water bucket, awl, knife, and clamps, as well as raw materials. Handcrafted baskets can be sold directly to consumers utilizing online marketplaces such as eBay, internet craft and gift malls, and your own web site, or you can sell to consumers in the bricks and mortar world utilizing venues such as flea markets, craft fairs, and gift shows.

AT A GLANCE

 INVESTMENT: Under $2K

 INCOME: $15+

 SKILL LEVEL: 1

 RESOURCES
—Basket Makers, industry information and resources, ♂ www.basket makers.org
—Basket Makers Catalog, supplies, ♂ www.basketmakerscatalog.com
—Basket Patterns, ♂ www.basketpatterns.com
—Handweavers Guild of America, ♂ www.weavespindye.org
—John C. Campbell Folk School, basket-making classes, ♂ www.folk school.com

---

Seashell Crafts

The call of the ocean, the lure of the beach, and the cry of the gull, few can resist buying seashell craft products. Cashing in on the demand for seashell products such as shell wind chimes, shell covered jewelry boxes, shell costume jewelry, and shell lamps is simple because shell craft products are easy to make, and even easier to sell. All you need to get started is an idea about the types of products you are going to make, a good supply of seashells, a glue gun, basic hand tools, and appropriate fasteners determined by the products you make. Combine these things with a bit of ingenious marketing savvy and you're in the seashell crafts manufacturing and sales business. Fortunately, making seashell craft products is not messy, so you can set up shop in just about any room of the house. There are numerous companies selling seashells in bulk at wholesale prices, such as the ones listed below. Sell your completed seashell creations online utilizing eBay, internet malls, and your own web site, as well as through offline sales venues, such as flea markets, arts and craft shows, and at community events. Another option is to sell your products wholesale to home décor, gift, and fashion retailers, or place products with retailers on a consignment basis.

AT A GLANCE

INVESTMENT: Under $2K

INCOME: $15+

SKILL LEVEL: 1

RESOURCES
—Sanibel Seashell Industries, seashell craft information and supplies, ☎ (239) 472-1603, ☌ www.seashells.com
—Shell Horizons Wholesale, ☎ (727) 536-3333, ☌ www.shell horizons.com
—The Shell Store, seashell craft information and supplies, ☎ (727) 360-0586, ☌ www.theshellstore.com
—U.S. Shell Wholesale, ☎ (956) 554-4500, ☌ www.usshell.com

Putting Green Installations

The advantages of synthetic surface backyard putting greens over real grass putting greens are obvious: no mowing, watering, fertilizing, or seeding. Synthetic putting greens are also way more durable and weather resistant, hold up in direct sunlight, and can be used year-round (weather permitting). These advantages have golf fanatic homeowners across the country lining up to have backyard putting greens installed. Designing and installing backyard synthetic turf putting greens is a wonderful full- or part-time opportunity that will appeal to golf-loving entrepreneurs. There are basically two types of backyard putting greens. The first is a sand-filled polypropylene (plastic) synthetic green that can be installed on a compacted aggregate or concrete base. Polypropylene synthetic turfs use fine silica sand to keep turf fibers in an upright position. The second option is synthetic nylon turf, which can also be installed on a compacted aggregate or concrete base, but because nylon turf has memory burned into it, the fibers stand upright without the aid of silica sand. Both can be installed for big profits, especially when you consider material costs are in the range of $3 to $4 per square foot and the greens retail for as much as $15 per square foot installed. Once established, referrals will become the main source of new business. Therefore, it makes sense to invite neighbors to come by to see and play each new installation.

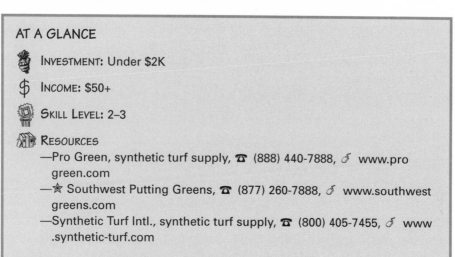

AT A GLANCE

INVESTMENT: Under $2K

$ INCOME: $50+

SKILL LEVEL: 2–3

RESOURCES
—Pro Green, synthetic turf supply, ☎ (888) 440-7888, ♂ www.pro green.com
—☆ Southwest Putting Greens, ☎ (877) 260-7888, ♂ www.southwest greens.com
—Synthetic Turf Intl., synthetic turf supply, ☎ (800) 405-7455, ♂ www .synthetic-turf.com

Solar-Powered Products

As the cost of energy continues to soar, the wave of the future is alternative energy sources. By starting a business selling solar-powered products, you will definitely be joining a growth industry. There are many types of solar and alternative energy products to sell: solar-powered interior and exterior lights, solar cell battery systems and chargers, wind-powered generators, rooftop solar panels, and any number of other solar cell power and storage systems. All can be purchased directly from manufacturers and wholesalers at deeply discounted wholesale prices. Who are your customers? They will include everybody who is currently or who wants to be off the grid, including remote property owners, boat owners, RV owners, campers, hikers, and anybody else that has a need for energy to power equipment, lights, and utilities. Solar-powered products can be sold directly from a home-based showroom supported by local advertising, as well as through consumer shows and online marketplaces catering to alternative energy enthusiasts.

AT A GLANCE

INVESTMENT: Under $10K

$ INCOME: $15+

SKILL LEVEL: 1

RESOURCES
—Alternative Solar Products Wholesale, ☎ (909) 308-2366, ♂ www.alter
nativesolar.com
—Solar Energy Industries Association, ♂ www.seia.org

Religious Products

Religion is a hot topic in North America and many parts of the world. Sales of religious products from books, to religious jewelry, to figurines generate billions in sales annually. Selling these products is a great way to supplement your retirement income, and there are a few ways you can go about it. Rent a retail storefront and open a well-stock religious products store. Open the store at your home, providing space and zoning permits. Sell religious products online, and at flea markets and religious-themed consumer shows and exhibitions. All have the potential to be very profitable. Religious products can be bought cheaply from wholesalers, distributors, liquidators, importers, and even factory direct from manufacturers. A few wholesale sources are listed below, but you can also visit manufacturer and wholesaler directories online to find many more sources for religious products. Naturally, you should follow your faith and concentrate your marketing efforts on the religion you know best.

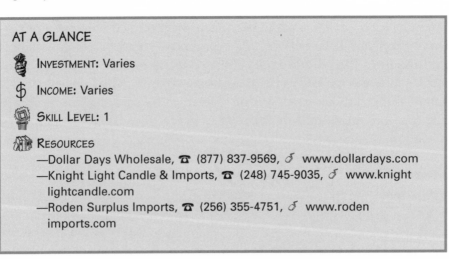

AT A GLANCE

INVESTMENT: Varies

$ INCOME: Varies

SKILL LEVEL: 1

RESOURCES
—Dollar Days Wholesale, ☎ (877) 837-9569, ♂ www.dollardays.com
—Knight Light Candle & Imports, ☎ (248) 745-9035, ♂ www.knight
lightcandle.com
—Roden Surplus Imports, ☎ (256) 355-4751, ♂ www.roden
imports.com

Home Tutoring

Dust off your degree in mathematics, biology, English literature, science, or history, and put it to work on a full- or part-time basis by becoming a private tutor. For parents who want their children to receive the best academic education, extracurricular in-home, one-on-one tutoring is usually the preferred teaching method. Utilizing your knowledge in your field of expertise means that you can start your own tutoring service and have the opportunity to earn $25 to $50 per hour, depending on your qualifications and your academic subject. Tutoring sessions can be held at your home or at your student's home. Low-income families can take advantage of tutoring programs for their kids in association with the No Child Left Behind Act, which provides tutoring funds for children who have learning disabilities. However, to qualify for these tutoring programs you need a teaching certificate. In addition to academic tutoring, English as a second language (ESL) tutoring has exploded in popularity in the past decade, both for new immigrants and foreign students who need to master English for job and study reasons. Once you've worked with a few clients, word-of-mouth advertising will spread, and you may be able to expand your business greatly and employ a number of private tutors.

AT A GLANCE

INVESTMENT: Under $2K

$ INCOME: $25+

SKILL LEVEL: 2–4

RESOURCES
—National Tutoring Association, ☌ www.ntatutor.com
—☆ Tutoring Club, ☎ (888) 674-6425, ☌ www.tutoringclub.com
—Tutor Nation, online portal bringing together tutors and students,
  ☌ www.tutornation.com

Customer Service Trainer

Everyone has received bad service in a business, over the phone, or in person. And it's probably happened a lot more than once, twice, or even ten times. The result of such frustrating encounters is usually a vow never to return to the business or to refer others. The adage, "a unhappy customer will tell ten people, but a happy one will tell no one," is as true today as the day it was coined. Rude or poorly trained employees cost companies millions of dollars every year in lost business and referral sales. But companies that take proactive steps to ensure that all employees receive professional customer service and appreciation training have a leg up on the competition. They wait in the wings with arms wide open to receive disgruntled customers when others screw up. You can earn incredible profits by starting a consulting service that offers customer service and appreciation training programs specifically designed to meet your clients' needs. The starting point is to choose a specialty, such as retail, food servers, or receptionists. Training and training curriculum and manuals can be based on your own expertise as well as that of other customer service professionals.

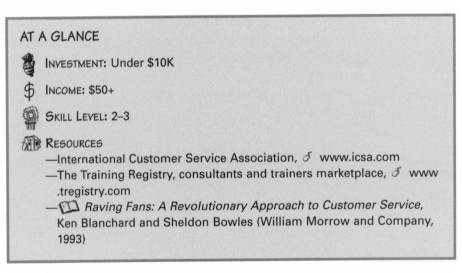

AT A GLANCE

INVESTMENT: Under $10K

INCOME: $50+

SKILL LEVEL: 2–3

RESOURCES
—International Customer Service Association, ♂ www.icsa.com
—The Training Registry, consultants and trainers marketplace, ♂ www .tregistry.com
— 📖 *Raving Fans: A Revolutionary Approach to Customer Service*, Ken Blanchard and Sheldon Bowles (William Morrow and Company, 1993)

Sales Trainer

Are you now or have you ever been recognized as a top-producing sales professional who knows how to prospect for new business, overcome all objections, win negotiations, and close the sale every time? If so, why not share your knowledge and experience and make huge profits in the process by training employees, managers, small business owners, and executives to also become top-producing sales professionals? Even if you are currently working in sales and don't want to rock the boat, you do not have to. You can train students online, via correspondence, with personal conference calls, and by way of evening and weekend workshops and seminars. This way you can make the transition into full-time sales training as your business and client list grows, which is the ideal scenario for people close to retiring from their current careers. Target customers will include small business owners, salespeople, retail clerks, and many others, that is, basically any person, manager, or business owner who wants to increase revenues and profits through increasing selling effectiveness.

AT A GLANCE

INVESTMENT: Under $10K

INCOME: $50+

SKILL LEVEL: 2

RESOURCES
—Sales and Marketing Executives International, ☎ (312) 893-0751, ♂ www.smei.org
—☆ Sandler Sales Institute, ☎ (800) 669-3537, ♂ www.sandler.com
—The Training Registry, consultants and trainers marketplace, ♂ www.tregistry.com
—📖 *Selling Power Magazine Online*, ♂ www.sellingpower.com

Dog Obedience Instructor

Dog obedience training is a multimillion dollar industry and growing by double digit gains every year as more and more dog owners realize the benefits of professional obedience training. Obedience training classes can be held at your home in a one-on-one or group format. If your home is not suitable, you can travel to a customer's home and train dogs and dog owners one-on-one. You can also strike deals with schools and community centers to hold dog obedience classes on weekends and nights. Many trainers are currently not certified by a recognized association, although that is changing. If you are serious about making dog obedience training your postretirement career, you should enroll in a professional training program and obtain a recognized dog obedience trainer certificate. The certification carries weight. Not only can it be used as a powerful marketing tool when it comes time to persuade people that you are the right trainer for their dogs, but having the proper credentials will also mean you can charge a premium for your services. Current rates for in-home training sessions are in the range of $30 to $50 per hour and many trainers create dog training packages for their customers that include a set number of training classes and course materials in print and video formats. You can contact either the Canadian Association of Professional Pet Dog

Trainers or the National Association of Dog Obedience Instructors through the contact information provided below to find out about certification programs offered in your area.

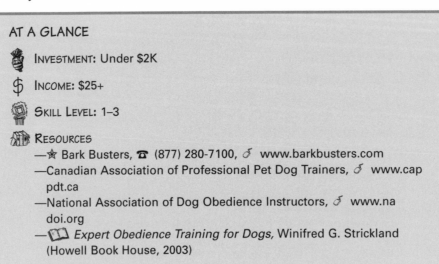

AT A GLANCE

INVESTMENT: Under $2K

INCOME: $25+

SKILL LEVEL: 1–3

RESOURCES
—☆ Bark Busters, ☎ (877) 280-7100, ♂ www.barkbusters.com
—Canadian Association of Professional Pet Dog Trainers, ♂ www.cap pdt.ca
—National Association of Dog Obedience Instructors, ♂ www.na doi.org
—📖 *Expert Obedience Training for Dogs,* Winifred G. Strickland (Howell Book House, 2003)

Personal Fitness Trainer

Calling all fitness gurus! The time has never been better than now to start your own personal fitness business teaching people from 5 to 95 how to live a more healthy life through exercise and nutritional programs. Although there are currently no universal certification requirements for personal trainers, anyone serious about operating this service should become certified. Contact the associations listed below for more information about certification programs offered in your area. Your target audience will include anyone who wants professional guidance. You can work one-on-one. You can specialize and train busy executives, kids, disabled people, moms-to-be, or seniors. Train at people's offices or homes. Open your own fitness studio, and offer one-on-one and group training programs. In addition to developing exercise programs to match each client's individual needs, personal trainers also conduct fitness assessments and provide nutritional coaching. Training in fitness clubs, community centers, retirement homes, hospitals, cruise ships, corporations, hotels, spas, resorts, camps, and schools are also other moneymaking options open to certified personal trainers.

AT A GLANCE

 INVESTMENT: Under $10K

 INCOME: $25+

 SKILL LEVEL: 2–3

 RESOURCES
—☆ Fitness Together, ☎ (303) 663-0880, ♂ www.fitnesstogetherfran chise.com
—International Fitness Professionals Association, (800) 785-1924, ♂ www.ifpa-fitness.com
—National Federation of Professional Trainers, (800) 729-6378, ♂ www .nfpt.com

Dance Instructor

Providing you now how to dance, regardless of the style—tap, highland, ballroom, ballet, swing, break, modern, disco, flamenco, or line dancing—there is big money to be earned teaching people aged 3 to 93 your smooth moves on the dance floor. If space is available, the most convenient way to get started is to open a dance studio right in your own home. If not, operate your dance classes in conjunction with a suitable partner or partners who do have the space, such as fitness and community center. Of course, you can also rent suitable studio space or even teach dance moves to students right in their own homes. There are lots of options. Expanding your dance business is as easy as hiring other dance instructors to teach students and work on a revenue-splitting basis. One-on-one instruction rates start at about $30 per hour. While group rates are less per student, you can earn more by teaching numerous people to dance at the same time. And, if you are really ambitious, classes can be filmed, and your dance instruction videos can be sold to people around the globe.

AT A GLANCE

 INVESTMENT: Under $2K

 INCOME: $25+

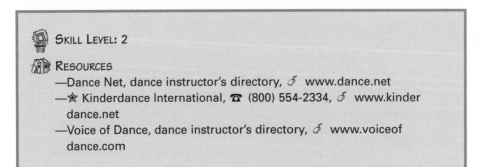

SKILL LEVEL: 2

RESOURCES
—Dance Net, dance instructor's directory, ♂ www.dance.net
—★ Kinderdance International, ☎ (800) 554-2334, ♂ www.kinder
dance.net
—Voice of Dance, dance instructor's directory, ♂ www.voiceof
dance.com

Music Teacher

The hills are alive with the sounds of music, and if you know how to sing or play any instrument well enough to teach others, what are you waiting for? Trade on your musical talents and earn a great full- or part-time income teaching students how to play your instrument of choice. Classes can be conducted one-on-one or in a group format; from your home, at the student's location, or from rented commercial space; or in conjunction with community programs, continuing education courses, or even an established music store. Expanding the business requires nothing more than hiring other experienced musicians to teach students. Fees are split. Basically, you find the students, your instructors teach the classes, and everyone benefits. Lesson rates vary depending on class size, skill level, and instrument. On average, group lessons cost students $10 to $20 per hour, and one-on-one lessons in the range of $40 per hour plus the costs of instrument rentals or purchases, course materials, and sheet music. Alternately, if you prefer to teach music without the added work of operating a business, then subcontract your musical teaching talents to an existing music school and earn in the range of $15 to $25 per hour.

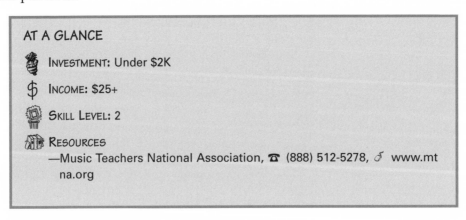

AT A GLANCE

INVESTMENT: Under $2K

INCOME: $25+

SKILL LEVEL: 2

RESOURCES
—Music Teachers National Association, ☎ (888) 512-5278, ♂ www.mt
na.org

—☆ Playtime Piano International, ☎ (877) 823-6664, ♂ www.play
timepiano.com

Arts and Crafts Instructor

Knitting, painting, print making, and many other arts and crafts are ever popular. People are more than willing to shell out their hard earned money to learn. If you have mastered an art or craft, why not be the person to train others and earn substantial profits for your efforts? Day, evening, or weekend classes can be taught from a homebased studio, rented commercial space, in partnership with a crafts retailer, community center, or school, or even at a park if weather permits. Promote your classes through arts and crafts retailers in your community, by running print advertisements in the newspaper, by networking at business and social functions, by posting notices on community bulletin boards, and by exhibiting at arts and crafts shows. Creative entrepreneurs may even choose to film the training classes and broadcast these via the internet to a worldwide student base, or produce and sell training videos or DVDs. The options are nearly limitless when you have a talent that other people want to learn. Rates vary depending on how many people are in each class and material and equipment requirements, but on average, arts and crafts instructors can expect to earn in the range of $25 to $50 per hour.

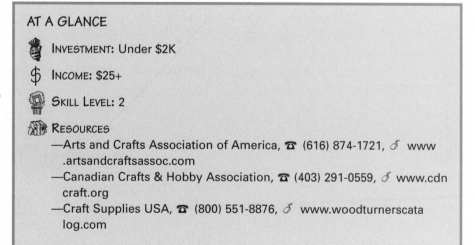

AT A GLANCE

💰 INVESTMENT: Under $2K

💲 INCOME: $25+

▦ SKILL LEVEL: 2

🏚 RESOURCES
  —Arts and Crafts Association of America, ☎ (616) 874-1721, ♂ www
    .artsandcraftsassoc.com
  —Canadian Crafts & Hobby Association, ☎ (403) 291-0559, ♂ www.cdn
    craft.org
  —Craft Supplies USA, ☎ (800) 551-8876, ♂ www.woodturnerscata
    log.com

Mobile Computer Trainer

The vast majority of computer training schools require students to come to their locations for classes. But for the countless numbers of companies that purchase or upgrade computers and software, this is often not practical, especially if there are five to ten, or even more, employees in need of training or retraining. Likewise, not everyone who purchases a new computer, software, or other hardware has time to attend classes to learn how to use the equipment. Herein lies the opportunity. Capitalizing on your computer, software, and marketing experience, you can start a mobile computer training service and train students one-on-one or in a group on their own equipment at their homes, businesses, or offices. The proliferation of technological advances, the constant new stream of software applications, and the variety of hardware devices means that there will always be lots of people in need of training or skills upgrading. Because students use their own computer equipment and software, the business can be started cheaply—basically for the cost of a notebook computer, software applications, marketing materials, and reliable transportation. Advertise your computer and software training services using promotional fliers and coupons, newspaper classified ads, Yellow Pages advertising, and networking at business and social functions. It also helps to build alliances with computer and software retailers that can refer your training services to their customers.

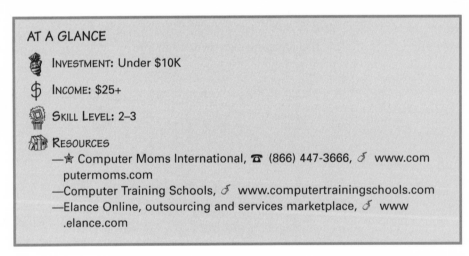

AT A GLANCE

INVESTMENT: Under $10K

INCOME: $25+

SKILL LEVEL: 2–3

RESOURCES
—☆ Computer Moms International, ☎ (866) 447-3666, ♂ www.computermoms.com
—Computer Training Schools, ♂ www.computertrainingschools.com
—Elance Online, outsourcing and services marketplace, ♂ www.elance.com

Homebased Sewing Classes

Calling all seamstress and hobby sewers! Starting a sewing instruction business is a fantastic opportunity to earn part-time profits right from the comfort of home.

With an investment of less than a few thousand dollars, you can purchase sewing machines and supplies to teach students sewing skills at your home. Charge each student $15 to $25 per hour for one-on-one training, or slightly less for a group format, but earn more overall by teaching multiple students at the same time. The rising cost of clothing is what makes this a great opportunity. After completing your sewing classes, students will have the skills to make their own clothing as well as other items, such as drapery and furniture slipcovers, at a fraction of what they cost at retailers. You will need to offer various levels of instruction, from beginner to advanced, and provide a sewing machine and related equipment for each student. Additional income can be earned by selling sewing supplies and patterns, as well as new and used sewing machines. Advertise locally in the newspaper, by posting promotional fliers on community bulletin boards, and by distributing literature at fabric shops.

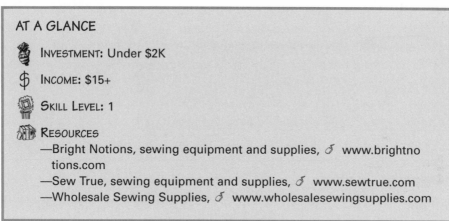

AT A GLANCE

INVESTMENT: Under $2K

$ INCOME: $15+

SKILL LEVEL: 1

RESOURCES
—Bright Notions, sewing equipment and supplies, ✄ www.brightno tions.com
—Sew True, sewing equipment and supplies, ✄ www.sewtrue.com
—Wholesale Sewing Supplies, ✄ www.wholesalesewingsupplies.com

Public Speaking Coach

The fear of speaking in public is universal. In fact, it is the number-one fear, shared by more people than fear of heights, claustrophobia, or even the fear of dying! Needless to say, if you have public speaking experience and can coach other people to become more effective and relaxed public speakers, then you not only have the potential to supplement your retirement income but also to earn huge profits. Why is the ability to speak in public important? There are many reasons, but number one is that by avoiding speaking in public, many people miss opportunities to advance their careers, businesses, educations, or personal lives. People may choose college courses, careers, or even partners in such a way as to avoid public speaking. Fortunately, you can help people overcome the fear of public speaking through coaching. You can train students one-on-one or in a group at your home or office, or at their homes, offices, or businesses using videotaped feedback and other proven step-by-step instructional techniques. Join professional and business associations, as well as social clubs, to help market your services by networking with members. Also initiate a direct mail campaign outlining the benefits of your coaching, and send this material to corporations, small businesses, and organizations. Once established, this is the type of business that thrives on referrals.

AT A GLANCE

INVESTMENT: Under $2K

INCOME: $50+

SKILL LEVEL: 2

RESOURCES
—Canadian Association of Professional Speakers, ☎ www.canadian speakers.org
—National Speakers Association, ☎ www.nsaspeaker.org
—Power Public Speaking, industry information portal, ☎ www.power publicspeaking.com

Management Trainer

According to the Association of Management Consulting Firms, management consulting and training generates more than $100 billion in annual revenues worldwide, and even better, management trainers earn an average of $150 per hour! Leadership management training is one of the fastest growing segments of the corporate training industry and for good reason. A corporation's or organization's management team needs the ability to lead, unite, and motivate all members of its team, including executives, employees, suppliers, and vendors, if the business is to succeed and survive in today's highly competitive global marketplace. Typically, management trainers coach clients in their own field of expertise—marketing, logistics, technology, international business, manufacturing, human resources, finance, and health care. You would be advised to do the same in order to establish a name and reputation as an expert in your specific discipline. The objective of the management trainer is to assess the client's management team and operational systems, identifying weakness and strengths, so that once the assessment is complete, a plan including recommendations, can be developed and implemented. It should reorganize, retrain, and refocus each individual as well as the entire management team as required to eliminate weaknesses and build upon strengths. Networking with business owners and executives to spread the word about the benefits of your services is one of the fastest ways to get started in the industry and build the business via referrals and repeat business.

AT A GLANCE

 INVESTMENT: Under $10K

 INCOME: $50+

 SKILL LEVEL: 2–3

 RESOURCES
—American Management Association, ♂ www.amanet.org
—Canadian Management Professionals Association, ♂ www.work place.ca
—☆ Leadership Management Inc., ☎ (800) 568-1241, ♂ www.lmi-bus.com

---

Small Business Coach

The need for small business coaching services is rapidly expanding, especially when you consider that in the United States and Canada more than 800,000 businesses are started annually. Combine this with the millions of small- to medium-sized businesses already operating, and you will agree the future looks very bright—and potentially profitable—for a small business coaching service. This hot opportunity will appeal to entrepreneurs who are past or present small business owners, business managers, and corporate executives, especially those with strong skills in specific areas like marketing, sales, administration, management, operations, logistics, and financial forecasting. Because there is a plethora of small business schools and courses offered by nonprofit government agencies and for-profit businesses in both countries, you will be well advised to specialize in a specific industry, such as retail, transportation, or food industries, or to offer clients a more personalized and hands-on, one-on-one coaching service. Small business coaches help new and existing business owners with any number of tasks: business start-up issues, business planning, import and export issues, product and consumer research projects, building and implementing marketing strategies, preparing financial budgets, logistics issues, technology issues, and expansion challenges.

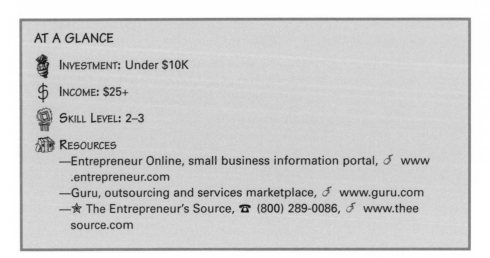

AT A GLANCE

💰 INVESTMENT: Under $10K

$ INCOME: $25+

🎖 SKILL LEVEL: 2–3

🏛 RESOURCES
—Entrepreneur Online, small business information portal, ♂ www
.entrepreneur.com
—Guru, outsourcing and services marketplace, ♂ www.guru.com
—★ The Entrepreneur's Source, ☎ (800) 289-0086, ♂ www.thee
source.com

Sports Coach

Amateur sports coaching is a growing industry in all areas of North America. If you have sports coaching or playing experience in the popular sports in your area, you can turn these experiences and skills into a profitable commodity by offering one-on-one coaching. Amateur athletes from 5 to 65 are turning to individual coaching to give them a competitive advantage on the field, course, ring, or pool. Parents are parting with up to $75 per hour to make sure their kids receive the coaching so they will not be left on the sidelines. Adult athletes are also enlisting coaches to help them improve their games, get more enjoyment from their sports, and decrease the risks of injury. Market your services by joining sports associations and clubs specific to your sport, and by networking with parents of kids involved in athletics and with adult athletes. Also develop a workshop or seminar on topics involving the benefits of your service and the sport you coach. It can be offered free to all, with the aim of recruiting students during and after the seminar.

AT A GLANCE

💰 INVESTMENT: Varies

$ INCOME: $50+

🎖 SKILL LEVEL: 2–4

RESOURCES
—Entrepreneur, small business information portal, ✆ www.entrepreneur.com
—Sports Workout, sports coaching training products and services, ✆ www.sportsworkout.com
—★ Velocity Sports Performance, ☎ (678) 990-2555, ✆ www.velocitysp.com

Desktop Publishing Service

The desktop publishing industry is experiencing double-digit growth, and with all the expected software and technological innovations, it will continue to flourish for years to come. This is a great business start-up with incredible upside growth potential for people of all ages. In fact, the Bureau of Labor Statistics estimates that more than 50,000 people are currently employed in the desktop publishing industry, and many of those are self-employed and working from home. Combining your graphic design and computer skills, you can provide clients with a wide range of desktop publishing services. With desktop publishing software programs from Adobe, ✆ www.adobe.com, and Corel, ✆ www.corel.com, as well as others, you can create and produce print and electronic promotional fliers, brochures, product catalogs, business reports, posters, presentations, coupons, and advertisements of all sorts. Create samples of your work and set up appointments with local business owners and professionals to present your talents and explain the benefits of your service. Attend business association meetings to network and spread the word about your services. You will need to invest in computer equipment, specialized software, a scanner, a digital camera, and a high-quality printer, but with desktop publishing rates in the area of $40 to $100 per hour, you can be assured of a very quick return on investment.

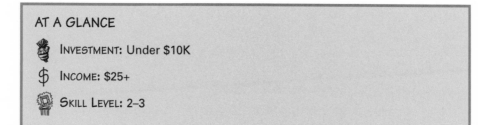

AT A GLANCE

INVESTMENT: Under $10K

INCOME: $25+

SKILL LEVEL: 2–3

RESOURCES
—Desktop Publishing Online, information and resources, ♂ www.desk
toppublishing.com
—Elance Online, outsourcing and services marketplace, ♂ www
.elance.com
—📖 *Layout Index: Brochure, Web Design, Poster, Flyer, Advertising,
Page Layout, Newsletter, Stationery Index*, Jim Krause (North Light
Books, 2001)

Web Designer

A huge opportunity exists in web design services. There are thousands of web
sites and web pages being posted on the internet every day. Even if you lack the
skills needed to design highly effective web sites and pages, you can take a crash
course in web design at your local community college or through private web
design schools. Alternatively, you can capitalize on your sales and marketing
skills and concentrate your efforts on finding new customers. Then hire a high-
tech wizard right out of school to take on design duties. Competition in web
design is steep, so you may want to take a more grassroots approach to marketing; start by servicing your local area while you build a name. Design a few sample sites to showcase your talents, and be sure to vary your samples with
e-commerce sites, information portals, and blogs. Next, initiate a letter, telephone,
and e-mail direct marketing campaign and accompany it with personal visits to
introduce your services to small business owners in your community that lack
sites or have one in need of improvement. Armed with your notebook computer,
you can meet business owners, present your sample sites, and explain the benefits of your services. Additional revenues can be generated by hosting sites, maintaining sites, providing content, and creating online marketing programs to meet
individual client needs.

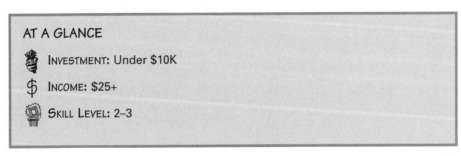

AT A GLANCE

INVESTMENT: Under $10K

$ INCOME: $25+

SKILL LEVEL: 2–3

RESOURCES
—Computer Training Schools, ♂ www.computertrainingschools.com
—Elance Online, outsourcing and services marketplace, ♂ www
.elance.com
—Web Design Developers Association, ♂ www.wdda.org
—★ WSI Internet, ♂ www.wsicorporate.com

eBay Consultant

eBay consulting is a very timely and exciting business opportunity with huge upside growth potential. With more than 100 million registered users, eBay generates billions of dollars in annual sales and, more importantly, enables small businesses to sell their products to consumers around the globe without having to break the bank on advertising and marketing. eBay in turn, has created a fantastic opportunity to start a consulting business training small business owners how to utilize the online marketplace giant to sell their goods and services. Marketing your consulting services requires nothing more than setting appointments with businesses that are not currently using eBay and explaining to them the opportunity they are missing. Then discuss the features of your service and why they should hire you as their eBay consultant. Teach business owners how to list goods for sale using one or more of eBay's seller's options, and how to increase interest in and promote their auctions, take online payments, and process and fulfill orders. Basically, you teach them everything necessary to get products listed on eBay, sell them, get paid, and have them delivered. There is a lot to know about eBay to truly take advantage of all of the programs and services provided. Therefore, be sure to educate yourself about everything eBay by reading books, spending lots of time on various eBay sites, and attending eBay hosting workshops and seminars. And, if you're already an experienced eBay seller, so much the better!

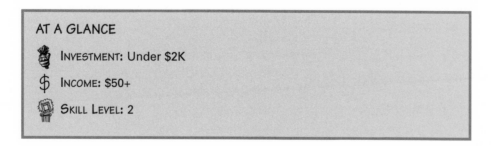

AT A GLANCE

INVESTMENT: Under $2K

$ INCOME: $50+

SKILL LEVEL: 2

RESOURCES

—eBay, ♂ www.ebay.com

—eBay Learning Center, ♂ http://pages.ebay.com/education/index.html

—eBay University, ♂ http://pages.ebay.com/university/index.html

—eBay Seller's Guide, ♂ http://pages.ebay.com/help/sell/index.html

—eBay Promotional Tools, ♂ http://pages.ebay.com/sellercentral/tools.html

E-Commerce Consultant

Doing business online and achieving any kind of e-profitable success are probably more difficult than in the bricks and mortar world. That's why webpreneurs of every size are enlisting the services of e-commerce specialists to help build, market, and maintain their businesses. Right now, and for the foreseeable future, there is an incredible opportunity to build a superprofitable e-commerce consulting business for entrepreneurs with web development, online marketing, e-commerce, and e-communications skills and experience. In short, if this describes you, the potential to earn $1,000 a day and more is presently available. And, if this doesn't describe you, don't fret. Instead, enroll in classes and become an e-commerce specialist; the financial rewards are well worth the investment. The Institute of Certified E-Commerce Consultants provides training, and students graduate with the professional designation of Certified E-Commerce Consultant. E-commerce specialists do much more than just show business people how to hawk their goods online. They also help businesses build or improve their web sites, develop productive database systems, manage electronic mailing lists, create efficient e-showrooms and checkouts, design e-mail communication systems and plans, increase search engine rankings, create effective advertising and pay-per-click promotions, and develop and implement order processing and fulfillment systems. Online sales are expected to top $1 trillion in 2005. The timing cannot get better for getting your piece of this very lucrative pie.

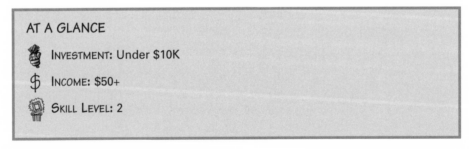

AT A GLANCE

INVESTMENT: Under $10K

INCOME: $50+

SKILL LEVEL: 2

RESOURCES
—E-Marketing Association, ☎ (401) 884-0614, ♂ www.emarketing
association.com
—Institute of Certified E-Commerce Consultants, ♂ www.icecc.com
—☆ Internet Marketing Group, ☎ (877) 803-3003, ♂ www.imgfran
chises.com
—☆ WSI Internet, ♂ www.wsicorporate.com

E-Zine Publisher

Thanks to the internet, starting a magazine no longer requires a million-dollar
investment. It is now possible to start and publish your own magazine on a shoestring investment of a mere few thousand dollars, but in electronic format instead
of print. In spite of the estimated 100,000 electronic publications being distributed to millions of readers monthly, there is room for lots of new starts-ups in the
e-zine publishing world. Why? Two reasons: the wide diversity of readers' interests and the fact that the e-zine publishing industry is nowhere near critical mass.
Develop your e-zine based on what you know and like—antiques, sports, family
issues, or just about anything else that tickles your informative fancy. General
information e-zines are typically free to subscribers and supported by advertising revenues, that is, by the businesses that rent space in your electronic magazine to advertise their products and services. For instance, if you publish and
distribute a monthly football e-zine, then logical advertisers would include
sports retailers and sports gaming businesses. Highly specialized e-zines can be
sold to subscribers, but the information featured must be truly beneficial to readers: make them lots of money, save them lots of money, or increase their business.
To stand out in the marketplace, aim to serve a well-defined niche market, provide interesting and informative content that readers cannot get anywhere else,
and build a large subscription base that will appeal to advertisers and marketers
that want to reach your audience.

AT A GLANCE

 INVESTMENT: Under $25K

 INCOME: $25+

 SKILL LEVEL: 1–2

RESOURCES
—Ezine Director, ezine delivery and management software, ♂ www
.ezinedirector.com
—Ezine Directory, lists over 2,400 electronic publications, ♂ www
.ezine-dir.com
— 📖 *The Columbia Guide to Digital Publishing*, William E. Kasdorf
(Columbia University Press, 2003)

Online Researcher

If you find yourself spending a lot of time surfing the web, and if you're are looking to supplement your income, consider starting an internet research service so
you can get paid for the time you spend surfing. Not long ago, this business was
referred to as information brokering, but with the introduction of the internet, the
name has changed. The business remains the same, however, as the information
that was once researched and compiled from newspapers, trade magazines, and
business and industry journals can now be found on online. An internet research
service operates in two fashions. First, collect data and facts relevant to a specific
topic or topics, and then sell the compiled data to individuals and businesses that
require the kind of information you have compiled. Second, business owners and
marketers often enlist the services of an internet researcher to find specific data
and facts relevant to their particular business, industry, or market. In both cases,
clients pay for information they are seeking. Billing rates for the services vary,
depending on how much research time is required to compile the data and related
costs, but expect to charge in the area of $25 to $35 per hour.

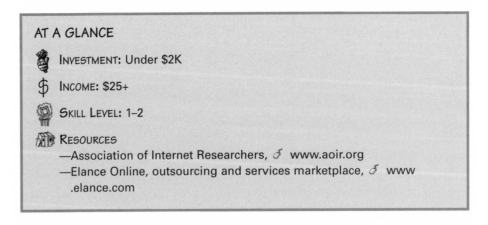
AT A GLANCE

💰 INVESTMENT: Under $2K

$ INCOME: $25+

🖲 SKILL LEVEL: 1–2

RESOURCES
—Association of Internet Researchers, ♂ www.aoir.org
—Elance Online, outsourcing and services marketplace, ♂ www
.elance.com

> — *Building & Running a Successful Research Business: A Guide for the Independent Information Professional*, Mary Ellen Bates (Cyberage Books, 2003)

Computer Repair Service

Now that you've slowed down, it's time to get busy again and get in on the multi-billion-dollar, ever-growing computer industry by starting your own computer repair service. You have lots of options: repair computers at home, repair computers on a mobile basis, rent a storefront or office, or partner with an existing computer retailer providing customers with computer and related technologies setup, repair, maintenance, and troubleshooting services. Market your services through traditional advertising formats such as the Yellow Pages and newspaper advertising, as well as through more direct methods such as networking at business functions and by creating and implementing a direct-mail campaign aimed mainly at commercial customers with multiple computer workstations. Don't worry if your computer troubleshooting skills are not up to par; there are a plethora of courses across the country appropriate to every skill level and budget. Some courses will have you up and running repairing computers in just a few short months. Best of all, computer repair technicians earn up to $50 per hour. As the world continues its push toward complete computerization, there will always be lots of computers to repair.

AT A GLANCE

 INVESTMENT: Under $10K

 INCOME: $25+

 SKILL LEVEL: 2–3

 RESOURCES
—Elance Online, outsourcing and services marketplace, ♂ www.elance.com
—Computer Training Schools, ♂ www.computertrainingschools.com
—★ Computer Troubleshooters, ☎ (877) 704-1702, ♂ www.comptroub.com

Computer Sales

Selling new and used computers is a great way to supplement your retirement income. In addition to computers, you can also sell computer accessories such as inkjet printers, laser printers, scanners, DVD and CD writers, LCD monitors, and wireless keyboards and mouse sets, as well as computer parts, including CDRW and DVD drives, hard drives, memory, audio and video cards, CPUs, and motherboards. New desktop and notebook computer systems, accessories, and parts can be purchased from wholesalers, liquidators, and distributors, and marked up by as much as 50 percent for resale. The options for selling computer systems are plentiful. You can develop your own web site for sales, sell via eBay and internet malls, open a retail computer store, or open a homebased computer showroom. There is also excellent profit potential selling secondhand computer systems, especially in-demand notebook computers, which hold their value much better than desktop computers. There are companies that even wholesale notebook computers for resale purposes. That's how big the demand and market is. Though the selling methods are the same as for new computers, the buying sources are not. To buy used computer systems, scan classified ads for bargains and attend auction sales, the preferred method. Many corporations, government agencies, and organizations replace their still otherwise good computer equipment on a scheduled basis. These computers can often be purchased for pennies on the dollar at auctions or tender sales.

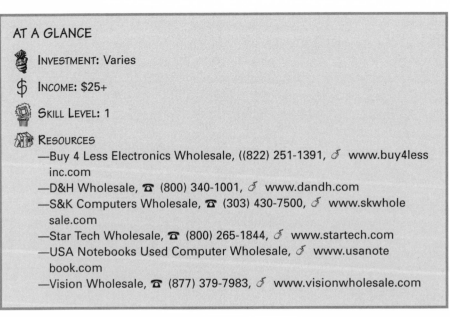

AT A GLANCE

INVESTMENT: Varies

$ INCOME: $25+

SKILL LEVEL: 1

RESOURCES
—Buy 4 Less Electronics Wholesale, ((822) 251-1391, ♂ www.buy4less inc.com
—D&H Wholesale, ☎ (800) 340-1001, ♂ www.dandh.com
—S&K Computers Wholesale, ☎ (303) 430-7500, ♂ www.skwhole sale.com
—Star Tech Wholesale, ☎ (800) 265-1844, ♂ www.startech.com
—USA Notebooks Used Computer Wholesale, ♂ www.usanote book.com
—Vision Wholesale, ☎ (877) 379-7983, ♂ www.visionwholesale.com

Community Web Site Host

Not all small business owners and professionals have the time, ability, or inclination to build, maintain, and regularly update a web site. But at the same time, many would still like to have some sort of presence on the web. Herein lies the opportunity for internet savvy entrepreneurs. Develop, maintain, and market a web site that services a specific area-neighborhood, town, city, or country and features local news and information, as well as participating businesses and professionals. Each business that joins receives space within the site to advertise, promote, and even sell products and services, a web address extension, private e-mail, and a host of additional web and commerce features. Think of it as a bricks and mortar mall, but in virtual space. You can charge each participating business a monthly fee that includes fixed services and additional fees for premium services such as content updating and web tools specific to their business. Promote the community web site locally using advertising fliers, print coupons, and print advertisements in newspapers. Offer clients a noncompetition clause to entice them to join. This means you will contract with only one car dealer, one roofer, one clothing retailer, or one chiropractor. Community web sites are truly a win-win-win situation. Participating businesses win by getting a fully functioning and regularly updated site for a fraction of what it would cost each individually. Community residents win by getting news and information localized to their specific area along with convenient online access to products and services offered by community businesses. And you win by building a successful and profitable business.

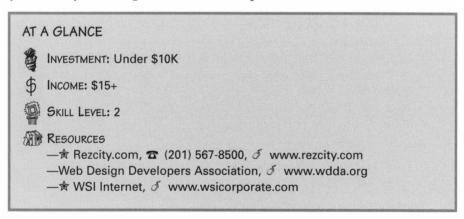

AT A GLANCE

INVESTMENT: Under $10K

INCOME: $15+

SKILL LEVEL: 2

RESOURCES
— ✶ Rezcity.com, ☎ (201) 567-8500, ♂ www.rezcity.com
— Web Design Developers Association, ♂ www.wdda.org
— ✶ WSI Internet, ♂ www.wsicorporate.com

eBay Business

Can you make big money selling stuff on eBay? Yes, you can, just like thousands of other people are already doing. The first decision you will need to make is to choose what types of things you are going to sell—new products, used products, or both. Of course, anything from toys to collectibles to DVDs can be sold on eBay for big profits, and all from the comforts of home. If you are going to sell new products, you will need to find a cheap and reliable source. Your options include buying in bulk from liquidators, wholesalers, importers, distributors, or directly from manufacturers. If you are going to sell used products, a little more leg work will be needed to maintain an inventory of saleable merchandise. Depending on the things you plan to sell, used products can be bought cheaply by scouring flea markets, garage sales, auction sales, and estate sales. Collectibles of every sort are always very popular items to sell on eBay. EBay is as wide as it is deep, so you should spend lots of time on the site, take advantage of its sponsored workshops, and read books about eBay selling to further your knowledge before you get started. Additional information about selling on eBay is found in Chapter 5.

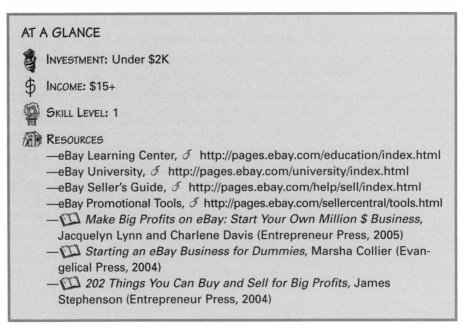

AT A GLANCE

INVESTMENT: Under $2K

INCOME: $15+

SKILL LEVEL: 1

RESOURCES
—eBay Learning Center, ♂ http://pages.ebay.com/education/index.html
—eBay University, ♂ http://pages.ebay.com/university/index.html
—eBay Seller's Guide, ♂ http://pages.ebay.com/help/sell/index.html
—eBay Promotional Tools, ♂ http://pages.ebay.com/sellercentral/tools.html
—*Make Big Profits on eBay: Start Your Own Million $ Business*, Jacquelyn Lynn and Charlene Davis (Entrepreneur Press, 2005)
—*Starting an eBay Business for Dummies*, Marsha Collier (Evangelical Press, 2004)
—*202 Things You Can Buy and Sell for Big Profits*, James Stephenson (Entrepreneur Press, 2004)

eBay Drop-Off Store

There are lots of people who would love to sell their unwanted stuff on eBay, but don't have the time or know-how to do it. Perhaps you are one of these people. Whether you are or not, some of the hottest new business opportunities are eBay drop-off stores. How does it work? Customers drop off items they want sold, and the eBay drop-off store does the rest—takes photographs, writes product descriptions, lists the item on eBay, packs and ships the item once sold, collects payment, and pays customers their portion, less the commission, which, depending on value, can be as high as 50 percent with listing fees. For people without the time or knowledge to sell the item themselves, paying the commission is well worth it. In most instances, the store will probably be able to sell the product for more because of better photographs, product descriptions, and marketing and exposure within the eBay site. Ideally, your eBay drop-off store should be located in a commercial retail storefront with set business hours. However, if you live in a small town or rural area where business volume is unlikely to support such expenditures, you can open and operate your store from home, and even go one step further and offer free and convenient pickup of items to be sold.

AT A GLANCE

INVESTMENT: Varies

$ INCOME: Varies

SKILL LEVEL: 1

RESOURCES
—eBay Learning Center, ♂ http://pages.ebay.com/education/index.html
—eBay University, ♂ http://pages.ebay.com/university/index.html
—eBay Seller's Guide, ♂ http://pages.ebay.com/help/sell/index.html
—eBay Promotional Tools, ♂ http://pages.ebay.com/sellercentral/tools.html
—☆ i-Sold it, ♂ www.i-soldit.com
—☆ Quick Drop, ♂ www.quickdrop.com

Art Dealer

Dealing in oil and watercolor paintings, ink drawings, sculptures in stone, wood, and iron, and a host of other fine art and folk art mediums can be the basis for a personally rewarding business and a great way to help supplement your retirement income. You can focus on either new art or resale and collector art. New original works of art can be purchased directly from local, national, or even world artists, as well as from companies that specialize in original art work wholesaling, such as the ones listed as follows. Previously owned and collectible original artworks can be purchased at auctions, estate sales, online marketplaces, and through private-seller classified ads. You may even stumble across the occasional rare and valuable piece of art at a garage sale if you are prepared to devote the time. Establish your own web site for promotion and sales, utilize eBay and other online marketplaces for sales, organize and host art auctions, and establish a homebased art gallery supported by local advertising and featuring weekly or monthly shows. Combine all of these selling methods to ensure maximum exposure and sales. When dealing in fine art and original folk art, you can never have enough knowledge. Therefore, invest in art value guides, study art books, join art clubs and societies, and network with artists and art dealers to learn as much as you can about the art world.

AT A GLANCE

 INVESTMENT: Under $2K

 INCOME: Varies

 SKILL LEVEL: 1–2

 RESOURCES
—Folk Art, folk art marketplace, ♂ www.folk-art.com
—Oil Painting Wholesale, ☎ (626) 308-0682, ♂ www.oilpaintingwhole sale.com
—The World Artist Directory, ♂ www.worldartistdirectory.com
—📖 *Davenport's Art Reference & Price Guide, Gordon's Art Reference,* ☎ (800) 892-4622, ♂ www.gordonsart.com

---

Homebased Rental Business

Rental businesses have long been a popular moneymaker for many reasons, but mainly because of cost. Most people can afford to shell out a few hundred dollars to rent an RV or front-loader for a week. That is the focus of this opportunity. Working from home you can earn big profits renting just about every type of product or equipment imaginable. Traditionally, the best items to rent for profits are things like tools, small watercraft, portable hot tubs, construction equipment, recreational vehicles, movie props, musical instruments, office furniture and equipment, computer hardware, especially items like notebook computers and power point projectors, canoes and kayaks, and camping equipment. Generally, rental items are things people need temporarily. The investment needed to start can be high depending on the types of products and equipment that you purchase for rent. However, you can minimize costs by purchasing items in good condition secondhand by scouring classified ads, business closeouts, auction sales, and liquidation sales. You may even elect to find owners of the products you want to rent and start a rental pool, keeping a percentage of the fees for providing management services. As a general guideline small items typically rent for 3 to 5 percent of their value per day, 10 percent per week, and 20 percent on a monthly rental.

AT A GLANCE

INVESTMENT: Varies

INCOME: Varies

SKILL LEVEL: 1

RESOURCES
—Entrepreneur Online, small business portal, ♂ www.entrepreneur.com
—☆ Party America, ♂ www.partyamerica.com/franchise_system.html

Antique Dealer

Replicas, inflated prices, and items in poor condition are a few reasons why you need to hone your knowledge and skills if you choose to buy and sell antiques as a business. But if you've had antique collecting as a hobby or take the time required to become a knowledgable antique expert, you may be rewarded with big profits and very gratifying work. The world of antiques is very broad, so pick an area in which to specialize—furniture, art, farm implements, or architectural antiques to maximize the potential for success. The best places to dig up antique treasures include garage sales, auctions, estate sales, and private sellers advertising in the classifieds. Secondary buying sources include flea markets, secondhand shops, and online marketplaces. Always take along your antiques hunter toolbox, which should include antique value guides, camera, flashlight, magnifying glass, angled mirror, and measuring tape. The best way to sell antiques for top dollar is directly to collectors via antique collector clubs, associations, and shows. Next to selling to collectors, antiques can also be sold through eBay and online antique buy-and-sell marketplaces, at flea markets, and directly from an antiques showroom at home, supported by community advertising, repeat business, and word-of-mouth referrals.

AT A GLANCE

 INVESTMENT: Under $10K

 INCOME: Varies

 SKILL LEVEL: 1–2

 RESOURCES
—Antique and Collectibles Dealers Association, ♂ www.antiqueand collectible.com/acda.shtml
—Go Antiques, buy and sell marketplace, ♂ www.goantiques.com
—The National Association of Antique Malls, ♂ www.antiqueand collectible.com/naam.shtml
—📖 *Kovels' Antique & Collectible Price List, 37th Edition*, Ralph Kovel and Terry Kovel (Random House, 2004)

Gift Basket Business

In terms of starting a gift basket business, you have two options: You can purchase pre-made gift baskets wholesale and resell them for a profit, or you can purchase all of the supplies to create unique one-of-a-kind gift baskets from your own designs and sell these for a profit. Your decision will depend on your budget, the types of gift baskets you want to sell, and your target customers. Don't fret if you decide to make your own. Gift baskets are easy to assemble, and all of the products and the baskets are readily available from any number of wholesale sources. Simply select items such as specialty foods, fashion accessories, or lingerie, arrange in attractive wicker baskets or similar containers, wrap in decorative foil or colored plastic, and the gift basket is complete. You should concentrate your marketing efforts on gaining repeat corporate clients: professionals, small business owners, and sales professionals, such as real estate agents. Basically, focus on individuals and companies that would have a reason to regularly send gift baskets to clients. Promote your baskets using a direct mail brochure and networking with your target audience at business and social functions in your community; places like the chamber of commerce are excellent. Also sell the gift baskets at community events, from rented mall kiosk, flea markets, and public markets on weekends and holidays.

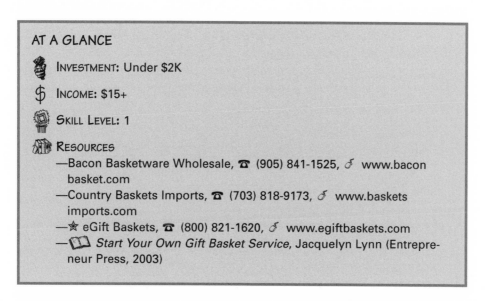

AT A GLANCE

INVESTMENT: Under $2K

$ INCOME: $15+

SKILL LEVEL: 1

RESOURCES
—Bacon Basketware Wholesale, ☎ (905) 841-1525, ♂ www.bacon basket.com
—Country Baskets Imports, ☎ (703) 818-9173, ♂ www.baskets imports.com
—★ eGift Baskets, ☎ (800) 821-1620, ♂ www.egiftbaskets.com
—📖 *Start Your Own Gift Basket Service*, Jacquelyn Lynn (Entrepreneur Press, 2003)

Flag Business

Believe it or not, flags are big business, generating millions of dollars in sales annually, and you can cash in on the craze by starting your own flag sales business. The choices are almost unlimited in terms of the kinds of flags that you can sell, from country, state, provincial, sports, marine, safety, historical reproduction, royal, military, organization, auto racing, handheld flags, windsocks, and, of course, flagpoles. Buy flags direct from manufactures and wholesalers, such as the ones featured below, or conduct a *Wholesale Flag* keyword search on any popular search engine or directory to find many more sources. There are almost as many ways to sell flags as there are different flags available. You can sell directly from home, via online marketplaces such as eBay and your own web site, and by renting booth space in malls, flea markets, consumers shows, and community events such as The Fourth of July and Flag Day celebrations. Additional income can be earned by selling flagpoles and flagpole installation services, which can be subcontracted to a local handyman on a revenue-splitting basis.

AT A GLANCE

INVESTMENT: Under $2K

$ INCOME: $15+

SKILL LEVEL: 1

RESOURCES
—American Flags Wholesale, ☎ (888) 719-9516, ♂ www.american
  -flags-wholesale.com
—National Independent Flag Dealers Association, ♂ www.flaginfo.com
—Patriotic Flags Wholesale, ☎ (866) 798-2803, ♂ www.patriotic-
  flags.com
—Sav-On Wholesale, ☎ (888) 662-1097, ♂ www.sav-on-wholesale.com

Coin Laundry

By the end of the year, all of that change customers have pumped into your coin laundry machines can add up to thousands of dollars in profit. Coin laundries have been around for decades, and in spite of the fact that washer and dryer sets can often be purchased for less than $1,000, coin laundries continue to thrive and earn big bucks for their owners. Why? Simply because not everyone has the space or the need to own laundry equipment, especially students, pleasure travelers, business travelers, and people living in small accommodations. The key to success in the coin laundry business is location, location, and location. You must set up your laundry in an area comprised mostly of your target audience. Therefore, think college and university districts, areas close to campgrounds and RV parks, and areas with many older style apartment buildings that do not have in-building coin laundries. Offering additional services such as a laundry drop-off, wash-and-fold, ironing, alterations, and a dry-cleaning depot can greatly increase revenues and profits. Likewise, selling products such as soaps and snacks from vending machines will add a few hundred dollars to the kitty each month.

AT A GLANCE

INVESTMENT: Over $25K

$ INCOME: Varies

SKILL LEVEL: 1

RESOURCES
—ACE Commercial Laundry Equipment, ♂ www.usedlaundryequip
  ment.com
—Best Buy Laundry, new and used coin laundry equipment sales,
  ☎ (800) 553-9788, ♂ www.bestbuylaundry.com
—📖 *Start Your Own Coin-Operated Laundry*, Mandy Erickson (Entre-
  preneur Press, 2003)
—United States Small Business Administration (SBA), ♂ www.sba.gov

Flower Kiosk

Diamonds may be a girl's best friend, but flowers are a close second. They cost a whole lot less. Providing you can secure the right high-traffic operating location(s), a fresh-cut flower vending business can be extremely profitable, as markups of 300 percent or more are common. One of the best ways to sell fresh-cut flowers is from a portable or fixed kiosk. Professional flower kiosks are available for purchase, or if you or someone in the family is a handyperson, one can be constructed for less than $1,000. Great operating locations include malls, transit stations, public markets, farmers' markets, and even a place near a larger retailer such as a grocery store or building supply retailer that does not sell fresh-cut flowers. Roses, mums, carnations, daisies, and other varieties of best-selling flowers can be purchased wholesale from flower distributors. Depending on the location, fresh-cut flowers can be sold full- or part-time, or seasonally during Christmas, Valentine's Day, Mother's Day, and Thanksgiving. If you are truly innovative, you can even combine travel and selling flowers by towing your kiosk behind your RV and selling flowers all around the country to fund your travel adventures.

AT A GLANCE

INVESTMENT: Under $2K

$ INCOME: $15+

SKILL LEVEL: 1

RESOURCES
—Anthuriums International, wholesale flower sales, ♂ www.flower
  sales.com

> —Carriage Works, vending cart manufacturer, ☎ (541) 882-9661,
>   🌀 www.carriageworks.com
> —Florabundance, wholesale flower sales, 🌀 www.florabundance.com

Flea Market Vendor

There are an estimated 750,000 flea market vendors peddling their wares at more than 10,000 flea markets, bazaars, and swap meets in the United States and Canada. Some flea markets attract crowds in excess of 25,000 a day. Flea market vendors are professionals and amateurs, working full-time, part-time, seasonally, or only occasionally. It is not unusual for vendors to earn as much as $50,000 a year working only a few days a week! Flea markets are everywhere. But don't judge a flea market by size alone. Instead, conduct research by visiting a few before deciding where to set up shop. Check out other vendors: What do they sell, how much are they charging, how much are they selling, and how many are selling the same things as you? Check out people in attendance: Are they buying or browsing, how many are there, and do they meet your target customer profile? There are also many types of flea markets—weekends only, everyday, summer only, outside under tent, open air, and inside in swanky buildings resembling mall retailing more than flea market vending. All have their pros and cons. Booth rents vary widely from a low of $5 per day to as much as $100 for single-day events. Other considerations include customer and vendor parking, electricity, phone lines for credit card and debit card terminals, on-site ATM machine, washrooms, food services, and overall organization. As a general rule, the best new products to sell are dollar store items: toys, hand and power tools, crafts, costume jewelry, sunglasses, auto parts, and novelty products, all of which can be purchased dirt cheap from wholesalers and liquidators. The best previously owned products to sell are glassware, antiques, collectibles, toys, tools, children's clothing, vintage clothing, and books. Finding these items for resale will require you to scour garage sales, auctions, and estate sales. In most cases, you will need a vendor permit and sales tax ID number, and some flea markets also require vendors to have liability insurance. Overall, flea market vending is an excellent way to supplement your retirement income, and you can even combine travel plans and sell your products at flea markets all over the country.

Vending Cart Business

Big bucks can be earned full- or part-time buying products such as T-shirts, crafts, art, jewelry, sunglasses, watches, souvenirs, umbrellas, and hats at dirt-cheap wholesale prices, and reselling them for a profit from portable vending carts. If you plan on selling from public lands and buildings, you will need to contact your local city or municipal government to inquire about street vending opportunities. On federally owned lands or buildings, contact the U.S. General Services Administration, at ☎ (877) 472-3779, ♂ www.gsa.gov, to inquire about opportunities. In addition to a vendor's permit, you may also have to obtain liability insurance, a health permit, and fire permit depending on goods sold. Vending permits are, however, usually not required if you operate from a privately-owned location such as lumberyard or car wash parking lots.

Before you decide what type of product(s) to sell, do the rounds. What are other vendors selling? Who is the busiest? Which days are they busiest? Who are their customers? Duplicating a successful business model is one of the easiest ways to eliminate or substantially reduce financial risk. Vendors can work from portable kiosks and pushcarts or right from a suitcase depending on what they sell. Depending on your budget, you can rent, lease, or purchase new and used pushcarts and kiosks, which come in many styles and price points. Some can be towed behind vehicles or placed on a trailer for transportation, some are motorized, and other are pedal powered. Also be sure to invest in wireless payment processing technology so you can accept credit cards and debit cards on site. This gives you a huge competitive advantage over vendors who do not offer these payment options, greatly increases impulse buying, and reduces the risk of theft because you have little cash on hand. Remember, vendors are never wallflowers. You must love what you do and what you sell and be extremely comfortable talking with people.

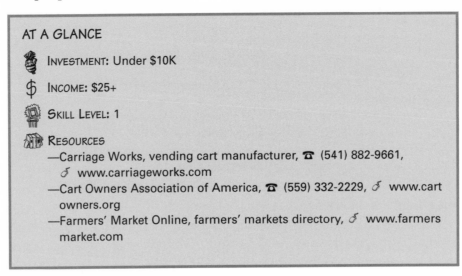

AT A GLANCE

INVESTMENT: Under $10K

INCOME: $25+

SKILL LEVEL: 1

RESOURCES
—Carriage Works, vending cart manufacturer, ☎ (541) 882-9661, ✄ www.carriageworks.com
—Cart Owners Association of America, ☎ (559) 332-2229, ✄ www.cart owners.org
—Farmers' Market Online, farmers' markets directory, ✄ www.farmers market.com

Garage Sale Business

An estimated 60 million people go garage sale shopping annually in the United States. If each spent $20, total sales would rack up more than $1 billion a year! Needless to say, starting a garage sale business has the potential to supplement your retirement income with big profits. A garage sale business is simple: Buy good quality used items at low prices by attending auction sales, flea markets, other garage sales, estate sales, and private seller classified ads, and resell these items at a profit at your own garage sales. You don't want neighbors calling city hall complaining every time you have a sale, so keep sales professional and noise to a minimum. A recent poll conducted by GarageSalePlanet.com asked garage sale enthusiasts what day of the week they liked best to go garage sale shopping. It was no surprise Saturday was number one by a landslide, but Friday beat out Sunday for the number-two spot. Of course, what you really want to know is what items sell the best. All products in good clean working order, but more specifically power tools, hand tools, toys, sporting goods, kitchen items, glassware, things for babies, lawn and garden equipment, crafts and decorations, collectibles, books, music and movie discs, kids clothing, and adult designer clothes. Professional merchandising is also important, and if you are going to regularly hold garage sales, invest in folding display tables, display cases with casters for easy transportation, and even a portable gazebo tent to keep both rain and sun off you, customers, and the merchandise. Skip having a garage sale every weekend, instead collect highly saleable items over time and hold a sale once a month. It won't take long for word to spread about your monthly sales of great merchandise; garage sale enthusiasts talk. Also, ask customers for their e-mail addresses so you can keep them informed when the next sale is taking place, as well as about the items for sale.

AT A GLANCE

 INVESTMENT: Under $2K

 INCOME: $15+

 SKILL LEVEL: 1

 RESOURCES
—Garage Sales Daily, U.S. garage sale directory, ♂ www.garagesale daily.com
—Garage Sale Planet, U.S. garage sale directory, ♂ www.garagesale planet.com
—Local Yard Sales, Canadian garage sale directory, ♂ www.localyard sales.com
—Yard Sales Search, U.S. garage sale directory, ♂ www.yardsale search.com

---

Party-in-a-Box Business

With everybody leading such busy lives, who has time to stop and buy all of the paper products and novelty items needed to throw one heck of a party? This reason alone is a strong argument for starting a party-in-a-box business. The concept is very straightforward. Prepare all of the products people would need to throw a party, all conveniently packaged in one box. Your customers simply open the box, decorate, and hand out the party favors to guests, and that's it. Depending on the theme of the party—children's birthday, adult birthday, retirement, anniversary, special achievement, bachelor, bachlorette, engagement, wedding, Christmas, News Years, Fourth of July, or any other event—each box can contain hats, flowers, banners, ribbons, balloons, pi–atas, invitations, streamers, glow sticks, noisemakers, games, confetti, and other party supplies.

All of these products can be purchased in bulk at deeply discounted wholesale prices from party product distributors, such as the ones listed below. Advertise in your local newspaper and by pinning promotional fliers to bulletin boards, and be sure to build working relationships with event and party planners, restaurants, and day-care centers, because all can be good sources for referral and repeat business. Let customers order by phone, fax, and e-mail, and offer free local delivery.

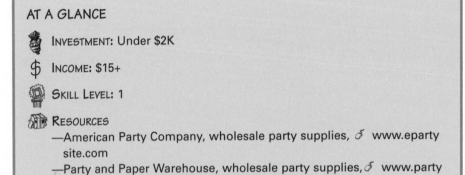

AT A GLANCE

INVESTMENT: Under $2K

INCOME: $15+

SKILL LEVEL: 1

RESOURCES
—American Party Company, wholesale party supplies, ☞ www.eparty site.com
—Party and Paper Warehouse, wholesale party supplies, ☞ www.party andpaperwarehouse.com
—Shindigz, wholesale party supplies, ☞ www.shindigz.com

Collectibles Dealer

Just think, throughout America, Canada, and much of the world, stuffed away in dusty attics or forgotten in dark basements are literally millions of collectibles worth many more millions of dollars to collectors around the globe. And you can cash in on the collectibles craze by becoming a collectibles dealer, buying low and reselling high. This is definitely one of the better ways to supplement your retirement income because there is huge profit potential and you can have a whole lot of fun in the process. Collectibles is a very broad subject, and can include items from vintage dolls, antique toys, comic books, trading cards, vintage advertising items, military collectibles, prints and posters, music memorabilia, and almost anything else people collect. Needless to say, you'll need to specialize. You will also need to invest in collectibles' pricing guides specific to the collectibles you buy and sell. Finding collectibles at rock-bottom prices is not overly difficult; it just requires you to invest time scouring garage sales, flea markets, estate sales, and auction sales in search of bargains. Selling collectibles is easy because there is a gigantic market for them. You can sell online via eBay and collectors' marketplaces, at flea markets, antique and collectors' shows, from a retail storefront, or from a home-based collectibles showroom.

AT A GLANCE

 INVESTMENT: Under $2K

 INCOME: Varies

 SKILL LEVEL: 1

 RESOURCES
—Antique and Collectibles Dealers Association, ♂ www.antiqueand
   collectible.com/acda.shtml
—Antiques Web, ♂ www.antiquesweb.com
—The National Association of Antique Malls, ♂ www.antiqueand
   collectible.com/naam.shtml
—The Online Collector, ♂ www.theonlinecollector.com

Vintage Clothing Dealer

How do you strike it rich in the vintage clothing business? You start by spending weekends at flea markets, garage sales, estate sales, and auctions looking for vintage clothing and fashion accessories, such as hats, shoes, handbags, and scarves. Just think, you could uncover a Chanel suit from the 1960s, which now can fetch up to $5,000, stumble across a pair of Levi blue jeans from the turn of the last century, which can net you $10,000, or happen to find a vintage Emilo Pucci dress, which sells for well into the five-figure range. You simply cannot go wrong buying vintage clothing and reselling it, providing you know what to buy and how much to pay. Consequently, you need to educate yourself about the value of vintage clothing and accessories. The best way to do this is by purchasing and studying vintage clothing pricing guides, such as the ones listed below. The items you purchase can be resold for a profit directly to collectors and vintage clothing retailers or through vintage clothing online marketplaces and eBay. You may also want to convert a spare room in your home into a vintage clothing boutique and advertise your products locally and by word-of-mouth via wedding and event planners.

AT A GLANCE

 INVESTMENT: Under $2K

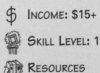

$ INCOME: $15+

SKILL LEVEL: 1

RESOURCES
—Antiques Web, vintage clothing collectors and retailers directory,
⚲ www.antiqueweb.com/links/clothingandfashion.html
—Linda White Antique Clothing, vintage clothing and accessories
buyer, ☎ (508) 529-4439, ⚲ www.vintageclothing.com
—📖 *The Official Price Guide to Vintage Fashion and Fabric*, Pamela
Smith (House of Collectables, 2001)
—📖 *The Vintage Fashion Directory: The National Sourcebook of Vintage Fashion Retailers*, Daniela Turdich (Streamline Press, 2002),
which lists every vintage clothing retailer in the United States

Used Sporting Goods Sales

Buying and selling used sporting goods is a business opportunity that is sure to be lots of fun and keep you active. It is potentially very profitable, especially if you specialize in high-end gear such as parasailing, scuba diving, or skiing equipment. But with that said, all types of used sports equipment can be bought and resold for a profit. Equipment such as treadmills, weight benches, golf clubs, hockey equipment, windsurfers, kayaks, canoes, bicycles, hunting equipment, trampolines, gymnastic mats, and tennis rackets are just the tip of the iceberg. Secondhand sports equipment can be purchased in many ways: garage sales, sports swap meets, estate sales, auctions, and private seller print and electronic classified ads. Used sporting equipment can be resold utilizing many of the same methods—online advertising, flea markets, sporting equipment swap meets, classified ads, and a well-stocked homebased business supported by repeat and referral business. There is also a big market for vintage and collectible sports equipment. If you have an eye for spotting good buys, then this is definitely an area to investigate further.

AT A GLANCE

INVESTMENT: Under $2K

$ INCOME: Varies

SKILL LEVEL: 1

Fishing Tackle and Bait Sales

For all you entrepreneurial fishing enthusiasts out there, great profits can be earned in the fishing tackle and bait business. On the tackle side of the business you can buy products such as rods, reels, lures, and anything else fishing related at wholesale prices from distributors or direct from tackle manufacturers. On the bait side, you can either purchase bait wholesale to resell or raise or catch your own bait to sell. Either way, a prerequisite is not to have an aversion to creepy, crawly things like worms and leaches because they will be two of your best income producers. Bait minnows, like shiners, can be caught in rivers and creeks using traps or a seine net. Or if you have the required space, you can install a minnow-breeding pond. If you catch or raise bait, a license issued by the Department of Fisheries is generally required, so be sure to check local regulations. Dew worms, aka night crawlers, are another bait. You can raise them in soil and moss boxes or purchase wholesale from worm farms and worm-picking crews working golf courses after the sun goes down. As mentioned, leeches are another bait that can be raised or purchased in larger quantities wholesale and resold in smaller quantities for a profit. The best ways to sell fishing tackle and bait are from a homebased tackle shop, selling online through eBay and fishing-related marketplaces, and at fishing and hunting shows. If you raise your own bait, you can also sell to bait shops in volume at wholesale pricing.

AT A GLANCE

INVESTMENT: Under $10K

$ INCOME: $15+

SKILL LEVEL: 1

RESOURCES
—Bait Net, industry information and links, ✆ www.baitnet.com

—Forked Tree Ranch, bait wholesale, ☎ (208) 267-2632, ♂ www.forked treeranch.com

—National Bait Wholesale, ☎ (905) 278-0180,♂ www.nationalbait.com

—Pokee Fishing Tackle Manufacturing, ☎ 8620-32234203 (China), ♂ www.pokeefishing.com

—Tackle Making, fishing tackle information portal, ♂ www.tackle making.com

—📖 *Shield Publications*, books on raising bait for profit, ♂ www.worm books.com

—📖 *The Complete Book of Tackle Making*, C. Boyd Pfeiffer (The Lyons Press, 1999)

Golf Ball Printing Business

Golf ball printing is a terrific moneymaking opportunity for just about everyone because all you need to get started in the multimillion dollar personalized golf ball industry is to purchase golf balls in bulk at wholesale prices and a simple and inexpensive pad printer. The rest is pretty easy. Market the business, take orders, print golf balls, and you're away and running. For those not familiar with personalized golf balls, they are nothing more than common golf balls that are printed with a person's name, a business name and/or logo, or the name of an organization. Personalized golf balls make fantastic gifts for the golf fanatic, as well as for businesses of all sizes to give to clients as appreciation gifts and at golf tournaments. This business is easy to start, and the low-mess and zero noise aspects of the printing equipment means you only need minimal working space, such as a spare bedroom, garage, or basement. Finding customers is not difficult because America is golf nuts and every golfer loves to have his or her name boldly printed on golf balls. Advertise locally in the newspaper, take online orders, exhibit at golf and recreation shows, and sell through golf retailers, pro shops, and golf courses on a revenue-share program. Landing business and corporate customers is as easy as designing and implementing a direct mail promotional campaign describing your products, prices, and ordering information.

AT A GLANCE

  INVESTMENT: Under $10K

 INCOME: $25+

> SKILL LEVEL: 1
>
> RESOURCES
>   —Apiona, golf ball manufacturer, ♂ www.apiona.com
>   —KingBo Golf, golf ball manufacturer, ♂ www.kingbo-golf.com
>   —Printex USA, golf ball pad printing equipment, ♂ www.printex usa.com
>   —Winon USA, golf ball pad printing equipment, ☎ (716) 400-8966, ♂ www.winonusa.com

Jewelry Dealer

Lots or cold hard cash can be earned buying and selling fine jewelry, especially secondhand jewelry purchased at distress prices. When money is needed in a hurry, often the first belonging people sell off at fire sale prices is fine jewelry— rings, watches, necklaces, bracelets, and diamond earrings. You see the ads all the time in the classifieds, "Diamond ring, must sell, worth $5,000 will take $1,000 or best offer." In addition to buying from private sellers through the classifieds, you can also purchase fine jewelry at auctions and estates sales. You will need to educate yourself about fine jewelry and values because when you are dealing in purchases of $1,000 to $10,000, the last thing you want to do is learn by trial and error. You can also specialize in costume jewelry sales. It has the benefit of reduced financial risk because except for antique costume jewelry, most sells for a fraction of the value of fine jewelry. Billions of dollars worth of costume jewelry is sold annually, especially earrings, rings, necklaces, and broaches. You can make a financial killing by purchasing costume jewelry at super low prices directly from manufacturers, wholesalers, and even local craftspeople and reselling for ten times your cost in some cases. Fine jewelry can be sold to collectors using classified ads, through auctions, and via online marketplaces. The best sales venues for costume jewelry are online marketplaces such as eBay, flea markets, kiosk sales in malls and markets, from a cart at community events, and hosting monthly costume jewelry parties.

> AT A GLANCE
>
> INVESTMENT: Under $10K

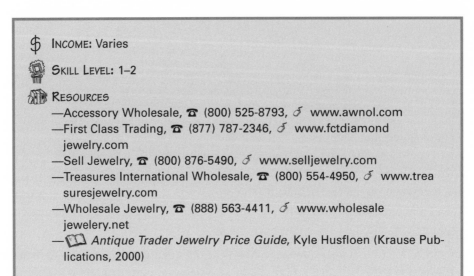

$ INCOME: Varies

SKILL LEVEL: 1–2

RESOURCES
—Accessory Wholesale, ☎ (800) 525-8793, ♂ www.awnol.com
—First Class Trading, ☎ (877) 787-2346, ♂ www.fctdiamond jewelry.com
—Sell Jewelry, ☎ (800) 876-5490, ♂ www.selljewelry.com
—Treasures International Wholesale, ☎ (800) 554-4950, ♂ www.treasuresjewelry.com
—Wholesale Jewelry, ☎ (888) 563-4411, ♂ www.wholesale jewelery.net
—📖 *Antique Trader Jewelry Price Guide*, Kyle Husfloen (Krause Publications, 2000)

Secondhand Furniture Sales

Strike it rich cashing in on the rising demand for good quality secondhand furniture. Start your own homebased used furniture sales business. There are numerous sources for good quality secondhand furniture: private sellers advertising in the classifieds, flier advertisements on community bulletin boards, estate, auction, garage, and moving sales, moving companies, and public storage businesses. In addition to selling used furniture from a homebased showroom, you can also utilize flea markets and even eBay if you happen to purchase a rare, cool, retro, or otherwise valuable piece of secondhand furniture that you know will command top dollar when exposed to a global audience of consumers. To maximize profitability on each sale, make sure all furniture is fit to sell by thoroughly cleaning everything before selling. The investment made in furniture polish, the odd repair, and an upholstery steam cleaning machine will be well rewarded with a higher selling price. You will also need to invest in suitable transportation such as a van or pickup truck and basic equipment such as a moving dolly.

AT A GLANCE

INVESTMENT: Under $2K

$ INCOME: $15+

SKILL LEVEL: 1

 RESOURCES
—Best Consignment Shop Inventory Software, ✂ www.bestconsign
mentshopsoftware.com
—Entrepreneur, small business information portal, ✂ www.entrepre
neurpress.com
—Flea Market USA, national flea market directory, indexed by state,
✂ www.fleausa.com

Used Building Products Sales

A small fortune can be made buying reclaimed building products such as bricks, lumber, kitchen cabinets, plumbing fixtures, windows, doors, hardware, ceiling tins, fireplace mantels, light fixtures, patio stones, and hardwood flooring cheap and reselling for a profit. The value of used building products has soared in recent years as the price of new materials has skyrocketed. Especially valuable are architectural antiques such as clear stock casings, stained glass windows, columns and capitals, claw-foot bathtubs, and cut-glass doorknobs. The primary buying sources for reclaimed building products are contractors specializing in renovations, flooring installers, window replacement companies, demolition companies, plumbers, and homeowners doing their own renovations. Build alliances with these companies so that you can get first dibs on the best and most valuable reclaimed building products as they become available. Equally valuable are barn board, barn timbers, and split cedar rail fencing. Go for a drive in the country and strike deals with farmers—they demolish old barns and you sell the products, splitting the proceeds on a 50–50 basis. Sell to homeowners, collectors, designers, and architects through online used building materials marketplaces and by advertising the materials offline in classified advertising and magazines catering to heritage home restoration. This is very much a business that is fueled by repeat customers and word-of-mouth referral. It does not take long to build a very substantial customer base, providing you can consistently source and offer excellent quality products for resale.

AT A GLANCE

 INVESTMENT: Under $2K

INCOME: Varies

 SKILL LEVEL: 1

RESOURCES
—Architectural Antiques, buy-and-sell marketplace, ✆ www.architec
turals.net
—National Demolition Association, ☎ (215) 348-4949, ✆ www.demolition
association.com
—The Used Building Materials Association, ✆ www.ubma.org
—Used Building Materials Exchange, buy-and-sell marketplace, ✆ www
.build.recycle.net

New and Used Book Sales

Book lovers take notice, buying and selling new, used, and rare books is a fantastic opportunity with incredible upside profit potential. You can buy new books from book distributors, wholesalers, liquidators, retailer returns, and direct from publishers at deeply discounted prices that can often reach 80 percent off cover price. One of the best ways to sell is on Amazon, right alongside the new books they sell, but for slightly less to entice people to buy yours. You can also hold monthly book sales by renting empty storefronts for a few days, through other online book marketplaces, at flea markets, and by renting mall kiosk space, especially close to Christmas. Specialty books can be sold by mail order supported by advertising in publications related to the book titles for sale. And if there is limited competition in your area, you can even convert a room in your home and sell new books right from home. Some new book sellers even go as far as selling their books online at cost plus listing fees or commissions and make their money on the shipping charges. Likewise, you also have the potential to hit the jackpot if you specialize in rare items such as first editions, antique books, and author autographed copies. There are an infinite number of used books available to be purchased at rock bottom prices. You can buy them at garage sales, flea markets, online marketplaces, auctions, estate sales, library sales, and secondhand shops. Few people take the time to find out the true value of the books they are selling, and because of this, many rare and valuable books can be purchased for little. You will want to invest in rare book pricing guides so you are armed with the resources needed to make wise purchasing decisions. Whether or not the books you sell are run-of-the mill used books for $10 or rare ones worth hundreds, the internet is your best marketing tool. List books for sale on Amazon, eBay, and Abebooks, the biggest used and collector book marketplace on the net. If you plan on volume selling, invest in barcode scanning software such as Scanner Pal ♂ www.scoutpal.com, which automatically scans all book information retrieved from the barcode for simple listing.

AT A GLANCE

🏺 INVESTMENT: Under $2K

$ INCOME: $15+

🗿 SKILL LEVEL: 1

📕 RESOURCES
—Abebooks, buy-and-sell marketplace, ♂ www.abebooks.com
—Baker & Taylor, new book distributor, ☎ (800) 775-1800, ♂ www.btol.com
—Independent Publishers Group, ☎ (800) 888-4741, ♂ www.ipgbook.com
—Ingram Book Group, new book distributor, ♂ www.ingrambook.com
—International Rare Book Collectors Association, ♂ www.rarebooks.org
—National Book Network, ☎ (717) 794-3800, ♂ www.nbnbooks.com
—Used Book Central, buy-and-sell marketplace, ♂ www.usedbookcentral.com
—📖 *Bookman's Price Index: A Guide to the Values of Rare and Other Out of Print Books*, Anne F. McGrath (Gale Group, 2004)

Home Medical Equipment Sales

As I have mentioned many times throughout this book, the trend in North America is toward an aging population. As a result, a terrific business opportunity is buying and reselling home medical equipment for a profit. Get started by converting your garage or basement into a lavish showroom stocked with the best quality previously owned home medical equipment. Best selling products include power and manual wheelchairs, walkers, mechanical lifts and slings, scooters, and bath safety products. Use your powerful negotiation skills to buy these products at low prices through online marketplaces and from private sellers advertising in classified ads, as well as at auctions and estate sales. In addition to selling medical products from home, you can also design a web site for online sales, display at health fairs, and sell through eBay and online used medical equipment portals. Thoroughly cleaning and tuning up all equipment, as well as providing a warranty, will greatly increase the value of your inventory and maximize the profitability on every sale. Also be sure to build alliances with doctors, therapists, and chiropractors, so they can refer your business to their clients in need of home medical equipment.

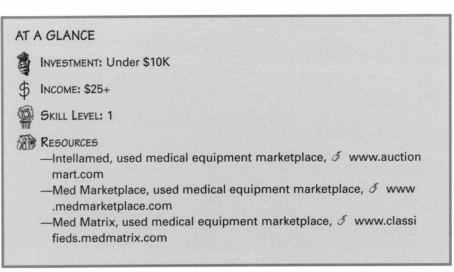

AT A GLANCE

INVESTMENT: Under $10K

INCOME: $25+

SKILL LEVEL: 1

RESOURCES
—Intellamed, used medical equipment marketplace, ♂ www.auction
    mart.com
—Med Marketplace, used medical equipment marketplace, ♂ www
    .medmarketplace.com
—Med Matrix, used medical equipment marketplace, ♂ www.classi
    fieds.medmatrix.com

Grocery Shopping Service

As the population continues to age, starting and operating a simple grocery shopping and delivery services is a very timely opportunity that is guaranteed to keep you busy and earning money. Your customers can fax, call in, or e-mail their supermarket orders to you. The rest is pretty easy: pick up their groceries at the supermarket and deliver the order. You will need reliable transportation, as well as a small cash float to pay for orders. Once the groceries have been delivered, you are reimbursed for costs plus your fee, which should be set as a minimum, perhaps in the range of $20 to $25. Keep in mind, seniors are not the only potential customers; anyone too busy or without transportation is also a potential customer. Advertise in classified ads, delivering fliers to homes, and posting fliers on community notice boards. Once word is out about your convenient, quick, and affordable grocery shopping service, you will probably have more work than you can handle. In addition to groceries, you can also providing shopping and delivery services for prescription medications, pet foods, wine and spirits, takeout food orders, and trips to the hardware store, especially if your vehicle is large enough to carry lumber.

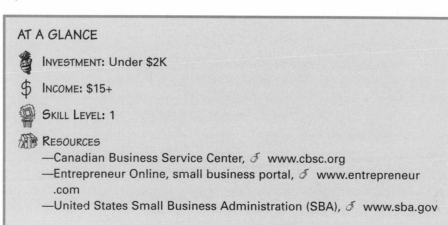

AT A GLANCE

💰 INVESTMENT: Under $2K

$ INCOME: $15+

🎛 SKILL LEVEL: 1

🏚 RESOURCES
—Canadian Business Service Center, ✂ www.cbsc.org
—Entrepreneur Online, small business portal, ✂ www.entrepreneur .com
—United States Small Business Administration (SBA), ✂ www.sba.gov

Catering

Turn your love of food and your incredible cooking skills into a gold mine by starting your own full-service catering business. Weddings, parties, corporate meetings, anniversaries, graduations, grand openings, product launches, tours and trips, and just about any other type of social function or business event can be catered for big profits. Catering is not a particularly easy business to start, especially if you want to do it right, because you will need to set up a fully equipped and permitted commercial kitchen in your own home or, if space or zoning do not allow, rent commercial space or strike a deal with a restaurant to share kitchen space in exchange for rent or a cut of the profits. Likewise, you will need to invest in cooking equipment, dishes, utensils, uniforms for staff, and a number of other items required to offer full-service catering. Cooking, serving, and bar staff can be hired on an as-needed basis. But catering can be a very profitable business venture for those truly motivated to succeed. Additional revenues can also be earned by providing valet parking services, coat-check services, and by renting party items such as tents, tables, chairs, and public address systems to your clients to create a more all-inclusive service.

AT A GLANCE

💰 INVESTMENT: Varies

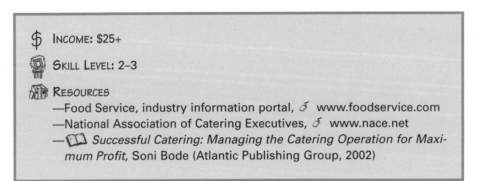

$ INCOME: $25+

SKILL LEVEL: 2–3

RESOURCES
—Food Service, industry information portal, ♂ www.foodservice.com
—National Association of Catering Executives, ♂ www.nace.net
—📖 *Successful Catering: Managing the Catering Operation for Maximum Profit*, Soni Bode (Atlantic Publishing Group, 2002)

Personal Chef

Take your pots and pans, cooking skills, and love of food mobile, and hit the road as a personal chef for hire. Prepare gourmet meals for people hosting house parties, special occasion events such as birthdays or anniversaries, and corporate luncheons—basically anywhere there is a kitchen on-site that you can use to create your mouth watering gourmet masterpieces. Personal chef services are quickly becoming a popular alternative for people who do not have the budget for a full-scale catered event and for others hosting small gatherings not requiring complete catering services. The advantages for start-up in comparison to a full-service catering business are apparent: low overhead and initial investment, full-time or part-time operating hours, and easy management from home. That may appeal to people who want to slow down, but at the same time want to have an excellent income doing something they love. Promote your personal chef services by joining business associations and community social clubs to network and spread the word about your business and menu. The service can easily be supported by word-of-mouth advertising and repeat business once established, providing the food is great and the service is second-to-none. Additionally, building alliances with party planners and event coordinators is also sure to land work. Rates vary according to factors such as the supply of food and the type of menu requested. However, average earning are $35 to $50 per hour.

AT A GLANCE

INVESTMENT: Under $2K

$ INCOME: $25+

SKILL LEVEL: 2–3

RESOURCES
—American Personal Chef Association, ☎ (800) 644-8389, ♂ www.per
sonalchef.com
—United Stated Personal Chef Association, ♂ www.uspca.com
—📖 *Become a Personal Chef: An Introduction to the Industry*, Brian
T. Koning (Authorhouse, 2004)

Mobile Cooking Classes

Does everybody rave about how great your cooking is? If so, why not put your extraordinary cooking skills to work by teaching others. Teaching students in your kitchen or theirs can help them learn how to prepare fantastic meals, desserts, and appetizers. And you can earn extra profits by selling cookware and kitchen utensils to students. Create and sell recipe books locally. One-on-one, students pay $20 to $30 per hour to learn how to prepare gourmet meals. Charge about half that amount when three to five are taught at the same time; less per student, but more income through volume. Needless to say, it does not take many students to earn an extra $1,000 per month working just a few nights and weekends. Start-up costs are also minimal because chances are you will already have everything you need in terms of cookware and other tools of the trade. Design, print, and post fliers in grocery stores, retail shops, and at your local butcher shop advertising your classes. This is the kind of specialized service about which word spreads fast, so don't be surprised if you are inundated in no time with more students than you can handle.

AT A GLANCE

 INVESTMENT: Under $10K

 INCOME: $25+

 SKILL LEVEL: 2

 RESOURCES
—⭐ Viva The Chef, ♂ www.vivathechef.com/franchise
—📖 *The Gourmet Cookbook: 1000 Recipes*, Ruth Reichl (Houghton
Mifflin Co., 2004)

Snack Vending Business

The snack vending business is a multibillion-dollar industry in North America and continues to grow annually. Fortunately, claiming your piece of the very lucrative snack vending pie is easy. Get started by finding the right location(s) before buying vending machine equipment and inventory. Do this by starting with friends and family members: Where do they work? Is there a vending machine present? If not, would the location support a vending machine? Failing this approach, strike out into the community and look for places that are busy with foot traffic or that have a large number of employees in the 25-plus-age range. These locations include car dealerships, factories, office buildings, fitness clubs, and laundries. But find out upfront if the property owners expect a fee, which can range from 10 to 20 percent of your gross sales, or a set amount each month, perhaps $50 to $100 for each machine. If you get lucky, you might find a few property owners who won't charge you to install a vending machine, but most will want some sort of financial compensation. Once you have found the perfect location and reached an agreement with the landlord or business operator to install the vending equipment, you will be in the right position to know which type of machine(s) to purchase and the kinds of snacks to stock—soda, chips, candy bars, gum, coffee, and even sandwiches. Typically, you can expect to mark up your product by 300 percent for vending. New vending machines are quite expensive, so consider purchasing secondhand machines or renting machines to get started. Expand the business from the profits you earn.

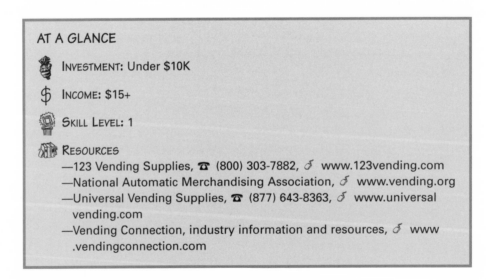

AT A GLANCE

INVESTMENT: Under $10K

INCOME: $15+

SKILL LEVEL: 1

RESOURCES
—123 Vending Supplies, ☎ (800) 303-7882, ♂ www.123vending.com
—National Automatic Merchandising Association, ♂ www.vending.org
—Universal Vending Supplies, ☎ (877) 643-8363, ♂ www.universal vending.com
—Vending Connection, industry information and resources, ♂ www .vendingconnection.com

Restaurateur

There is a perception that restaurants are easy to start, operate, and profit from. While it may be true that anyone and everyone is qualified to start a restaurant, the fact remains that less than 10 percent of new independent restaurants stay in business past five years. The percentage of franchise restaurants that stay in business that long is significantly higher. This is not meant to deter you. It is more than possible to start a very successful restaurant as proven by the untold numbers of successful restaurateurs. After all, a chap with the last name of Sanders made it big in the restaurant game after age 70, and so can you. I grew up in the restaurant business, and my family has a long history of restaurant ownership all the way back to the 1930s. Based on my experiences, I can tell you that the keys to restaurant success are careful research, meticulous planning, the right location, and the three "greats"—great food, great service, and great staff. You will also need to decide what type of restaurant to start (tavern, seafood, steakhouse, breakfast, buffet, pizza parlor, sub shop, vegetarian, family, fine dining, café, fast foods, or ethnic foods restaurants, and coffee houses and internet cafés). This decision should be based on your research into the marketplace and competition rather than the food you enjoy eating. The National Restaurant Association is a good place to start your research. Also be sure to attend restaurant trade shows, buy and read lots of books about starting a restaurant, and talk to lots of restaurant owners and managers to get firsthand feedback about the pros and cons of becoming a restaurateur because the level of investment warrants a lot of homework.

AT A GLANCE

INVESTMENT: Varies

INCOME: Varies

SKILL LEVEL: 1–2

RESOURCES

—Alliance Auction, restaurant equipment auctioneers, ♂ www.alliance auction.com

—National Restaurant Association, ♂ www.restaurant.org

—Plan Magic, restaurant business plan software, ♂ www.planmagic.com/ business_plan/restaurant_business_plan.html

—Restaurant Operator Online, information and resources, ♂ www.restau rantoperator.com

—📖 *The Complete Idiot's Guide to Starting Your Own Restaurant*, Howard Cannon and Brian Tracy (Penguin Putnam, 2001)

Mobile Food Business

Incredible profits can be earned on weekends, or any other day of the week for that matter, by starting and operating a mobile food business. You options are nearly limitless—sell hot dogs, ice cream, mini-donuts, hamburgers, French fries, cotton candy, and any food that fits. The best locations to set up a mobile food vending cart, trailer, or converted van are any places where there are lots of people, such as community events, parades, transit stations, sporting events, concerts, auction sales, flea markets, corporate events, rodeos, fairs, family reunions, parks, retailer special sales events, and even weddings. So what do you need to start making big money in the mobile food business? The list is actually very short. You will need to purchase a new or used food vending cart or trailer, a vendor's permit, a health board certificate, and food and beverage stock. Expect to invest anywhere from $5,000 to $25,000 depending on the type of mobile food business you start. But don't worry, return on investment is quick. It is not uncommon for ice cream, hot dog, and snow cone vendors to earn as much as $1,000 per day in a busy location and retain half that amount after expenses.

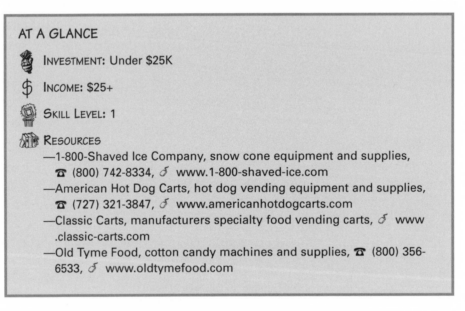

AT A GLANCE

INVESTMENT: Under $25K

$ INCOME: $25+

SKILL LEVEL: 1

RESOURCES
—1-800-Shaved Ice Company, snow cone equipment and supplies, ☎ (800) 742-8334, ♂ www.1-800-shaved-ice.com
—American Hot Dog Carts, hot dog vending equipment and supplies, ☎ (727) 321-3847, ♂ www.americanhotdogcarts.com
—Classic Carts, manufacturers specialty food vending carts, ♂ www.classic-carts.com
—Old Tyme Food, cotton candy machines and supplies, ☎ (800) 356-6533, ♂ www.oldtymefood.com

Cake Baking and Decorating

Making, decorating, and selling one-of-a-kind cakes for occasions ranging from birthdays to weddings to anniversaries is a great opportunity for the hobby baker to pursue, and one that is potentially very profitable. On a small scale, by baking and decorating cakes in your own kitchen, you can get started on shoestring promotional budget. Contact wedding planners, photographers, bridal shops, event coordinators, restaurants, and catering companies to let them know about the specialty cakes you bake and sell. But don't forget to bribe them with an occasional cake to make sure they send business your way. Likewise, you can rent kiosk space at farmers' markets, public markets, and community events. On a large scale, you can rent commercial kitchen space so you have enough room to mass produce cakes that can be sold wholesale to restaurants and grocery stores. Baking and decorating specialty cakes can be very profitable, as ingredient costs are only about 15 to 20 percent of the retail selling price.

AT A GLANCE

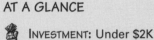 **INVESTMENT:** Under $2K

 INCOME: $15+

 SKILL LEVEL: 1–3

 RESOURCES
  —A.J. Winbeckler Enterprises, wholesale cake making equipment, supplies, and decorating classes, ♂ www.winbeckler.com
  —Baking Tools, baking equipment and supplies, ☎ (509) 468-8691, ♂ www.bakingtools.com
  —The International Cake Exploration Society, ♂ www.ices.org
  —📖 *The Wedding Cake Book*, Dede Wilson (John Wiley & Sons, 1997)

Herb Grower

Fresh herbs are always in demand, which creates a fantastic homebased business opportunity for growing and selling herbs for big profits. Start-up costs are minimal, and even a small backyard herb garden can generate a substantial extra income. Herbs are divided into three primary categories: culinary herbs, such as basil and sage; fragrant herbs, such as tansy and clove; and medicinal herbs, such as borage and valerian. The first step is to educate yourself about herbs and herb gardening by reading books, joining clubs, and obtaining information online. Next, devise a plan outlining the types of herbs you will grow and how each will be marketed. The plan does not have to be sophisticated; it just has to outline the basics such as production costs, marketplace and potential, pricing, and selling methods. Herbs can be sold in a wide variety of ways, including direct to the customer as plants or as a finished product, wholesale sales to retail stores and bulk herb buyers, and direct to restaurants and catering companies. This is a simple business that will appeal to people who love to garden and that want to earn an extra few thousand dollars every year doing nothing more than playing in the soil in their own backyards.

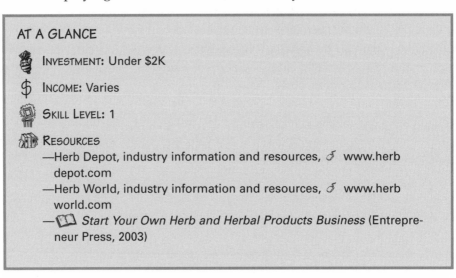

AT A GLANCE

INVESTMENT: Under $2K

$ INCOME: Varies

SKILL LEVEL: 1

RESOURCES
—Herb Depot, industry information and resources, ♂ www.herb depot.com
—Herb World, industry information and resources, ♂ www.herb world.com
—📖 *Start Your Own Herb and Herbal Products Business* (Entrepreneur Press, 2003)

Used Restaurant Equipment Sales

Restaurants and food-related businesses are one of the most common new business start-ups, but unfortunately they also have one of the highest failure rates, with only about 10 percent of new restaurants remaining in business past five years. This staggering statistic does, however, create a fantastic opportunity for entrepreneurs to buy secondhand restaurant equipment, such as grills, deep fryers, and coffee machines for a song and resell for a handsome profit. When a restaurant goes out of business, simply purchase the equipment and fixtures for a fraction of their original retail value. When a new restaurant opens, sell the same equipment to them at a profit. In addition to restaurant closures, equipment can also be purchased cheaply at auctions and bankruptcy sales. Once you have accumulated some equipment, it is time to advertise in online marketplaces, in specialty restaurant publications, by developing your own web site linked with other restaurant information sites, and by contacting current and soon-to-be restaurateurs to inquire about their equipment needs. The business can easily be operated from home, providing you have adequate storage space. Local delivery companies can be hired for pick up and deliveries.

> AT A GLANCE
>
> INVESTMENT: Under $10K
>
> INCOME: Varies
>
> SKILL LEVEL: 1
>
> RESOURCES
> —Alliance Auction, restaurant equipment auctioneers, ♂ www.alliance auction.com
> —National Restaurant Association, ♂ www.restaurant.org
> —Restaurant Operator Online, information and resources, ♂ www.restau rantoperator.com

On-Call Bartender

There are lots of people willing to hire people with excellent bartending skills and pay them for it. Even if you are not 100 percent up-to-speed on the latest drink recipes or the finer aspects of working behind a bar, fret not. Across the country in cities large and towns small, there are a multitude of schools providing bartending training. What is needed, however, is an outgoing and sociable personality. Tending bar on weekends, evenings, and even on a full-time basis is a great way to earn a terrific living or some spare cash to help cover living expenses. You can market your services as a freelance bartender to catering companies, event and wedding planners, private residential parties, corporate events, charity events, banquet halls, hotels, and any place that needs the drinks to flow. Earn upwards of $300 per day when you tally up your wages and tips. To expand the business, simply employ other bartenders on an as-needed, on-call basis.

> AT A GLANCE
>
> INVESTMENT: Under $2K
>
> INCOME: $15+
>
> SKILL LEVEL: 2–3
>
> RESOURCES
> —American Bartenders Association, ♂ www.americanbartenders.org

—World Bartender Training Organizations, ♂ www.wbto.net
—📖 *The Bartender's Best Friend: A Complete Guide to Cocktails, Martinis, and Mixed Drinks*, Mardee Regan (Wiley, 2002)

Restaurant Service Businesses

Restaurants are the number-one new business start-up, so supplying restaurant owners with services such as consulting, menu design, take-out delivery service, and cleaning has the potential to make you rich. In fact, there are so many restaurant service businesses that an entire book could easily be devoted to the subject. Space limitation do not permit for such detail here, so listed here and on the following pages are a few of the better restaurant services businesses that you can start to supplement your retirement income.

Restaurant Consulting

Restaurant consulting is a red-hot opportunity that will appeal to experienced, retired restaurateurs. Restaurant consultants assist clients with any number of tasks, such as restaurant start-up issues, business planning, restaurant design, menu planning, staffing, building and implementing marketing strategies, preparing financial budgets, technology issues, and expansion challenges. Expect to earn in the range of $75 per hour or more.

Take-Out Delivery

Equipped with nothing more than a cellular telephone to handle incoming and outgoing customer calls and reliable transportation, you can offer restaurants in your community fast and convenient take-out food delivery services. Getting started requires nothing more than setting appointments with restaurant owners and managers to pitch the benefits of your food delivery services. Expect to earn in the range of $15 per hour, plus gratuities.

Knife Sharpening

Restaurants, catering companies, and butcher shops are all potential customers for a knife sharpening service. Depending on the type of sharpening equipment you purchase, you can either sharpen knives at the customer's location working from a mobile workshop, or take knives to a homebased workshop to be sharpened and returned when complete. Expect to earn in the range of $20 to $30 per hour.

Washroom Sanitizing

Next to bad food, the number-one reason people will not return to a restaurant is dirty washrooms. This fact alone can be used as your greatest sales and marketing tool for convincing restaurant owners and managers that they need your washroom sanitizing services. Concentrate your marketing efforts on busy fast-food restaurants, family restaurants, coffee shops, and donut shops with a high turnover of customers—businesses that would stand to benefit the most from a daily washroom sanitizing service. Outside of reliable transportation, basic cleaning equipment and a strong work ethic are all that are needed to start. Expect to earn in the range of $15 to $20 per hour.

Exhaust Hood Cleaning

In many regions of the United States and Canada, restaurants are required by health board regulations to have their kitchen exhaust hoods and filters cleaned on a regularly scheduled basis to prevent bacteria growth and to eliminate the potential for grease fires. Given the vast number of restaurants in North America, an incredible opportunity exists to start a restaurant exhaust hood cleaning service and cash in big time. To become a certified hood cleaner only requires a few weeks of classroom training. You can contact the Certified Hood and Duct Cleaners Association, ✆ www.chdca.com, to find out about training in your area. Hood cleaning rates vary by size, access, and frequency, but average between $30 and $50 per hour.

Kitchen Cleaning

Restaurant kitchen cleaning is a booming industry. Cashing in on the demand is relatively easy because if you know how to clean, you're qualified. The only downside to restaurant kitchen cleaning and sanitizing is that in most cases cleaning must be performed nights after the restaurant closes. Rates tend to be higher for restaurant kitchen cleaning compared to residential or office cleaning because work is performed at night and is more labor intensive. Expect to earn in the range of $20 to $30 per hour, plus specialized supplies.

AT A GLANCE

🏭 INVESTMENT: Varies

$ INCOME: $15+

SKILL LEVEL: 1–3

 RESOURCES
—☆ Aire-Master, washroom sanitizing, ☎ (800) 525-0957, ✂ www
.airemaster.com
—☆ Dine-In Delivery, ☎ (303) 604-6840, ✂ www.dine-indelivery.com
—☆ Knife, sharpening services, ☎ (877) 956-4339, ✂ www.knifex.com

Vegetable Stand

Whether it's a roadside stand along a busy highway, a stand in front of your own home, a rented booth at a farmers' market, or portable kiosk set up at a local flea market, selling fresh in-season fruits and vegetables can be very profitable. Like any type of retail venture, the key to success is location, location, and, you guessed it, location. With that goal in mind, excellent locations for a vegetable stand include gas stations, industrial parks, busy intersections, and along roadways leading to popular attractions like the beach, garden centers, and public parks. Even right in front of your own home works, providing zoning permits and visibility to passing traffic is excellent. The stand you work from needs to be nothing more than a basic framework covered by a nylon tarp to keep the sun and heat off the veggies. Of greater importance, however, are the signs needed to advertise your products and business. Signs should be large, colorful, and compel passing motorists to stop, with screaming statements such as, "Stop 100 yards ahead for the best deals on fresh vegetables!" Be sure to place your signs well ahead of your stand to give motorists ample warning so they have time to stop safely. Buy vegetables directly from farmers or farmer's co-operatives in your area, or from produce wholesalers. Regardless of your buying sources, sell only the highest-quality and freshest products available.

AT A GLANCE

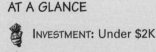 INVESTMENT: Under $2K

$ INCOME: $15+

 SKILL LEVEL: 1

RESOURCES
—Eden Valley Growers, ☎ (716) 992-9721, ♂ www.edenvalleygrow ers.com
—Seminole Produce Distributing, ☎ (800) 745-1102, ♂ www.freshveg gie.com
—Today's Market Prices, ♂ www.todaymarket.com

Tropical Fish Sales

You can make a small fortune from the comforts of home by turning your garage or basement into a well-stocked tropical fish showroom. In addition to selling fresh-water and salt-water tropical fish, you can sell supplies and related accessories such as glass and acrylic fish tanks and stands, canopies, and filters. All of these items can be purchased at deeply discounted prices from manufacturers, wholesalers, and tropical fish farms. Additional sales options include online sales via tropical fish marketplaces, eBay, and your own web site. Bricks and mortar sales options include pet shows and direct to businesses and offices for great conversation pieces. Market your business and products utilizing classified advertising, online advertising, and ads in publications catering to tropical fish hobbyists. Of course, in time, word of mouth referrals and repeat business will go a long way in supporting the business financially. Be aware that there are laws and regulations on importing and exporting tropical fish, so research will be required if you are planning these activities.

AT A GLANCE

 INVESTMENT: Under $2K

 INCOME: $15+

 SKILL LEVEL: 1

 RESOURCES
—Florida Tropical Fish Farms Association, ♂ www.ftffa.com
—Tropical Fish Net, industry information and links, ♂ www.tropical-fish.net
—Uncle Ned's Fish Factory, ☎ (508) 533-5969, ♂ www.unclenedsfish farm.com

Security Product Sales

We live in a violent society. People want to protect themselves and their families, businesses, and homes against crime. The best way to do both is to be proactive and get the security devices that get the job done. Thus, the time has never been better to start a business selling personal security products such as mace, sirens, whistles, and stun guns, as well as home security products such as window security bars and roll shutters, home alarm systems, surveillance equipment, security lighting, and motion detector dog barkers. Security products can be bought at rock-bottom wholesale costs and resold to security-crazed consumers for big profits. Who can blame people for being security crazed—muggings, personal attacks, and road rage have many people scared to death. Although many people refuse to have a gun, these same people are more than willing to use personal and home security products. Online marketplaces such as eBay are perfect selling venues. You can also set up sales displays at consumer shows and in malls. Organize safety seminars with experts talking about personal safety and home security issues. You then sell security products during and after the seminar. Security product sales to business owners who want to protect their shops, employees, customers, and livelihoods are also possible.

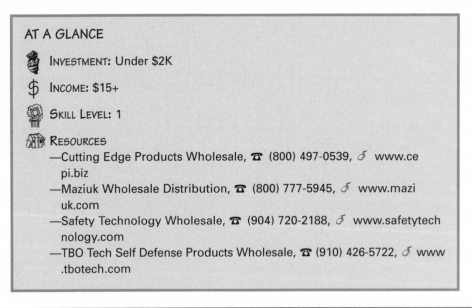

AT A GLANCE

INVESTMENT: Under $2K

INCOME: $15+

SKILL LEVEL: 1

RESOURCES
—Cutting Edge Products Wholesale, ☎ (800) 497-0539, ♂ www.cepi.biz
—Maziuk Wholesale Distribution, ☎ (800) 777-5945, ♂ www.maziuk.com
—Safety Technology Wholesale, ☎ (904) 720-2188, ♂ www.safetytechnology.com
—TBO Tech Self Defense Products Wholesale, ☎ (910) 426-5722, ♂ www.tbotech.com

Security Mirror Business

In spite of the popularity of security video cameras, security mirrors will always be a popular choice for merchants because they enable shopkeepers to keep an eye on their valuable inventory as they assist other customers. Security and safety mirrors come in many styles and price points, ranging from inexpensive 18-inch convex mirrors, which retailers can purchase for about $75, to four-foot ceiling dome mirrors for large surface viewing, which can cost upwards of $400. Even the large mirror is still substantially less than a video surveillance camera and arguably more of a deterrent to would-be shoplifters. Even though the retail prices are reasonable, you can easily generate 30 to 50 percent gross profit on each sale, and anyone with a stepladder and cordless drill can install a security mirror in about 20 minutes. The best way to market security mirrors is to design a simple brochure highlighting all the benefits and features and call on businesses directly. Talk with shopkeepers, and let them know that you are there to save them money. Security mirrors are not a hard sale: If they deter just one thief from shoplifting, there is a good chance they have already paid for themselves, and if they deter ten shoplifters a month, the shopkeeper will be ahead thousands of dollars every year, which is a pretty persuasive sales pitch. Additional locations where safety and security mirrors are needed include warehouses, parking lots and garages, construction sites, and factories. Listed below are a few wholesale sources for security mirrors.

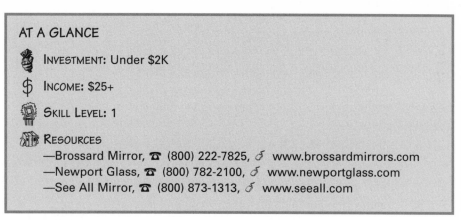

AT A GLANCE

INVESTMENT: Under $2K

$ INCOME: $25+

SKILL LEVEL: 1

RESOURCES
—Brossard Mirror, ☎ (800) 222-7825, ✆ www.brossardmirrors.com
—Newport Glass, ☎ (800) 782-2100, ✆ www.newportglass.com
—See All Mirror, ☎ (800) 873-1313, ✆ www.seeall.com

Shuttle Service

Starting and operating a quick-trip shuttle service in your community is a terrific way to supplement your retirement income. You can help out all sorts of people without transportation and earn great money in the process. For instance, offer to shuttle seniors to medical appointments, the grocery store, or social engagements, or provide safe transportation for kids to school, music lessons, and sports practices. Start-up costs vary depending on your transportation needs. If you already have a suitable car or van, the business can be kicked into high gear cheaply, basically for the cost of a cell phone, initial advertising, and permits. In addition to advertising your shuttle service using classified ads and fliers posted on bulletin boards, build alliances with businesses and professionals that can refer your service to their clients. These would include places such as medical offices, schools, day-care centers, seniors' homes, pharmacies, and grocery markets. Special licenses, permits, and increased liability insurance may be required to operate a community shuttle service in your area, so be sure to check regulations before you get started.

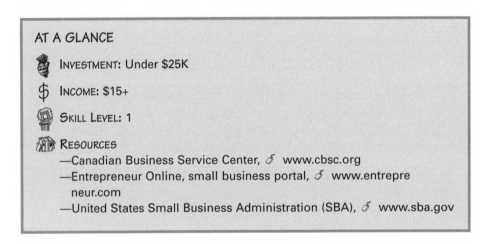

AT A GLANCE

INVESTMENT: Under $25K

$ INCOME: $15+

SKILL LEVEL: 1

RESOURCES
—Canadian Business Service Center, ♂ www.cbsc.org
—Entrepreneur Online, small business portal, ♂ www.entrepreneur.com
—United States Small Business Administration (SBA), ♂ www.sba.gov

Car Wash Business

North America's unflinching love affair with the automobile almost guarantees success for entrepreneurs who take the leap of faith and open a car wash business. There are basically three types of car wash businesses that can be started—full service, automated, and self-serve—all have advantages and disadvantages. For instance, a full-service car wash generates the highest per wash value, but because people are needed to wash and detail cars, labor costs are high. An automated car wash has very low labor costs because it can be operated by one attendant, but it is also the most expensive to start. While a self-serve wand-style car wash is relatively cheap to start, it also generates the lowest per wash sales value. Ultimately, your investment budget and the amount of hands-on management you are prepared to invest will determine the right option for you. One characteristic that all car washes share is that location is the key to success. The location has to be highly visible, easily accessed, and very convenient for customers. Also be sure to purchase and install coin-operated vending machines such as soda and snack machines and coin-operated vacuum cleaners to increase sales and profits.

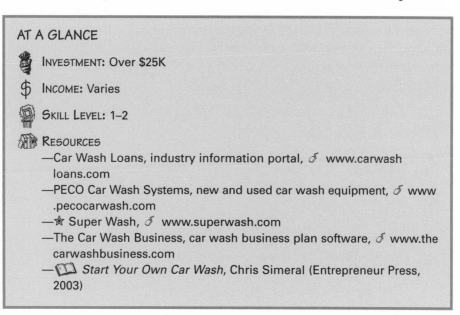

AT A GLANCE

INVESTMENT: Over $25K

INCOME: Varies

SKILL LEVEL: 1–2

RESOURCES
—Car Wash Loans, industry information portal, ♂ www.carwash loans.com
—PECO Car Wash Systems, new and used car wash equipment, ♂ www .pecocarwash.com
—☆ Super Wash, ♂ www.superwash.com
—The Car Wash Business, car wash business plan software, ♂ www.the carwashbusiness.com
—📖 *Start Your Own Car Wash*, Chris Simeral (Entrepreneur Press, 2003)

Used Vehicle Sales

Buying and reselling used cars or motorcycles, recreation vehicles, and classic cars is a good way to supplement your income, but because mechanical repairs are very expensive, this is a business that is definitely best left to people who have mechanical aptitude and can thoroughly inspect vehicles to ensure they are in good working order before buying. Used vehicles can be purchased at auctions, from private sellers, and from car dealers who take in trades, but only resell late model vehicles on their own lots. To maximize profits, try to buy off-season— SUVs in the spring and summer, convertibles and sports cars in the fall and winter, and motorcycles in the winter. Doing so can net you an additional 10 percent or more. Also go out of you way to clean up every vehicle prior to selling—polish the glass, vacuum the carpets, touch up the paint, and steam clean the upholstery. Such little actions can also increase the sales value by 10 percent or more. Buying and selling antique and classic cars generates really big profits because classic car enthusiasts are prepared to pay top dollar to relive their youth or reward themselves for years of hard work by buying the car of their dreams. And because demand is high, prices have exploded into the high five- and, in some cases, six-figure range for prized classic cars, such as 1969 L–89 Corvette in mint condition that now sells for more than $100,000. Buying and selling any type of vehicles, especially classic cars is not for the faint of heart or romantic types. You need to be educated about cars, especially about the condition, mechanical soundness, and value of collector cars. It should be noted, some areas in the United States and Canada have laws that prohibit nonlicensed car dealers, often referred to as curbsiders, from buying and selling cars. Check into the legal issues in your area prior to getting started.

AT A GLANCE

 INVESTMENT: Under $25K

 INCOME: Varies

 SKILL LEVEL: 1–2

 RESOURCES
—Buy Classic Cars, buy-and-sell marketplace, www.buyclassic cars.com
—Used Cars, buy and sell marketplace, ☌ www.usedcars.com
—📖 *Blackbook National Auto Research*, automotive pricing guides, ☎ (800) 554-1026, ☌ www.blackbookusa.com
—📖 *NADA Guides*, classic car price guide, ☎ (800) 966-6232, ☌ www .nadaguides.com
—📖 *The Used Car Money Machine*, Robert Cohill (Dorrance Publishing, 2003)

Boat Broker

Highly ambitious entrepreneurs with a love for boating have the potential to cash in big time on the boating boom by starting a boat broker service. But before you get too excited by the prospect of selling boats, you should know that some states require boat brokers to be licensed. You can contact the boat broker associations that follow to find out licensing regulations in your state. Or, enroll in the National Yacht Brokers Certification Program, ☎ (410) 263-1014, ☌ www.cpyb.net, but only people with prior boat sales experience are eligible for this training program. The cost and time to obtain a license in your state may still be a wise investment because thousands of pre-owned motorboats, sailboats, and personal watercrafts are bought and sold annually, generating billions in sales. Securing just a tiny portion of this very lucrative market may be easier than you think, especially when you consider that you can operate from home and travel to marinas to list, show, and sell, enabling you to keep start-up costs to a minimum. Or, if investment funds are plentiful, you can lease space at a marina without a boat brokerage and offer full brokerage services on-site. Generally, boat brokers or boat sales consultants charge a 10 percent commission fee upon the successful sale and transfer of the boat to the new owner. The commission rate can be as high as 25 percent for boats with a value of less than $5,000 and as low as 3 percent when selling boats in the million-dollar price range.

AT A GLANCE

INVESTMENT: Varies

INCOME: $50+

SKILL LEVEL: 3–4

RESOURCES
—United States Boat Brokers Association, ☌ www.usboatbrokers.com
—Yacht Brokers Association of America, ☌ www.ybaa.com
—📖 *American Marine Publishing*, powerboat value and price guides, ☎ (231) 933-0827, ☌ www.powerboatguide.com
—📖 *NADA Guides*, sailboat price guides, ☎ (800) 966-6232, ☌ www.nadaguides.com

Valet Parking Service

The three most important tools needed to start a special events valet parking service are a driver's license, the ability to obtain third party liability insurance, and an outgoing, friendly personality. If you can meet these requirements, you are qualified to start a valet parking service. The business can be started with minimal cash, and the profit potential is excellent. Rates for valet parking services are in the range of $50 to $70 per hour for a two- to three-person car parking crew, and cash tips can really add up. Market your valet parking services directly to consumers hosting parties, corporations hosting events, and through entertainment industry professionals, such as event and wedding planners, tradeshow organizers, and charity groups for their special functions. Uniforms worn by all staff and emblazoned with your business name and slogan, along with incredible customer service with a smile, will make a favorable impression on customers that is sure to secure lots of repeat business and word-of-mouth referrals. Beyond that, there is not much you need to know and operate a valet parking service. This is one of those rare opportunities in which just about everyone is qualified and has the potential to earn substantial full- or part-time profits.

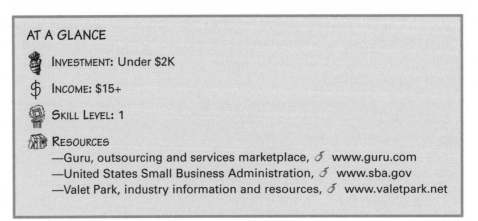

AT A GLANCE

INVESTMENT: Under $2K

INCOME: $15+

SKILL LEVEL: 1

RESOURCES
—Guru, outsourcing and services marketplace, ♂ www.guru.com
—United States Small Business Administration, ♂ www.sba.gov
—Valet Park, industry information and resources, ♂ www.valetpark.net

Limousine Service

Limousines are no longer limited to stretched Cadillac and Lincoln automobiles. Today's limos include mile-long Hummers, vintage Rolls Royces, stretched Minis, and theme vehicles with built-in hot tubs, grand pianos (complete with a pianist), and even disco themes complete with the mirror ball and mini dance floor. In most areas of the United States and Canada, a special business and driver's license, a chauffeur's license, is required to operate a limousine service and drive the vehicle. Therefore, be sure to check into regulations in your area before making any investments. If you cannot acquire a limousine plate, you may be able to purchase one, but expect to shell out up to $100,000. Limousine plates and licenses are in high demand because it is not uncommon for operators to earn six-figure incomes. Advertising in newspapers, Yellow Pages directories, and school newspapers before graduation is sure to get the telephone ringing. Likewise, contact hotels, nightclubs, wedding and event planners, celebrity handlers, and larger corporations to drop off business cards and fliers and to let them know about the limo services you provide, so they can have their guests and clients whisked around town in style.

AT A GLANCE

INVESTMENT: Over $25K

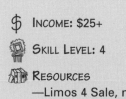

$ INCOME: $25+

SKILL LEVEL: 4

RESOURCES
—Limos 4 Sale, new and used limousine marketplace, ☎ www.limos4
sale.com
—National Limousine Association, ☎ www.limo.org
—★ Racing Limos, ☎ (866) 746-5466, ☎ www.racinglimos.com

Mobile RV and Boat Detailing

If you are an avid recreational vehicle adventurer or boater, this is the business for you. They are actually two separate, but equally potentially profitable business opportunities. Mobile RV detailing and mobile boat detailing are grouped together because the businesses share similar characteristics. They enable operators to combine their love of recreation vehicles or boating with a simple and profitable business. In both instances, equipment and supplies needed to start are basic and cheap, and better, no real experience is needed. Offer customers detailing and cleaning services such as interior and exterior washing, upholstery steam cleaning, and chrome polishing at RV campgrounds or marinas. In terms of boat detailing, additional money can be earned by also offering clients services such as in-the-water bottom cleaning, sailboat rigging, haul-out bottom painting, and woodwork or brightwork refinishing, providing you have the skills and equipment needed. The best way to market the service is to simply design, print, and distribute promotional fliers describing the various detailing services you offer, and rate and contact information.

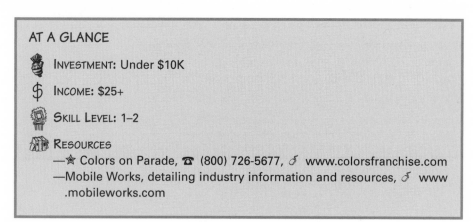

AT A GLANCE

INVESTMENT: Under $10K

$ INCOME: $25+

SKILL LEVEL: 1–2

RESOURCES
—★ Colors on Parade, ☎ (800) 726-5677, ☎ www.colorsfranchise.com
—Mobile Works, detailing industry information and resources, ☎ www
.mobileworks.com

—⭐ Super Clean Yacht Service, ☎ (949) 646-2990, ✂ www.superclean yachtservice.com

Small Engine Repair

Mechanically-inclined entrepreneurs who have the time, skills, space, and tools required can make fantastic full- or part-time cash repairing outdoor power equipment and small engines, right from a fully equipped homebased workshop or small commercial storefront. Even if you do not have previous small-engine repair experience, there are numerous schools offering in-class and correspondence small-engine repair training, such as the ones listed below. Once trained, the list of equipment you can repair is almost unlimited: lawn mowers, outboard marine engines, gas trimmers, lawn tractors, snowmobiles, snow blowers, leaf blowers, and chainsaws are only the tip of the iceberg. There are also three additional revenues sources as well. The first is to become a certified warranty repair depot for outdoor power-equipment manufacturers, which generally only requires a short training course at the manufacturers' locations to qualify. The second is to buy secondhand outdoor power equipment in need of repair at dirt-cheap prices at auction sales, from classified advertisements, and at garage sales, fix it, and resell it for two, three, or even ten times your cost. The third additional revenue source is to rent outdoor power equipment and tools to local homeowners and contractors. Combine the three with the repair side of the business and you could easily generate in excess of $100,000 per year in sales.

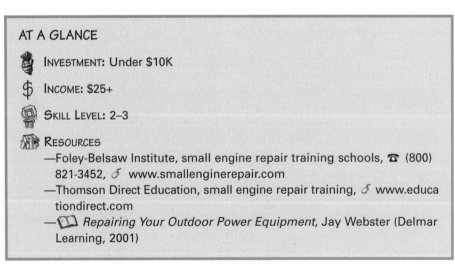

AT A GLANCE

INVESTMENT: Under $10K

$ INCOME: $25+

SKILL LEVEL: 2–3

RESOURCES
—Foley-Belsaw Institute, small engine repair training schools, ☎ (800) 821-3452, ✂ www.smallenginerepair.com
—Thomson Direct Education, small engine repair training, ✂ www.educa tiondirect.com
—📖 *Repairing Your Outdoor Power Equipment*, Jay Webster (Delmar Learning, 2001)

Town Delivery Service

Starting and operating a town delivery service requires no special skills or previous experience. Equipped with nothing more than a cellular telephone to handle incoming and outgoing customer calls, coupled with reliable transportation, you can offer clients in your community fast and convenient delivery and/or pick up services for spirits, fast foods, medications, event tickets, or just about anything else imaginable. In fact, you'll probably find you quickly have more deliveries than you can handle, which is okay because the business is easily expanded simply by putting your marketing and management skills to work. Concentrate on promoting your services and securing new customers, while hiring subcontracted drivers with their own automobiles to handle the pick-ups and deliveries on a flat fee per call basis. Maximize the efficiency of the operation by installing two-way radios linked to a central dispatcher in each vehicle, thereby limiting downtime and nonproductive travel time. In addition to advertising with promotional fliers, in the newspapers, and with direct-mail coupons, also be sure to strike deals with retailers to handle their delivery services.

AT A GLANCE

💰 INVESTMENT: Under $10K

$ INCOME: $15+

SKILL LEVEL: 1

RESOURCES
—⭐ Dine-In Delivery, ☎ (303) 604-6840, ♂ www.dine-indelivery.com
—Entrepreneur Online, small business portal, ♂ www.entrepreneur.com
—United States Small Business Administration (SBA), ♂ www.sba.gov

Rubbish Removal Service

Let's face it, trash isn't pretty, but cleaning it up and removing it can put you on the road to riches. The big requirement for starting a rubbish removal service is physical fitness. This is not easy work, so if your health is a concern, look for other moneymaking opportunities or hire others to do the physical work. Providing you are in good health, the only other requirements are a reliable truck, shovels, rakes, gloves, and a few garbage cans. Rubbish removal rates are by the hour, truckload, or quotation before removing the junk, but on average you can expect to earn in the range of $25 to $40 per hour, after expenses and dumping fees. Providing home and business owners fast and convenient rubbish removal services at competitive prices is without question the best way to build a reputable business quickly, one that can largely be supported by repeat business and word-of-mouth referrals. Still, be sure to build alliances with people who can refer your trash removal services to their clients or become regular customers. These would include real estate agents, residential and commercial cleaners, home service companies such as carpet cleaners, construction contractors, and residential and commercial property managers. In terms of a low-cost business start-up that requires little in the way of special skills or experience, a rubbish removal service is a good choice.

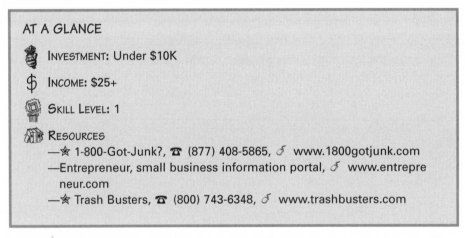

AT A GLANCE

INVESTMENT: Under $10K

$ INCOME: $25+

SKILL LEVEL: 1

RESOURCES
—☆ 1-800-Got-Junk?, ☎ (877) 408-5865, ♂ www.1800gotjunk.com
—Entrepreneur, small business information portal, ♂ www.entrepreneur.com
—☆ Trash Busters, ☎ (800) 743-6348, ♂ www.trashbusters.com

Snowplowing

Depending on how much money you have to invest, how much money you want to earn, and your level of health and fitness, there are two options in terms of starting a part-time snowplowing business. The first and most expensive option is to purchase a four-wheel drive truck outfitted with a professional snowplow. This option could easily set you back $40,000, but it is the best and most profitable way to move snow. The second option is to purchase a walk-behind, self-propelled snow blower, which will also require a truck or trailer to move from job to job. This is a good option for people with a limited investment budget or people wanting to earn extra money nights and weekends. A good quality self-propelled snow blower will cost about $500 to $800 plus the cost of transportation. There is not much to know about snowplowing or marketing a snowplowing service. Print and deliver fliers in your area to inform people about your service, and drop in and talk to business owners with parking lots. Another option is to subcontract for plowing companies with contracts with malls, schools, and residential homes. This route typically pays about $25 to $30 per hour, with you responsible for supplying the equipment. Even though this is a seasonal and weather-dependant opportunity, it is common for snowplow operators to earn $1,000 a day or more when the snow blows.

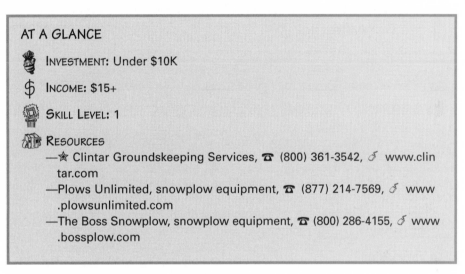

AT A GLANCE

INVESTMENT: Under $10K

$ INCOME: $15+

SKILL LEVEL: 1

RESOURCES
—★ Clintar Groundskeeping Services, ☎ (800) 361-3542, ♂ www.clin tar.com
—Plows Unlimited, snowplow equipment, ☎ (877) 214-7569, ♂ www .plowsunlimited.com
—The Boss Snowplow, snowplow equipment, ☎ (800) 286-4155, ♂ www .bossplow.com

Driveway Sealing

A driveway sealing business is the perfect opportunity for people looking to stay active, work flexible hours, and earn an excellent income. Sealing or coating asphalt driveways is very easy: edge the driveway, removing grass, weeds, and loose debris, fill cracks with cold asphalt compound, power sweep, compressor blow or power wash the surface clean, and finally apply the premixed asphalt sealer. There is self-propelled and tank-fed spraying equipment available at relatively reasonable costs, which makes the job go quickly and is less labor intensive. For entrepreneurs on a tight start-up budget, you can use the good old strong arm method and roll on the sealer straight from a five-gallon bucket using a coarse roller or squeegee. And forget about just plain old black asphalt sealer. New age acrylic driveway coatings are available in a wide range of colors so you can match your clients' driveway colors to trim, siding, or even hair color if they want. Therefore, you are not limited to sealing only older driveways in need of spruce-ups. Any driveway is a potential candidate if the homeowner would like to change its color. You will find all of the necessary supplies and equipment available at most major building centers or online. On average you can earn between $25 and $40 per hour sealing driveways on a full- or part-time basis, which makes this the perfect service for students, retirees, and weekend entrepreneurs.

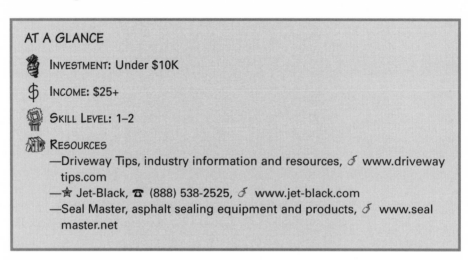

AT A GLANCE

INVESTMENT: Under $10K

$ INCOME: $25+

SKILL LEVEL: 1–2

RESOURCES
—Driveway Tips, industry information and resources, ✆ www.driveway tips.com
—★ Jet-Black, ☎ (888) 538-2525, ✆ www.jet-black.com
—Seal Master, asphalt sealing equipment and products, ✆ www.seal master.net

Waiting Service

I am sure many of you are wondering what exactly is a waiting service? The answer is simple: you charge clients fees to stay at their homes and wait for a delivery, the plumber or electrician, or the telephone or cable company to come by and install a service. Waiting services are starting to flourish for obvious reasons—most working people cannot afford, or even get permission, to sit around all day waiting for a delivery or the repairperson. Start-up costs are low, a little bit of money for marketing materials like fliers and business cards and an investment in bonding insurance. You can charge clients anywhere from $8 to $20 per hour for this service, and if clients want additional services performed such as feeding pets or watering plants, you can charge extra. You will also definitely want to charge a minimum for the service; $25 for the first hour and your regular rate for each additional hour on the job is recommended. Promote the service by establishing alliances with companies that typically require people to wait, such as the telephone company and repair people. That way, the next time one of their customers tries to pin them down to an exact time, they can simple refer your service. Expanding the business is as easy as hiring additional contract waiting staff and booking jobs for a portion of their fees.

> **AT A GLANCE**
>
> INVESTMENT: Under $2K
>
> INCOME: $15+
>
> SKILL LEVEL: 1
>
> RESOURCES
> —Canadian Business Service Center, ☎ www.cbsc.org
> —Entrepreneur Online, small business portal, ☎ www.entrepre
> neur.com
> —United States Small Business Administration (SBA), ☎ www.sba.gov

Auctioneer

Have fun and makes lots of money in your postretirement years by starting and operating an auction service. Training is required, and each U.S. state and Canadian province has its own criteria for auctioneer licensing. There are dozens of auctioneer schools across the United States and Canada to help you get that training, and you can contact the trade associations listed below to inquire about auctioneer training and licensing requirements in your area. Auctioneers are more than just fast talkers. Auctioneers are also expert marketers who have an excellent knowledge of the products they sell, the demand for these products, and the target audience of buyers, because without buyers in attendance it doesn't matter what's up for auction. That is why most auctioneers specialize in one or two types of goods, such as real estate, heavy equipment, antiques, art, inventory liquidation, automobiles, boats, livestock, or general household goods. Starting an auction service also requires relatively deep pockets unless you contract your auctioning services to other auctioneers. It is a costly business to establish because you have to pay upfront to advertise, promote, set up, and run the auction before you get paid. Your commissions are based on the total value of the goods sold at auction and are typically 10 percent, plus fees for transportation, storage, and additional services requested by the seller. Auctioneers also commonly charge buyers a fee as well, typically 5 percent of the value of goods purchased.

> **AT A GLANCE**
>
> INVESTMENT: Over $25K

$ **INCOME:** $50+

SKILL LEVEL: 4

RESOURCES
—Auction Guide, industry information portal, ♂ www.auction guide.com
—Auctioneers Association of Canada, ☎ (866) 640-9915, ♂ www.auctioneerscanada.com
—National Auctioneers Association, ☎ (800) 662-9438, ♂ www.auctioneer.org

Residential Safety Consultant

Statistically speaking, the largest percentage of accidents causing injuries do not happen on the job, on the roads, or on the playing field, but right at home. Falls, accidental poisonings, burns, cuts, broken bones, and other types of injuries take place in thousands of homes across the country every single day. The vast majority of these injuries are preventable through education and by taking proactive steps to eliminate or reduce harmful risks around the home. Working as a residential safety consultant, you can conduct inspections of your clients' homes, noting all of the potential hazards inside and outside. The next step is to write a report outlining these hazards and the recommendations required to remove, repair, or reduce these hazards. At this point and at a client's request, you can either carry out the recommended corrective measures, hire a handyperson to do the work, or refer your client to people who can do the work. What are these potential hazards around the home that can cause harm to kids, pets, seniors, and all occupants? A few include trip hazards on exterior walkways, window blind cords, lack of grab bars and anti slip surfaces in washroom, unsafe storage of cleaning solvents, and lack of child-proof latches on cabinets and cutlery draws.

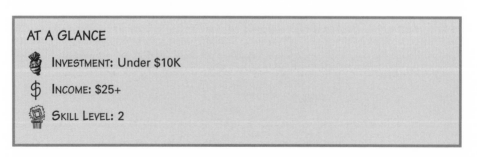

AT A GLANCE

INVESTMENT: Under $10K

$ **INCOME:** $25+

SKILL LEVEL: 2

On-Call Notary Public

Notary publics are legal officers with specific judicial authority to administer oaths, certify affidavits, and take depositions. Notaries prepare wills, mortgages, and other legal documents, which they certify with an official seal, as well as provide official witnessing of signatures. There is a growing need for notaries public to work in financial, real estate, business, insurance, and law fields. Imagine the flexibility that being an on-call notary public affords. You can work from a home-based office and on an on-call mobile basis, going where your clients want you to notarize documents and witness signatures. These locations can include real estate offices, private homes, businesses, insurance offices, or even the airport to meet with clients on tight schedules. In a nutshell, if you are prepared to invest in the training required to become a notary public, you have lots of options in terms of how you operate your on-call business once certified. Notary Public Online, ✆ www.notarypublic.com, provides state-by-state notary public training and certification requirements. In addition to traditional advertising in the Yellow Pages and newspapers, the most successful notaries public are the ones who build a broad network of business alliances with professionals that often require notary public services, such as real estate brokers, health care providers, insurance brokers, and professional service providers. The only equipment and tools you'll need to operate the business is a cellular telephone and reliable transportation.

AT A GLANCE

INVESTMENT: Under $25K

$ INCOME: $50+

SKILL LEVEL: 4

RESOURCES
—National Notary Association, ☎ (800) 876-6827, ✆ www.national notary.org
—The American Society of Notaries, ✆ www.notaries.org
—The Society of Notaries Public of BC, ✆ www.notaries.bc.ca

Business Broker

To legally market and sell businesses in Canada, you require a real estate license. In the United States at the time of writing, only 17 states require people to obtain a real estate license to start and operate a business brokerage. These states include AK, AZ, CA, FL, GA, ID, IL, MI, MN, ME, NV, OR, SD, UT, WA, WI, and WY. The exciting news is that an estimated 1,000,000 businesses are for sale at any one time in the United States. Needless to say, there is potential to earn enormous profits listing, marketing, and selling businesses. Even if you must invest the time and money to obtain a real estate license, the potential rewards easily justify the effort. What exactly do business brokers do to earn these big profits? The short answer is they sell lots of businesses. The long answer is they source people wanting to sell their businesses, prepare a business valuation to establish a fair market value for the listing price, list the business for sale, market the business, qualify potential buyers, show the business, answer questions, work on behalf of their clients to negotiate a mutually agreeable selling price, and assist in all matters relating to closing the sale and transferring ownership. In other words, a business broker looks after everything that is required to sell a business, taking all of the stress and work off the seller's shoulders. You might also want to consider specializing in selling specific types of businesses such as restaurants, hotels, retail, or manufacturing. Specialization is the fastest way to become known as an industry expert and to increase repeat and referral business.

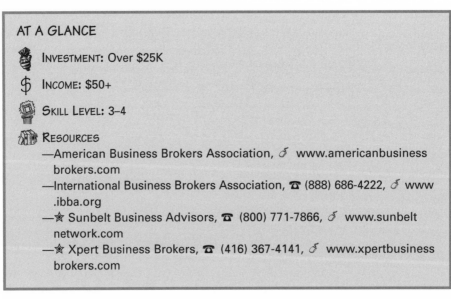

AT A GLANCE

INVESTMENT: Over $25K

$ INCOME: $50+

SKILL LEVEL: 3–4

RESOURCES
—American Business Brokers Association, ♂ www.americanbusiness brokers.com
—International Business Brokers Association, ☎ (888) 686-4222, ♂ www.ibba.org
—✫ Sunbelt Business Advisors, ☎ (800) 771-7866, ♂ www.sunbelt network.com
—✫ Xpert Business Brokers, ☎ (416) 367-4141, ♂ www.xpertbusiness brokers.com

Nonmedical Home Care

It's no secret the 50-plus age group is the fastest expanding demographic in North America. Generally speaking, as people age they tend to need more personal attention than younger folks, which is why the nonmedical home care industry is exploding. People who are reliable, compassionate, and care about the welfare of others will thrive in this field. The business is easy to start because there are minimal skill and experience requirements, and start-up costs are low. In fact, it is possible to get started for well under $10,000, including the cost of reliable transportation. Nonmedical home care services provide clients with services specific to each individual's needs. These services often include companionship, meal preparation, medication reminders, light housekeeping duties, laundry, running errands, trips to doctors and other appointments, and shopping for groceries and personal needs. In addition to seniors, nonmedical home care workers also provide similar services for moms-to-be, new moms, people with disabilities, and people of all ages recovering from injury or illness. Although there are no across-the-board certification requirements for nonmedical home care providers, although all services and workers are required to carry insurance and be bonded.

AT A GLANCE

 INVESTMENT: Under $10K

 INCOME: $25+

 SKILL LEVEL: 1–3

 RESOURCES
—American Association of Retired Persons (AARP), ♂ www.aarp.org
—Canadian Association of Retired Persons (CARP), ♂ www.50 plus.com
—★ Home Instead Senior Care, ♂ www.homeinstead.com/Franchise_Opp.asp
—★ Homewatch Caregivers, ☎ (800) 777-9770, ♂ www.homewatch-intl.com
—National Private Duty Association, ☎ (317) 844-7105, ♂ www.private dutyhomecare.org

Renovation Project Manager

Turn your knowledge of construction and home renovation into big bucks by starting a renovation project-management service focused on helping clients manage their homes, offices, or store renovations. It is especially in demand in the red-hot residential home improvement industry. Regardless of whether a homeowner tackles his own renovation job or if a renovation company is hired to perform the work, an unbiased remodeling project-management service to oversee the complete job can potentially save clients thousands of dollars, while ensuring all work is performed to code and the highest-quality products and installations are used. This is especially true for homeowners doing their own work: What permits do they need, and where do they get them? In what order is the job completed? And the granddaddy of them all, how much will the entire project cost, including potential extra costs to deal with unforeseen circumstances? These are common questions that project managers answer as they contact and screen potential trades, establish budgets, sign off on materials and labor, and keep the project on-time and on-budget. Remuneration is by way of a pre-quoted flat fee to oversee all or part of a project, or a percentage of the total project value.

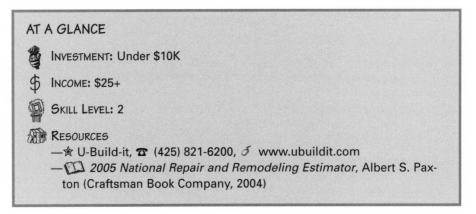

AT A GLANCE

INVESTMENT: Under $10K

$ INCOME: $25+

SKILL LEVEL: 2

RESOURCES
—★ U-Build-it, ☎ (425) 821-6200, ♂ www.ubuildit.com
—📖 *2005 National Repair and Remodeling Estimator*, Albert S. Paxton (Craftsman Book Company, 2004)

Decorating Service

A myriad of popular television programs aimed at home decorating, such as "Trading Spaces," "Designers Guys," and "While You Were Out" have fired up people's imaginations about how they can dramatically change the look of their homes over a weekend on a relatively small budget. But there is a hook; in order to do this, someone must have a creative flair for decorating and design, and the skills and tools necessary to pull it all together. Not all homeowners have these skills and talents. But if you do, operating a decorating service might be right up your brightly colored faux finished alley. For budget-minded clients, you can spend time at garage and estate sales, scrounge through flea markets, and scan local newspaper classified ads for wacky decoration items, recycled building materials, and unique home furnishing. All can be purchased and resold to clients at a profit as you redecorate rooms or entire houses. For your well-heeled clients, stick with designer and brand-name products to transform their homes and offices into designer masterpieces. Market your decoration and design service by exhibiting your talents at home and garden shows and by creating colorful before-and-after brochures illustrating your decorating talents that can be distributed to home and business owners. It generally only takes a few well-received jobs to build a solid reputation in the decorating world. Therefore, consider doing the first few jobs at cost, so you can begin to build the portfolio that can be used to attract new business.

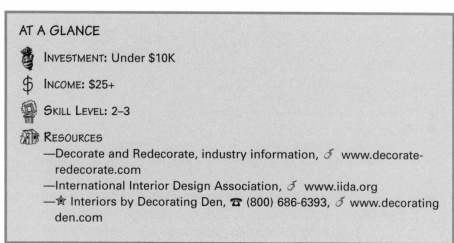

AT A GLANCE

INVESTMENT: Under $10K

INCOME: $25+

SKILL LEVEL: 2–3

RESOURCES
—Decorate and Redecorate, industry information, ♂ www.decorate-redecorate.com
—International Interior Design Association, ♂ www.iida.org
—☆ Interiors by Decorating Den, ☎ (800) 686-6393, ♂ www.decorating den.com

Home Inspector

People retiring from the construction industry or engineering profession who are prepared to invest some money and time in a training course that will qualify them as a certified home and property inspector can earn a very good living operating a home and property inspection service. How good a living? Many home and property inspectors routinely earn six-figure annual incomes after business expenses and as much as $40,000 per year working part-time. Millions of homes and properties are bought and sold each year in North America. As a condition of sale, most buyers, and often mortgage lenders, insist the property be professionally inspected to ensure the building does not have major structural or mechanical problems. Doing so is a safeguard for the investment. Home and property inspection rates range from $150 for a small residential home to as much as $10,000 for large commercial buildings. Training and certification is required in most areas of the United States and Canada to be recognized as a professional home and property inspector. You can contact the associations listed below to find out about available training classes and certification requirements in your area. Be sure to build alliances with real estate companies, mortgage brokers, property appraisers, lawyers, notary publics, and insurance agents, all of whom can refer their clients to you.

AT A GLANCE

INVESTMENT: Under $10K

$ INCOME: $25+

SKILL LEVEL: 4

RESOURCES
—☆ Amerispec Home Inspection Services, ☎ (800) 426-2270, ♂ www
.amerispecfranchise.com
—Canadian Association of Home and Property Inspectors, ♂ www.ca
hi.ca
—National Association of Home Inspectors, ♂ www.nahi.org
—📖 *Start Your Own Home Inspection Service*, Claire Ginther (Entrepreneur Press, 2003)

Rental Accommodations Finder Service

Face it, finding a new home or apartment to rent can be time consuming and frustrating: scanning countless rental ads, booking appointments, viewing properties, and completing applications. That's why many people needing to rent a home enlist the services of a professional apartment and house finder service. This is a great opportunity for the recently retired to tackle because the service can easily be operated from home with the aid of a web site and requires no previous experience. There are basically two ways to earn money. First, charge clients a fee to find the right rental accommodation, or second, charge landlords a fee to list their rental accommodations with your service. The "home finder" industry is competitive, especially in large urban centers. Consequently, specialization in one or two types of rental accommodations will enable you to serve a specific target audience very well. You could specialize in roommate listings, short- or long-term furnished and unfurnished accommodations, executive accommodations, "pets allowed," and any other logical category.

AT A GLANCE

INVESTMENT: Under $10K

INCOME: $15+

SKILL LEVEL: 1

RESOURCES
—American Association of Small Property Owners, ♂ www.aaspo.org
—Building Owners and Managers Association of Canada, ♂ www.boma canada.org
—National Apartment Association, ♂ www.naahq.org
—National Property Managers Association, ♂ www.npma.org

Real Estate Appraiser

Real estate appraisers specialize in estimating the value of land and the structures inhabiting the land. Real estate appraisals are commonly required when people buy a home, sell a home, or apply for/or renew a mortgage, for insurance purposes, to settle estates and divorce cases, and for all other situations when the value of a property is needed. The job of the real estate appraiser is to prepare a written description and diagram of the property noting structures, verifying legal descriptions of the property with county or city records, and preparing an estimated market value for the property. Calculating fair market value is based on factors such as property condition, values of homes in close proximity, and building replacement costs using building valuation manuals and professional cost estimators. The key to success in real estate appraisal is alliances. You need to build working relationships with other professionals that commonly need real estate appraisal services for themselves or their clients. These professionals include mortgage brokers, bankers, real estate brokers, real estate agents, and real estate lawyers. Providing real estate appraisal services is an excellent way to supplement a retirement income because the opportunity provides great flexibility—work part-time, full-time, or only seasonally. Contact the real estate appraisal associations listed that follow to find out about training and certification requirements in your area.

AT A GLANCE

INVESTMENT: Under $25K

INCOME: $50+

SKILL LEVEL: 4

RESOURCES
—Appraisal Institute of Canada, ☎ (613) 234-6533, ♂ www.ai canada.ca
—National Association of Real Estate Appraisers, ☎ (320) 763-7626, ♂ www.iami.org
—The American Society of Appraisers, ☎ (703) 478-2228, ♂ www .appraisers.org

Real Estate Investor

There are two ways to earn big profits in real estate investing. The first is to buy properties at less than market value and resell for a profit; the second is to purchase income-producing properties and hold on for long-term equity gain. Many savvy entrepreneurs earn seven figure incomes buying and selling real estate. As a rule, they look for three types of buying opportunities: foreclosures, motivated sellers, or paint, putter, and profit opportunities. The best real estate buys occur when you can purchase a foreclosed property for far less than market value. You negotiate an incredibly low price because the seller is very motivated by health, finances, or another reasons. Or, you buy the worse house on the best street, well undervalued, and carry out minor repairs and cosmetic fix-ups so you can flip the property for a profit. There are also things these same savvy entrepreneurs do not do. They never buy vacant land because it cannot generate income (rent) until resold or held for long-term equity gain. They use everyone's money but their own through mortgage takeovers, vendor financing options, equity leverage, and 100 percent lending options. And they never sell for less than they have invested because they do the required homework before buying, negotiate the lowest price, and prepare the house to be resold for top dollar before listing, or fix up the property to acquire top rents. There are literally hundreds of real estate buying books, programs, and seminars available to show you how to buy and sell for a profit, or hold and rent for a profit. It should be noted that real estate investing is not for the faint of heart, and you cannot just simply jump in with both feet and hope for the best. You have to acquire the knowledge needed to make smart investments that can be easily resold or rented to return your investment and show a profit. This takes time, research, and education to accomplish, but is well worth the investment of time and money.

AT A GLANCE

 INVESTMENT: Over $25K

 INCOME: Varies

 SKILL LEVEL: 1

 RESOURCES
—Foreclosure Free Search, online database listing REO, HUD, VA, Fannie Mae, Bank, and mortgage company real estate foreclosures indexed by state, ♂ www.foreclosurefreesearch.com
—Real Estate Foreclosures, online database listing REO, HUD, VA, Fannie Mae, Bank, and mortgage company real estate foreclosures indexed by state, ♂ www.realestateforeclosures.net
—Real Estate Investing, online community serving small real estate investors with industry information, resources, and links, ♂ www.realestateinvesting.com
—📖 *Flipping Properties: Generate Instant Cash in Real Estate*, Robert Dahlstrom and William Bronchick (Dearborn Trade Publishing, 2001)
—📖 *Making Big Money Investing in Foreclosures*, David Finkel and Peter Conti (Dearborn Trade Publishing, 2003)

Mortgage Broker

Working as an independent mortgage broker, you can help people fulfill their dreams of home ownership and earn an excellent income in the process. The primary function of a mortgage broker is to bring together people who want to borrow money to buy real estate with lending institutions that advance funds for the purpose of real estate purchases. The rules and policies for obtaining a mortgage broker's license differ among states and provinces, but you can contact the National Association of Mortgage Brokers in the United States and the Canadian Institute of Mortgage Brokers and Lenders via the contact information listed as follows to find out about training and licensing requirements in your area. Once a mortgage broker has received an application from a client and checked credit and work references, the next step is to send the application to one or more lending institutions for acceptance or rejection. Mortgage brokers are typically paid a commission by the lending institution that advances the mortgage funds, ranging from a few hundred dollars to thousands of dollars, depending on the mortgage amount. Sometimes, however, in more difficult funding scenarios—second mortgages, third mortgages, or bridge financing, for instance, a mortgage broker will also charge the borrower a fee to cover the extra work involved in securing suitable financing. Most mortgage brokers handle finding residential mortgages for their clients, but you can also work with clients who want to refinance their mortgages, increase their mortgage amounts, take out second or third mortgages, use equity for bridge financing, or purchase commercial properties, vacant land, income properties, or vacation properties. This is very much a business that thrives on referral and repeat business, so be sure to build working relationships with numerous real estate brokers and agents.

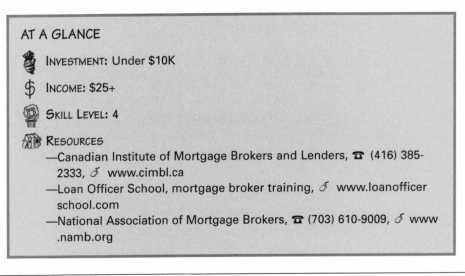

AT A GLANCE

INVESTMENT: Under $10K

INCOME: $25+

SKILL LEVEL: 4

RESOURCES
—Canadian Institute of Mortgage Brokers and Lenders, ☎ (416) 385-2333, ♂ www.cimbl.ca
—Loan Officer School, mortgage broker training, ♂ www.loanofficer school.com
—National Association of Mortgage Brokers, ☎ (703) 610-9009, ♂ www .namb.org

Property Management Service

Starting and operating a property management service is ideal for people with previous experience in real estate, project management, construction management, or property administration. However, anyone can start this venture on a small or part-time basis and gain valuable on-the-job experience, which can be leveraged to grow the business. Residential and commercial property managers are busy people because they have lots of work to do on behalf of their clients. These duties often include preparing annual management plans; preparing budgets and monthly financial statements; maintaining good tenant-owner relations; organizing trades to conduct repairs; negotiating, preparing, and executing leases;

and managing deposit accounts, just for starters! The Building Owners and Managers Association of Canada, and the National Property Managers Association in the United States offer property management training and certification programs. Although certification is not mandatory, it is a wise investment, especially for people who want to make a professional postretirement career of property management. Property management fees vary depending on the residential or commercial property being managed as well as on the services provided, but you can expect to earn in the range of $25 to $40 per hour.

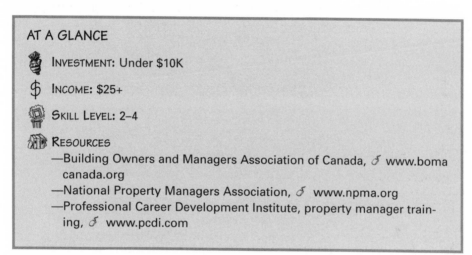

AT A GLANCE

INVESTMENT: Under $10K

INCOME: $25+

SKILL LEVEL: 2–4

RESOURCES
—Building Owners and Managers Association of Canada, ☎ www.boma canada.org
—National Property Managers Association, ☎ www.npma.org
—Professional Career Development Institute, property manager training, ☎ www.pcdi.com

Relief Apartment Building Caretaker

Working as a relief apartment building caretaker is a wonderful way to supplement your retirement income. Building managers and caretakers may need time off for any number of reasons, from vacations to family emergencies, and when they are away, someone is needed to take their places. Building managers and caretakers perform a number of duties, from rent collection, to preparing apartments for rent, to light housekeeping and exterior maintenance. Depending on the length of the relief duty, you may not even be needed on-site, just on-call in case of emergencies. Therefore, you will need to develop a fee scale covering on-call fees, daily fees, and a long-term weekly or monthly fees. If you do not have previous apartment building management or caretaking experience, there are training programs available, or you may even elect to become a Certified Apartment Manager (CAM) via a program offered by the National Apartment Association. This program teaches fundamental and advanced techniques in modern apartment management, all presented with the goal of developing the knowledge and skills to manage a successful, quality apartment community in a professional manner. However, if you have some previous building management and maintenance experience, this type of training is not required. To get the word out about your service, contact property management firms and landlord associations.

AT A GLANCE

 INVESTMENT: Under $2K

 INCOME: $15+

 SKILL LEVEL: 2–3

 RESOURCES
—Building Owners and Managers Association of Canada, ♂ www.boma canada.org
—National Apartment Association, ♂ www.naahq.org
—National Property Managers Association, ♂ www.npma.org
—Resident Managers' Training Institute, ♂ www.rmti.ca
—The Caretaker Gazette, industry information portal, ♂ www.care taker.org

---

House Refitting for Seniors and the Disabled

Many seniors and people living with physical disabilities often find life's simplest tasks, such as cooking dinner or doing laundry, stressful and daunting. The housing requirements for many seniors and disabled people are much different from those for people without disabilities. Doorways must be wide enough to accommodate wheelchairs, light switches must be lowered, and electrical sockets raised, for example. Likewise, kitchens and bathrooms generally must be customized to suit each person's specific needs. Changes such as the installation of ramps, chair lifts, and safety handrails are common refits. Starting a business that specializes in refitting homes for seniors and disabled persons can be a rewarding enterprise. If you have basic carpentry skills and tools, you can do much of the work yourself and hire out alterations requiring certified trades such as plumbing and electrical. House refitting is much more involved than providing simple handyman or even renovation services because much consultation must take place with the senior or disabled homeowner to assess his or her individual needs to ensure the changes are beneficial and improve his or her quality of life. Traditional advertising combined with building alliances with medical care and service providers as well as retailers of home medical equipment is the best way to get started. With 78 million baby boomers in the United States, the future for this business opportunity is bright.

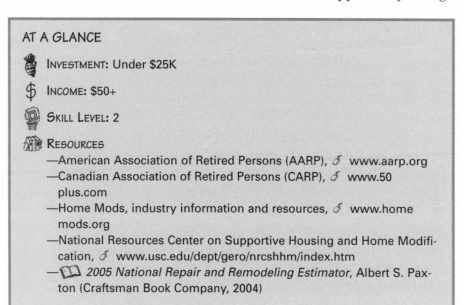

AT A GLANCE

💰 INVESTMENT: Under $25K

$ INCOME: $50+

🖳 SKILL LEVEL: 2

🏠 RESOURCES
—American Association of Retired Persons (AARP), ♂ www.aarp.org
—Canadian Association of Retired Persons (CARP), ♂ www.50 plus.com
—Home Mods, industry information and resources, ♂ www.home mods.org
—National Resources Center on Supportive Housing and Home Modification, ♂ www.usc.edu/dept/gero/nrcshhm/index.htm
—📖 *2005 National Repair and Remodeling Estimator*, Albert S. Paxton (Craftsman Book Company, 2004)

Dog Biscuit Bakery

One of the best ways to supplement your retirement income was saved for last. The fastest growing, and arguably most profitable, segment of the pet food industry is gourmet dog treats. There is a lot of money to be made in this business because the profit margin is very high and people are willing to pay for the best dog treats money can buy. You may well be one of them. As people become more health conscious with their own diets, they begin to scrutinize their pets' diets as well. Many are turning to naturally made biscuits for their dogs, even though all-natural handmade biscuits cost as much as ten times more than commercially produced dog ones. Making dog biscuits at home is easy; all you need to get started are dog biscuit recipes, healthy ingredients, biscuit molds (bones and cats are dog favorites), a catchy name, and packaging materials. Baking and selling specialty dog biscuits is a fantastic opportunity for pet-loving entrepreneurs who want to work from home and have a lot of fun, and selling options are plentiful. Sell to independent and chain pet food retailers on a wholesale basis or directly to consumers via online pet products marketplaces, at pet fairs, and from your home supported by word of mouth advertising, which is very easy to get if dogs love your treats.

AT A GLANCE

 INVESTMENT: Under $2K

$ INCOME: $15+

 SKILL LEVEL: 1

 RESOURCES
—American Dog Owners Association, ♂ www.adoa.org
—American Pet Products Manufacturers Association, ♂ www.app
ma.org
—Gourmet Sleuth Recipes, ♂ www.gourmetsleuth.com/recipe_dog
biscuit.htm

INDEX